Dancing Spirit,
Love, *and* War

DANCE STUDIES ASSOCIATION

The Dance Studies Association (DSA) advances the field of dance studies through research, publication, performance, and outreach to audiences across the arts, humanities, and social sciences. As a constituent member of the American Council of Learned Societies, DSA holds annual conferences; publishes new scholarship through its book series, proceedings, and *Conversations across the Field of Dance Studies*; collaborates regularly with peer institutions in the United States and abroad; and presents yearly awards for exemplary scholarship.

DSA President: ANNE FLYNN, University of Calgary

DSA Editorial Board

Chair: SARAH DAVIES CORDOVA, University of Wisconsin–Milwaukee

Chair-Elect: CLARE CROFT, University of Michigan

SHERRIL DODDS, Temple University

NORMA SUE FISHER-STITT, York University

JENS RICHARD GIERSDORF, Marymount Manhattan College

ELLEN GRAFF, The New School, New York

VIDA MIDGELOW, Middlesex University

RAMÓN RIVERA-SERVERA, Northwestern University

REBECCA ROSSEN, University of Texas at Austin

LINDA TOMKO, University of California–Riverside

Dancing Spirit, Love, *and* War

Performing the Translocal Realities of Contemporary Fiji

Evadne Kelly

THE UNIVERSITY OF WISCONSIN PRESS

This research was supported by the Social Sciences and
Humanities Research Council of Canada.

Social Sciences and Humanities Research Council of Canada   Conseil de recherches en sciences humaines du Canada   Canada

The University of Wisconsin Press
1930 Monroe Street, 3rd Floor
Madison, Wisconsin 53711-2059
uwpress.wisc.edu

Gray's Inn House, 127 Clerkenwell Road
London ECIR 5DB, United Kingdom
eurospanbookstore.com

Copyright © 2019
The Board of Regents of the University of Wisconsin System
All rights reserved. Except in the case of brief quotations embedded in
critical articles and reviews, no part of this publication may be reproduced,
stored in a retrieval system, transmitted in any format or by any means—digital,
electronic, mechanical, photocopying, recording, or otherwise—or conveyed
via the internet or a website without written permission of the
University of Wisconsin Press. Rights inquiries should be
directed to rights@uwpress.wisc.edu.

Printed in the United States of America

This book may be available in a digital edition.

Library of Congress Cataloging-in-Publication Data

Names: Kelly, Evadne, author.
Title: Dancing spirit, love, and war : performing the translocal realities of
contemporary Fiji / Evadne Kelly.
Other titles: Studies in dance history (Unnumbered)
Description: Madison, Wisconsin : The University of Wisconsin Press, [2019] |
Series: Studies in dance history
Identifiers: LCCN 2018046895 | ISBN 9780299322007 (cloth : alk. paper)
Subjects: LCSH: Dance—Fiji. | Dance—Social aspects—Fiji. | Folk
dancing—Fiji.
Classification: LCC GV1728.F5 K45 2019 | DDC 793.319611—dc23
LC record available at https://lccn.loc.gov/2018046895

ISBN 9780299322045 (paperback)

Contents

List of Illustrations	vi
Acknowledgments	viii
Note on Orthography	xii
Introduction: Fijian by Decree	3
1 Meke in a Changing Imperial World	34
2 Governing Meke: Choreographing Pasts, Expressing Futures	67
3 Meke in Multicultural Canada	100
4 Spiriting Meke: Generating Stability, Tension, and Transformation	124
5 Generating Efficacy: Countervailing Rhythms of a Contemporary Meke	145
6 Performing Indeterminacy: Performance of *Mekhe ni Loloma*	173
Glossary	185
Notes	187
Bibliography	219
Index	233

Illustrations

Figure I.1	Map of Fiji	7
Figure I.2	Oceania Dance Theatre Meke Fusion	11
Figure I.3	Map of the Pacific	26
Figure I.4	Yaqona ceremony, Bau, 1945	29
Figure 1.1	Anna Qumia with Hilary White Nunn, Suva, Fiji, circa 1943	50
Figure 1.2	Anna Qumia with Hilary White Nunn, Suva, Fiji, circa 1968	51
Figure 1.3	Men's meke wau, Nasova, 1948	56
Figure 1.4	Women's meke, Beqa, 1949	57
Figure 1.5	Women's vakamalolo, Nasova, 1948	58
Figure 1.6	Men's meke wau at Beqa, 1948	58
Figure 1.7	Men's meke wau at Beqa, 1948	59
Figure 1.8	Women's meke iri, Beqa, 1948	59
Figure 1.9	Men's meke iri, Nanukuloa, 1944	60
Figure 1.10	Women's meke iri, Nanukuloa, 1944	60
Figure 1.11	Women's seasea meke, Beqa, 1949	61
Figure 1.12	Tourists watching meke (children), Savusavu, 1963	62
Figure 2.1	"Teivovo," University of the South Pacific, Suva, June 3, 2012	83
Figure 2.2	Meke ceremony, Bau, 1945	85

Illustrations vii

Figure 2.3 Meke wau, Bau, 1945 — 85
Figure 2.4 Fiji Dance Group performing at the opening of Fijian Cultural Center in Pacific Harbour, 1978 — 90
Figure 2.5 Women walking over hot stones during a firewalking ceremony, Laucala Island, 1978 — 91
Figure 3.1 Pearl of the South Pacific performing meke at Greek Fest, Victoria, BC, September 3, 2011 — 114
Figure 5.1 *Mekhe ni Loloma* rehearsal, Pacific Harbour, Fiji, August 2012 — 161
Figure 5.2 Damiano Logaivau in rehearsal of *Mekhe ni Loloma*, Suva, Fiji, October 2012 — 161

Acknowledgments

The development of this manuscript has been a long process, with intellectual and technical support from many. Rebecca Rossen, former chair of the editorial board of the Dance Studies Association, has patiently provided exceptional guidance and dedicated much thought, time, and energy to draw out the best possible manuscript. I am grateful to be part of the Dance Studies Association's inaugural mentorship program for first-time authors. Rachmi Diyah Larasati provided a high level of feedback that will continue to impact my thinking and writing. I also thank Clare Croft, Royona Mitra, the other members of the editorial board and the two anonymous reviewers who, as a community of scholars committed to building dance studies as an interdisciplinary field of inquiry, provided critical provocations and feedback throughout the process.

I respectfully acknowledge and thank those who have accelerated the development of this book. Adrienne Kaeppler, Danielle Robinson, Ken Little, and Patrick Alcedo each brought crucial support and guidance that helped me work through a politically challenging and nuanced topic. Norma Sue Fisher-Stitt was a steady advocate along the way. Participation and mentorship at the 2015 Mellon Dance Studies Summer Seminar (at Northwestern) provided pivotal workshop opportunities to develop the writing. And Damian Tarnopolsky (of Slingsby and Dixon Editorial Communications) and Samantha Mehra provided excellent early formatting and editing support. During the production phase, I thank the many members of the University of Wisconsin Press, including Sheila McMahon, Jennifer Conn, Ryan Pingel, and Amber Rose, copyeditor Mary Magray, and Derek Gottlieb of Scholarly Indexing.

Acknowledgments

I thank all the funding bodies that generously supported this research. In particular, I thank the Dancers Transition Resource Center, and Social Sciences and Humanities Research Council of Canada. I am grateful to the Canadian government for the system of parental support, which provided my partner with paternity pay for the duration of our time in Fiji. This enabled me to travel to Fiji with my partner, our young son, Eagon, and our newborn daughter, Imogen.

I am filled with gratitude and respect for the South Pacific Islanders on Vancouver Island and in Vancouver who contributed their knowledge to this study and patiently read interview transcripts, research summaries, and portions of the manuscript. In particular I thank Sefo Avaiki; Peni Tavutonivalu; Noa, Janet, and Sipili Molia; Emori Ralisa; Joe Fuailefau; Jack Morris; Isaac Bainivalu; Sala Alfred (Adi Salaseini Seruvatu Veikoso); and Mua Va'a. Most importantly, I thank Sefo and Sala for being an important part of my lifelong development as a person and for sharing their knowledge of Rotuma and Fiji and their love of the Pacific with me. I extend a deep thanks to Lavonne Gucake Donu, her husband, Matai, and Bavai Batibasiga in Vancouver for helping me meet with friends, family, and key meke organizations in Fiji. My project was enriched by their knowledge and the connections they enabled. I also thank individuals at the Fiji Canada Association (Rosy Pal, James Madhaven, Shane Dalwood, and Vincent Prakash), who helped me locate Fijians in Vancouver knowledgeable about meke.

On Vancouver Island, I thank the Pacific Peoples' Partnership and, in particular, April Ingham for introducing me to a broader base of Fiji scholars working around the globe. Ingham's efforts enabled important links to S. Aporosa, who, via email, introduced me to Sekove Degei Bigitibau, the past director of the iTaukei Institute of Language and Culture in Fiji. I appreciate the time these individuals took to explain the ethics of doing research among iTaukei (Indigenous Fijians).

In Fiji, I thank the library staff at University of the South Pacific's Pacific Collection, especially Lavenia Sau, who went out of her way to help me locate images and titles on meke as well as introduce me to the archivists at the National Archives of Fiji. At the national archives, I would like to acknowledge many past and current archivists, including Apakuki Pita Toga (past director), Director Opeta Alefaio, Josaia Nanuqa, Arieta Buliruarua, Jemesa Baleijamani, Vaciseva Levu, Timoci Balenaivalu, and Titilia Vusoniyasi, who were from beginning to end extremely helpful, thorough, and quick. At the iTaukei Institute for Language and Culture, I extend my sincere appreciation to Pita Tagicakirewa (past director) and especially Simione Sevudredre for supporting my research and taking time to discuss meke with me. As well, I thank Sachiko Miller (artistic director and founder of VOU Fiji dance company), Iosefo Kaliova (Cultural Center), Jiuta Tokula and members of the Nasikawa Meke Group, Kelera Batibasaga (Namatakula), and Master Lai Veikoso and his dancers (Conservatorium of Music) for sharing their knowledge, insights, and passion for meke.

I am most grateful to a number of individuals at University of South Pacific's Oceania Center for Art, Culture, and Pacific Studies. Vilsoni Hereniko and Peter Rockford Espiritu, who were at the Oceania Center during my time in Fiji and at the University of Hawai'i at Mānoa during my time in Hawai'i, deserve my deepest gratitude and respect. They generously welcomed me and my family and made us feel a part of the action at the Oceania Center, continuing to extend that generosity in Hawai'i and throughout the research and writing of this book. Hereniko and Espiritu introduced me to photographers Naoki Takyo and Konrad Thorpe, who have generously provided photos of Oceania Dance Theatre performing meke and meke fusions for this book. Hereniko also introduced me to Master Damiano Logaivau, one of my most important sources for understanding meke. I am indebted to Logaivau for his tireless efforts to share his extensive knowledge of meke, especially through his creating a meke for me to take back to Canada. I extend my respect to his partner Akeneta Dulunaqio Logaivau and children Mary Joseph D. Logaivau and Maria Paulo D. Logaivau. In addition to Logaivau, Dave Lavaki, Igelese Ete, and the artists and performers at the Oceania Center (Nisimere Bola, Jolame Cagi, Sorpapelu Tipo Fatiaki, Katalina Fotofili, Paula Liga, Glenville Lord, Saunikalou Qolivicicia, Fumaru Fatiaki, Ledua Peni, Kim Rova, Tulevu Soronakadavu, Etueni Tagivakatini, Epeli Tuibeqa, Sadrishan Velaidan, Peter Waqavonovono, Moira Samisoni, Benji Patel) were so welcoming, and many of these individuals have generously looked over dialogue, research summaries, and writing excerpts to ensure the accuracy of my understanding and analysis.

I continue to thank my mother for introducing me to Fiji and making the affective dimensions of loloma (kindly love), bula (to live, life) and vinaka vaka levu (deep gratitude and respect) part of my upbringing. I desire to say thank you to Anna Qumia from Namosi Province, who, wittingly or not, shared her care with my mother and, by extension, my family and has motivated this entire project. I would also like to recognize the Sisters at the Home of Compassion in Tamavua and Tarisi Vunidilo and her husband for helping me to share my appreciation with Qumia's surviving family members in Fiji.

I reserve my deepest gratitude to my family. My children (Eagon and Imogen) were so patient and provided much needed critical distance daily, and my dad, stepmom, and parents-in-law (Geoff Fulton, Lynn McDonald, and Jack and Judy Kelly) offered extensive childcare support throughout this research and writing process. My partner, Aaron Kelly, invested his own heart, soul, time, and energy in order to support, understand, and share in the work. His partnership in life has kept me thriving throughout this project.

My deepest thanks and gratitude to all! Vinaka vaka levu!

Note on Orthography

Generally, the Fijian alphabet follows the English one with the following exceptions:

    b is pronounced mb.
    c is pronounced th as in them.
    d is pronounced nd.
    g is pronounced ng as in sing.
    q is pronounced ngg as in anger.

Dancing Spirit,
Love, *and* War

Introduction

Fijian by Decree

It was July 2012 and I was in Fiji researching a Fijian song-dance tradition called meke. As a white Canadian citizen and daughter of a Fiji-born Canadian, I grew up on Vancouver Island, British Columbia, in constant contact with songs and dances of the South Pacific, including meke, with its geometric unison movements to the quick and percussive rhythms of chanting voices, clapping hands, and a slit drum. My (now deceased) mother strongly identified with her childhood memories of living in Fiji. But British colonialism structured her memories, as my Australian grandfather worked for the British colonial administration as a Fiji civil servant.

In Suva, Fiji's capital city, I was invited to attend and video-record the Conservatorium of Music's relatively new, but already nationally celebrated, meke performing group called Kabu ni Vanua, meaning morning mist of the land. Hearing beautiful voices singing from down the street, I followed the voices and entered a space in the Fiji Arts Council building where their rehearsal was in full swing. Master Lai Veikoso, the founding artistic director of the Conservatorium, was quickly becoming recognized as an expert on meke. The group regularly performed meke for tourists nationally and internationally as well as for the national stage in Fiji and abroad at large intergovernmental meetings. They had just returned home after representing Fiji at the Melanesian Spearhead Group meetings as part of Commodore Voreque (Frank) Bainamarama's entourage. Prime Minister Bainamarama had become the head of Fijian governance after his controversial military takeover in 2006.[1]

After entering the space, Master Lai warmly and generously introduced me to the Indigenous Fijian students and performers. Because my mother was born in Fiji, Master Lai said to the group and to me that I was also "Fijian." Critically aware of my family's colonial relation to Fiji, Master Lai's comment surprised me. Perhaps his words could be understood as aligning with the recent multiracial policies and discourses of the Fijian military government and the decree that all citizens of Fiji be referred to as "Fijian." The performers cheered and smiled in response to his statement. But the communication of joy seemed controlled and even forced and, as much as I would have loved to feel included, I know that I am not "Fijian." Instead, the hospitality of inclusion reminded me that my white body brought with it a colonial legacy that haunts Fiji's current political climate. I did not yet know it, but this haunting would impact everything I learned and wrote about meke.

The meke group practiced in a space indicative of the economic circumstances of Fiji's postcoup military state. The parking lot of the Fiji Arts Council building provided them with the space they needed. A single flood light lit the lot and the pavement was cracked and broken. Tourists would see a different image of meke: Indigenous Fijians performing in a romanticized imagining of the past with lush tropical paradise scenery. Despite the conditions, the chanters and dancers rehearsed for the next three hours with terrific force and energy.

During rehearsal, bodies were expressive in multiple ways. In one meke, the live polyphonic vocal chanting, cup-clapping of hands, and slit-drum rhythms began with a slower tempo.[2] The dancers gradually separated themselves from the ensemble of chanter/singers to sit and form two straight rows on the pavement facing the ensemble. Once the dancers were seated with legs crossed, upright spines, lengthened arms, and fists resting on knees, there was a moment of stillness. Then the central dancer called out, "meke," from his chest to signal to the group to begin. A high-pitched voice cut across the space from another direction to add to the energy and focus of the group. One voice from the ensemble began to sing and a second voice, pitched two tones higher, joined almost immediately for eight slow beats. On the last two beats, the dancers moved together quickly and sharply in unison to curve their spines, with wide elbows. They pounded their fists to the pavement over one knee and over the other. As the dancers moved, a low-pitched sound emanated from the chest of one of the dancers, which punctuated the force of the movement. While bodies moved together, the sounds sprang from varying points in the group, darting across the space in ways that spontaneously heightened the spirit and energy while connecting the group across time and space. Then, for four more slow beats, all the voices of the ensemble joined to build intensity in the feeling of suspension that was already thick in the air. Dancers slowly lifted their heads, letting their torsos follow their upward gaze to add to the four-beat anticipatory thickening. Then there was a feeling of freefall as the entire ensemble sang with incredible speed in close harmony while the dancers performed quick and rhythmically percussive movements in unison. The ensemble added levels of lightness and heaviness to the chant, generating a layered, visceral resonance while the dancers punctuated every beat with their bodies to build the chant's intensity. Pounding the broken pavement with their bare feet, legs, and hands, the dancers were precise and fast, fully synchronized with one another in their energy, enthusiasm, and muscular sharpness. Their spirit and energy were magnetic and electric.

After sustaining this energy and commitment for the duration of the rehearsal, they joined in a circle and held hands (as they later explained to me) to share with one another and create group spirit and respect on Christian terms. They said a Christian prayer and sang a hymn. Some of the dancers told me the group chose to finish rehearsal in this way because they were worried about the pre-Christian origins of the meke they had just rehearsed.

The group were to perform this meke for the upcoming 2012 national Fiji Day in celebration of Fijian independence. It was an interesting choice considering, I was told, that the meke was created around the time when Fiji was ceded to Britain in 1874. Despite the seemingly contradictory significance, watching them in performance at the Fiji Day celebrations, they were just as inspiring and exhilarating. As representative of Fiji's original settlers and landowners, who were now by decree "iTaukei," they were a strategic choice for the national Fiji Day celebrations.[3] They generated the spirit and feelings with which iTaukei viewers might want to identify: proudly Christian, living life to the fullest, generous, welcoming, and full of kindness and joy. Their meke articulated a celebration of Christian joy and national pride within the shadow of colonialism.

Dancing Spirit, Love, and War draws from my experiences growing up amid an Oceanic diaspora in Canada as well as fieldwork in Canada and Fiji in order to explore meke, Fiji's rich and powerful song-dance tradition, in relation to legacies of British Christian colonialism and post-2006-coup changes in Fijian governance.[4] Contemporary meke expresses Indigenous ownership, pride, and spirituality, while navigating government censorship, anti-meke sentiment from a growing evangelical Christian community, and racialized tensions between Indigenous Fijians and Fijians of Indian descent.

This book, and my experience researching and writing it, is also embedded within the fraught relations informed by my family's colonial history with Fiji and Fijians. Impacted by close to a century of British colonial rule (1874 to 1970), Fiji has had a tumultuous independence with four coups d'état since 1987. In that time, firm categories of race, ethnicity, and culture have governed gendered categories of citizenship and national belonging. My family, who lived in Fiji between 1937 and 1945, is implicated in Fiji's colonial history, as my grandfather worked for Fiji's British colonial administration as a mining engineer and inspector. With this history in mind, *Dancing Spirit, Love, and War* aims to decenter colonial legacies that seek to control and contain bodies, identities, and cultures through processes of governance. As I hope the opening account begins to reveal, however, I remain suspicious of the particular knowledge my own fraught position and perspective might produce and invite readers to do the same. Thus, this book also centralizes uncertainty and research as a site for change and exchange to pose a challenge to ownership over knowledge.

The racialized body politics of negotiating identity in postindependence Fiji have created tensions that have divided dance forms.[5] In light of Fiji's most recent 2006 military coup in the name of multiracial harmony and antiracism, Fijians have been renegotiating "Fijianness" in performances of meke that sometimes blur and other times maintain race-based boundaries. In the context of shifting biopolitical terrains of power—whereby heritage and body politics interconnect in new categories of citizenship and national belonging—this book explores how and why meke plays a role in the postindependence politics of Fijian identity formation.[6] It places meke in relation to Fiji's evolving political and religious landscape, while also considering the significant role of meke in Fijian tourism and diasporic identity.

Members of Fiji's disparate diaspora in multicultural Canada are renegotiating these political and historical contexts. Because Canada has one of Fiji's oldest diaspora populations, which has grown significantly because of the coups, the relations and migrations between Fiji and Canada are ongoing and part of a continuing renegotiation of Fiji Canadian identity.[7] Throughout, I aim to demonstrate the migratory relationship between

Canada and Fiji as it is laden with political struggles for nation-state inclusion. Therefore, most chapters weave back and forth between Fiji and Canada as a reminder of this migration and to demonstrate the relationships, hauntings, and reciprocities as they occurred in my research. Culture and identity, although emerging out of particular experiences, are not fixed and bounded by geographic sites but renegotiated translocally—across time and space.

The linchpin of this exploration is that meke experiences and expressions (as relationally felt and sensed) activate and transform political tensions and identifications with nation, ethnicity, and culture for practitioners of meke in Canada and Fiji. Using original ethnographic and archival research

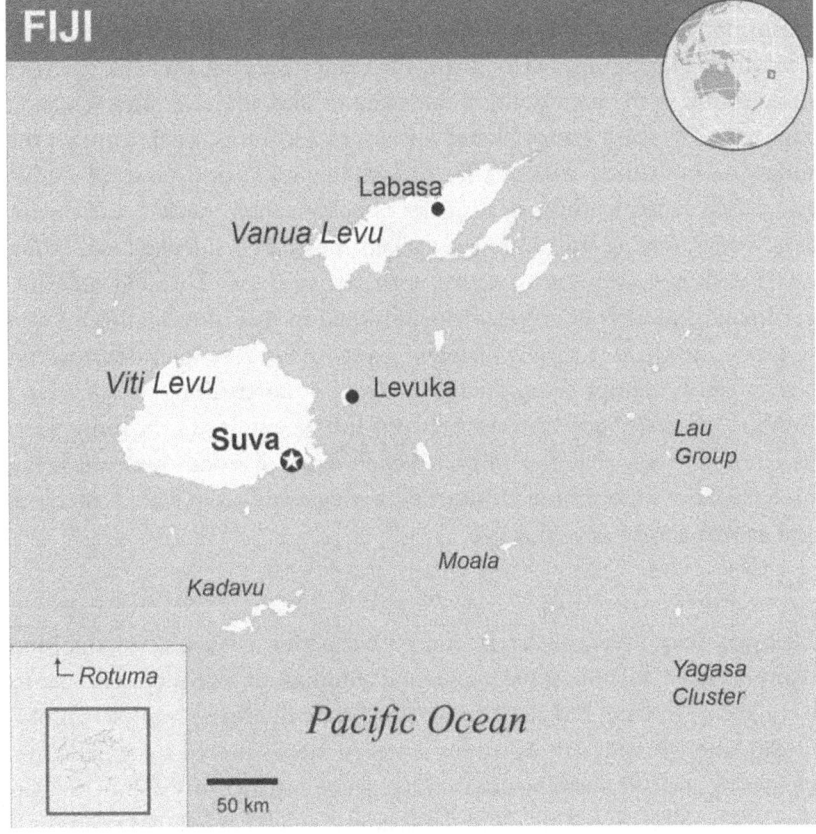

Figure I.1. Map of Fiji. Based on OCHA (UN Office for the Coordination of Humanitarian Affairs) map. Wiki Commons.

conducted in Viti Levu, Fiji, the largest of Fiji's islands (figure I.1), and among Fiji's diaspora between 2011 and 2015, I examine examples of meke that show how expressions, such as spirit, love, and war, go beyond mere reflections and surface representations of culture and ethnicity and instead expose how they actively generate culture and identity. In addition, I explore how and why meke enables Fijians to move through, with, and against Christian colonial narratives and discourses that divide Fijians by treating them as ethnically and racially homogenous yet distinct groups. Ultimately, these examples show that, while felt memories and Christian colonial legacies haunt, Fijians generate and express new articulations of identity through meke that emerge in relation to new connections to place and/or new political spaces and maneuvers.

Despite the cultural, historical, and political significance of meke as a performance practice, there is very limited scholarly writing on meke, and what little writing does exist leaves the reader wanting more in terms of understanding the sociopolitical, kinesthetic, and affective intricacies and nuances of its form transnationally. I aim to address this gap through the following multisited, kinesthetic, autoethnographic, and political study.[8] Each chapter works through histories of colonization, racism, and migration, while moving toward Fijian dancers' postindependence reclamation of danced expression as an active, relational process. Through reflexive, yet fraught, models of engagement (outlined in this introduction), I aim to create a space for ongoing dialogue—a space for questions, debates, and challenges. I attempt to productively expose countervailing pressures and rhythms of reciprocity at work between Indigenous and non-Indigenous exchange in ways that also impact meke—at a crossroads between being understood as an object of culture and heritage and as an active, effective, and evolving expressive practice.

Meke: A Choreographic and Strategic Tradition

Meke is a ubiquitous and diverse Indigenous performance practice tradition that predates Christian missionaries and colonial contact and continues to be linked to shifts in Fijian identifications. As with other Melanesian, Polynesian, and Micronesian dance forms, missionaries played a dramatic role in altering and often wiping out the knowledge and memory of much Fijian dance. Therefore, it is difficult to assess how much the missionary and colonial presence in Fiji altered meke.[9] Authenticity, however, is not necessary for people to engage a practice or attitude in order to affirm a national or local identity with ties to the past that feels authentic. In other words, what becomes traditional or customary are not simply persisting beliefs and practices that have remained the same for a long period of time. Instead, as Oceania scholar Nicholas Thomas argued, they are "selective construct[s] defined partly in opposition to foreign ways or intrusions."[10] Bodies performing meke generate emergent meaning grounded in the current realities of what it feels like to be Fijian in Fiji and diaspora. Using choreography as an analytical framework for understanding the social and political relations of bodies in motion, this book shows how meke configures shifting identifications and social membership.[11]

Expanding on studies of Fijian and Oceanic customs of practice, I understand performed expressions in and around tradition in Fiji as politically and strategically choreographic and actively stabilizing and destabilizing culture and identity.[12] Meke, as a staged performance of tradition, is part of negotiating local and national identities, sovereignty, and notions of belonging.[13] This approach to cultural convention counters earlier writing that romanticized meke as a form of essentialized cultural authenticity. For example, in writing about a traditional Fijian men's spear dance called meke wesi in the late 1970s, dancer and critic Beth Dean Carell wrote: "The eerie excitement developed is such that as rhythms grow faster and faster the symbolic atmosphere of the spear thrust movements takes on a timelessness as though it were all a kind of subconscious record, the imprint in ancient memory of a single mighty thrust by one great antediluvian warrior who overcame all adversaries."[14] While this performance may have been choreographed to give spectators the impression of a larger-than-life iTaukei warrior fixed in a precontact past, Carell's writing erases the politics and economics of making the antediluvian iTaukei warrior through performance as well as the unique context in which the meke was created and performed. Although Carell wrote to centralize the meaning and importance of Indigenous dance practices, here I share a concern with dance scholar and ethnographer Rachmi Diyah Larasati about the violence that vanishes in nation-state representations of "traditional" dance, which, in this case, is compounded by Carell's description of the meke.[15] Indeed, meke for the national and international stage has largely supported a conservative Christian ethnonational notion of Fiji, erasing over 130 years of Indo-Fijian presence and influence. To mitigate this, I follow dance and Pacific studies scholar Katerina Teaiwa's work on "choreographing difference" in Fiji to examine how dance in Fiji choreographs the past as a way to strategically express particular histories and postcolonial identities.[16] Teaiwa's work on popular dance in Fiji and Fiji's New Zealand diaspora is also instructive for the ways she demonstrates dance as a medium for moving beyond divisive postcolonial politics.[17] My exploration of meke demonstrates how the cultural conventions of meke are not immutable but shift to suit the needs of Fijians living in particular times and places, which are constantly changing owing to a myriad of global forces (such as migration, Christian colonialism, neoliberal economic adjustments, transnational nongovernmental organizations [NGOs], and evangelical church networks).

Although meke differ widely, and it is not the aim of this book to generate singular notions of meke, there are some features, trends, and shifts worth noting for the purposes of understanding the current negotiations of identity this book explores. Throughout this book, meke refers to a traditional dance genre involving the performance of rhymed verse, animated through song and choreographed movement with instrumental accompaniment. While the term also refers generally to the act of dancing, meke is commonly understood not to include European-derived music and Western popular dance.[18] In a calibration of rhythmic verse, sounds, and movements, dancers perform (often in unison) to live polyphonic vocal chanting and rhythms often set by a single lali (slit drum) or bamboo tubes and cobo (cup-clapping the hands). Meke can be done sitting, standing, and with or without fans, spears, and clubs. In particular, this book examines examples of the ways in which meke wesi (spear meke), meke wau (club meke), meke iri (meke with a fan), seasea (women's standing meke), and vakamalolo (sitting meke) carry meaning and significance that moves with and beyond nominalized representations and objectifications of Fijian culture and heritage. These examples show how expressive bodies, while situated in time and place, also extend in relation to time, place, spirits, and human and nonhuman bodies.

The organization of bodies in performances of meke suggests the complex ways in which notions of power, culture, and identity are changing for Fijians. In Fiji, it is not uncommon to have several dozens of Fijians doing meke at once on an open field, called rara, using sounds, rhythms, and movements to connect across time and space. In Canada and in Fiji's tourist resorts there are fewer performers, who often need to fit onto a small stage. Whereas gender and race once strictly divided meke performances, today some performances of meke appear to transcend these boundaries, as exemplified in the image of a 2012 contemporary meke performed by

Oceania Dance Theatre (figure I.2).[19] Yet within post-2006-coup choreographic renderings of inclusion and harmony (including a Fiji Day military parade and the transnational migrations of bodies), kinesthetic bodies also generate choreographies of ethnonational power and politics that perpetuate firm boundaries of race, in part through the performance of gender.

Meke were (and continue to be) created for social and ceremonial purposes involving many protocols that are customary yet changing to adjust to new circumstances.[20] Meke can be performed at social and political events as entertainment, in connection with ritual, and in the recounting of stories (formal, informal, real, and fictional). Meke traditions are not unified but vary from village to village and province to province because they are based on specific pre-Christian ties to ancestral gods called kalou vu, from which lines of common descent are traced and customs are informed.[21] As a result, although there are larger governing confederacies that have become culturally dominant voices for tradition and custom (such as Bau—the preeminent ruling chiefdom when Britain ceded Fiji), there is not one set of meke that are considered true, authentic, and original to Fiji as a whole. Each province has its own choreographic aesthetic and its own harmonic, stanza, and strophic style. Despite the variances, Fijians have frequently

Figure I.2. Oceania Dance Theatre Meke Fusion. University of the South Pacific, Laucala. Photo by Naoki Takyo.

explained to me that if someone wants to perform a meke they need to approach the daunivucu (meke choreographer/composer) who created it, or the chief of the village from which the meke came, and make a proper request by following certain protocols involving gift exchange. While some protocols such as this are still practiced, meke serve different purposes and involve new protocols when they are also performed for staged productions, national and intergovernmental events in Fiji and abroad, in diaspora, for tourists in Fiji, and for Fiji tourism promotion internationally.

My understanding of meke as a tradition that shifts to suit present processes of identity and culture formation may be in opposition to certain ethnonational and international objectives (such as UNESCO) that seek to define, safeguard, and utilize unified notions of Fijian cultural heritage. Taking an approach that shows the constructedness of meke as a tradition runs the risk of undermining iTaukei rights movements and perpetuating a legitimating of white postcolonial authority. Yet, as I hope to show in the following sections, equally insidious is the act of turning cultural heritage into a static, unified object of culture, as this perpetuates legacies of British Christian colonialism that diminish the processes through which culture emerges and privileges one voice over many.

New Biopolitical Terrain

The post-2006-coup shifts in Fiji's political, religious, and economic ecology have changed the way power operates in Fiji. With new categories of citizenship imposed by decree, renegotiating identity has to do with a process of generating new feelings and sensations of Fijianness. Meke is central to this renegotiation.

A brief understanding of Fiji's unique colonial history helps situate meke within shifting political relations of power. Fiji encountered close to a century of British colonial rule from 1874 to 1970. From the establishment of the Colonial Sugar Refinery in 1880 until 1916, Indian indentured laborers were brought to Fiji and the refinery exploited their labor.[22] By 1921 the Fijian population had declined dramatically due to disease introduced by Europeans (between 1879 to 1921 the total population dropped by approximately twenty-five thousand people to roughly eighty-five thousand), the Indian population had reached over sixty thousand in roughly forty years, and the ruling European population had reached just under four thousand.[23] The 1930s and 1940s (when significant amounts of gold were discovered) marked the increased presence of British subjects with mining expertise and their families.[24] This is the context in which my grandfather and grandmother came to Fiji from Australia. By the 1940s Indians and Fiji-born Indians outnumbered iTaukei Fijians.[25] But for the most part, only those considered native to Fiji could own land, an enduring policy that continues to impact land ownership today.[26] Such policies of land ownership inform a continuation of racially charged political dynamics for Fijians in Fiji and its Canadian diaspora. Many Fijians and Fiji scholars place tensions involving "ethnic" identity at the center of political instability in Fiji, together with the inheritance of British colonial strategies and legacies of governance and control.[27]

Church and state have historically been closely allied in Fiji, in part through Fijian customs of practice.[28] In its early days in Fiji, the Wesleyan Methodist Church, which sent some of the first Christian missionaries to Fiji, interwove itself within the vanua (iTaukei customs and practices of the land) and reconfigured Fijian identities and their connections to the vanua as Christian.[29] During colonial rule, the power of this link between Wesleyan Methodism and Fijian custom supported a hegemonic hierarchy; colonial administrators and primarily Methodist chiefs held positions of power, and the chiefs were representative of the vanua.[30] Until recently, traditional practices and protocols, including meke, have maintained this hierarchical formation of power. But Bainimarama's 2006 coup has changed this structuring of power.

Fiji's post-2006-coup military government and current democratically elected government, both led by Frank Bainimarama in the name of multiracial harmony, "good governance, anti-racism, and anti-corruption," claim to be striving toward governance based on a new biopolitical arrangement.[31] Since Bainimarama's 2012 Fiji government decree that shifted the definition of "Fijian" to include all citizens of Fiji regardless of descent but, at the same time, sustained a racial distinction by insisting all Indigenous Fijians be referred to as iTaukei, body politics appear to have been rearranged. As Giorgio Agamben has argued, the tethering of bodies to categories of identity enables the governance of bodies by formations of hierarchical power.[32] Yet, while the decree aims to fix and actualize Fijians by their definitions in new categories for new forms of top-down governance, the most recent application of the terms "Fijian" and "iTaukei" destabilizes and challenges previously established race-based categories of citizenship and puts into motion new targets of inclusion and exclusion. Changed boundaries of belonging develop through a narrative process of decontextualizing culture and identity by removing sociopolitical histories of colonialism and then reterritorializing, or widening, culture and identity on the latest multiracial terms that celebrate harmony through diversity. This shifting biopolitical terrain creates a space for political maneuvering, where new possibilities to feel and sense one's identity emerge in and around Fijian customs, such as meke.

Both Canada and Fiji, through discourses of multiculturalism and multiracialism, respectively, have encouraged the objectification of culture and cultural heritage as part of identity-forming and nation-building narratives of belonging. While there is a difference in the tactics of inclusion and exclusion in these two separate locales, with one based on ethnicity and the other based on racial hierarchy, Canadian and Fijian governments use narratives of belonging as a strategy to mend deep colonial divides formed along lines of ethnicity and race by generating common identifications with the nation-state and its narratives of diversity. Events that showcase multicultural or multiracial diversity, such as cultural heritage festivals, often function in this way. Nevertheless, such events cluster immigrants and minorities into homogenous, distinct groups and then marginalize those who do not fit into the parameters of accepted societal norms upon which discourses of belonging are based.[33] In Fiji and, to a lesser extent, Canada, inclusion reflects a predominantly Christian ethos, thereby excluding Fijians who are not Christian, particularly those of Indian descent who are mostly Hindu or Muslim. Additionally, in relying on ethnic or racialized bodies as homogenous representations and significations of past times in other places and cultures, multicultural and multiracial discourses and practices in some ways perpetuate British colonial hierarchies that stereotype the ethnic and racialized homogenous Other rooted in pastness. The result is a failure to acknowledge and theorize how cultures and identities merge and change, while bodies continue to be read through cultural heritage practices as racially fixed.

In addition to new categories of multiracial citizenship in Fiji, whereby the governance of bodies continues to be imposed as a vertical and hierarchical formation of power, horizontal governance also organizes bodies. While church and state still co-constitute much of the way power organizes itself, there are redistributive forces at work in redirecting power to transnational organizations that, as anthropologist Charles Piot has said, govern without government.[34] Specifically, the hierarchical governance of the Great Council of Chiefs, Methodist Church pastor, and dictator (turned prime minister) is giving way to the horizontal governance of transnational organizations. These organizations include NGOs, which are involved in human rights issues, self-help, and family planning; intergovernmental organizations (such as the Pacific Islands Forum, the Asian Pacific Bank, and the Commonwealth), which eventually suspended Fiji from participation prior to Fiji's most recent democratic election in 2014; and evangelical and charismatic churches (such as born-again Christians, Assemblies of God, The Apostles, and New Methodists, among others), which encourage democratic, interpersonal, and small-group worship as well as transnational mission work. Thus, in 2012 bodies in Fiji were governed by externally imposed military rule as well as more horizontal formations of power emerging from transnational organizations and churches that were generating moral and social reforms through self-governance.[35] But biopolitics in Fiji are also contradictory in that bodies are not only controlled by formations of power rooted in the past but are also agentive and generative of not-yet charted futures through relational contact with other bodies.

Governance in Fiji is also relational, or transcorporeal, in the realm of performed experience and expression. By experience I refer to the body as inextricably linked with other phenomena.[36] Expressing here refers to a body that transmits or communicates by extending toward another. In particular, affects—intensities, energies, and emotions—expressed kinesthetically in the visceral sensibilities, movements, rhythms, and sounds emerging between bodies are central to the ways in which bodies communicate.[37] In meke, stable signs and signifiers, which depend on prior knowledge to generate meaning, do not reduce the body to the past and knowable, categorical flesh. Instead, kinesthetically visceral and transcorporeal experiences and expressions have generated culture and identity and yet have remained to a degree "in(sinew)ated with power relations" that permeate the body, its practice, and its performance.[38] Governance through expression occurs through relationally felt and sensed intensities, making the directionality of power more horizontal. This is not to say that horizontal formations of power have removed inequities but that control happens through relational encounters that produce, reproduce, and distribute power. In focusing on the body as generative of power relations and not just an effect of power that has been inscribed on the body, this book explicates how meke involves multidimensional relations out of which something more thick emerges. The muscular effort, rhythms, and sounds of meke are part of securing

Fiji's future as a tourists' paradise, an Indigenous Christian nation-state, and an economically prosperous multiracial democracy.

Expressing Spirit, Love, and War

As part of understanding power and politics in relation to bodies performing meke, this book focuses on examples of meke that generate power between bodies through expressions of spirit, love, and war. Spirit, love, and war, as the primary affective through lines to this book, are actively and socially distributing and disrupting Fijian normative values and are expressions by which power locally and translocally organizes and governs. Through these dynamic articulations, postcolonial meke governs, generates, and transcends differences in power and material circumstances. As performance studies scholar José Esteban Muñoz has argued, national norms are activated through the affective performance of ethnic and racial normativity.[39] The meke this book explores theatricalizes cultural change, power, resistance, and agency through modes of feeling Fijian in a world still organized by the cultural legacies of white, British, Christian colonialism that aim to contain and control bodies, cultures, and identities.

Despite colonial and postcolonial attempts to substantivize and nominalize it as an object of Fijian culture and heritage, meke exists at the crossroads of competing and changing views, interests, and interpretations.[40] In meke, the body and its movements, experiences, and expressions are linked with emergent meaning and are, therefore, generative of culture and identity. With this in mind, I trace expressions not as fixed categories but as shifting and indeterminate operations of power entwined with identity and culture in Fiji and Fiji's diaspora.

The notion of spirit in relation to meke exemplifies the colonial and postcolonial restructuring of the form as a substance or thing as well as what transmissions of spirit in meke do. While missionaries translated the Bible into Fijian and, in the process, nominalized and substantivized spirits into a supernatural substance,[41] spirit performed in meke challenges dominant religious politics by showing that despite the Christian concern in Fiji with separating the spirits of ancestors (whom missionaries named as devils and demons in the Fijian Bible) from the living, body and spirit are not bifurcated. In the context of growing religious anxieties in Fiji, the porous relationship between flesh and spirit results in a constant and political negotiation of proximity and distance with felt and sensed spirit. In meke, spirit is relational and ephemeral when it excites, instigates, or stirs up an audience. Communications of spirit can cause hairs to stand on end and unknowable or unnerving feelings that disrupt the status quo. Some Fijian dancers and daunivucus are reclaiming the Fijian spiritual life-energy concept of mana as a source of immediate action and efficacy in meke. This approach to mana supports an understanding of the expressive body in relation to the world as generative of power and political authority. The notion that meke generates mana demonstrates power emerging between bodies in motion. Yet, in meke, performative expressions that emerge between bodies can also be implicated in colonial and postcolonial formations of power, making mana in meke a political site for social change.

I use the concept of haunting to refer to unresolved colonial systems of abusive power that materialize in and around the performance of meke. Hauntings animate the violence of colonialism—a violence that tried to diminish the enabling power of ancestor spirits and retain only the culture and heritage aspects that served dominant colonial modernity and social evolutionary discourses. But the haunting presence of ancestor spirits blurs distinctions between life and death, material and nonmaterial, human and nonhuman, and disrupts bodily containment and the firm categories of identity and being established by colonialism. Living memories that resist such legacies also disrupt the present in the transmission of meke movements, protocols, and techniques. Additionally, as Diana Taylor has argued, ghosts and specters take on a life of their own in performance.[42] In other words, hauntings and memories carry no fixed meanings but change according to current circumstances. In the meke this book explores, I focus on how the past lives, is active, and has efficacy in the moving, expressive body to impact future outcomes.[43]

Through a process of generating spiritual efficacy, meke also reclaims the notion that bodies extend across time and space in relation to other bodies.[44] Tongan scholar 'Okusitino Māhina and Fijian scholar Unaisi Nobobo-Baba have affirmed the notion that bodies are part of a continuum between past and future in relation to spiritual and environmental realities.[45] Such a view of the body as indistinguishable from the world allows for an analysis of relational and integrative bodies, as opposed to a self-contained, concrete, and predetermined category of being. Movement and sound do not originate in, belong to, or become contained by individual bodies. Rather, in meke, the body is always in a state of emergence through its movements and sounds (such as the spontaneous vocal calls I describe in the opening that connect bodies across space) in relation to other human and nonhuman bodies (such as animals, plants, costumes) and ephemera (such as sounds, light, memories, spirits, visceral feelings and sensations, and future potentials). Meke has an integrative character with respect to its environment that includes material and nonmaterial co-presences. The source of movement and sound in meke is the incorporation of these phenomena.[46]

Notions of love, or Fijian loloma, are equally laden with power and politics. For example, the definition of loloma I read about in the work of the anthropologist Martha Kaplan, although somewhat binary and romanticizing, suggests loloma comes from "indigenous readings of the missionary tenet of kindly love . . . , the term with which Fijians nowadays characterize 'life in the way of the land'" and as a freely given gift explicitly in opposition to European or Indo-Fijian "life in the way of money."[47] While loloma was once a powerful part of a gift economy that iTaukei used to distinguish themselves from the perceived selfishness of foreigners, now, because of larger liberal economic forces, loloma has widened to take on additional meanings that produce new effects. With shifts in power and economics, loloma is embedded within larger transnational market forces that influence meke. Loloma expressed in meke makes the song-dance appealing and marketable for the tourist industry. In some contexts, loloma contributes to a Christianized "us" versus heathen "them" mentality. In other multicultural or multiracial contexts, loloma widens to include all regardless of religion and descent in Fiji and as it migrates to diaspora. In each of these contexts, loloma continues to shape the core of how iTaukei perceive their traditions and culture.[48]

Expressions of war can be viewed as equally central to iTaukei (and larger Oceanian) perceptions of culture, identity, tradition, and national belonging. In a meke war challenge, or bole, the ancient power and physical strength of the masculine iTaukei warrior is rendered in the muscular strength, range of motion, sharpness, force, and readiness as well as the heightened spirit and aggressiveness of the challenge. Through such referrals to the past, gendered expressions interconnect with nationalist ones to imagine and affect Fiji's future. Sometimes the past is romanticized as a time of great and powerful antediluvian warriors. Other times, warriors of the past are considered with reverence and respect as powerful role models for battling the present-day challenges of life. Some, who view the past as a time of heathenism, reject all meke associated with war. Renditions of the powerful warrior, described by interlocutors as "aggressively masculine" also migrate to Canada in performances of meke in ways that generate a sense of belonging,⁴⁹ while expressions of warrior ancestors are believed to be innately part of the iTaukei body. At the same time, in the space of political maneuver opened up by Fiji's post-2006 coup and in diaspora, such transmissions are contradictory. Recently, transgendered iTaukei, Fijians of Indian descent, and other peoples of Oceania are performing war meke for the national stage, thereby troubling firm categories of race, sex, and gender. Insofar as three of the four postindependence coups d'état were military takeovers, I treat the coups and other national stagings of military might as postcolonial expressions of war.

I have paid close attention to moments of indeterminacy when affects were not performed within normalized registers of comportment—when my interlocutors explained that their autonomic responses were the result of too much spirit, too much sad, or too much fear and not enough sharp, fast, muscular rhythmic punctuation and readiness to express a sanctioned amount of spirit, love, and war. These ephemeral responses, as the "glimmers, residues, and specks of things," have a subversive potential to work against the sanctioned registers of Christian, gendered, and racialized comportment.⁵⁰ This is not to say that bodies are dichotomous or stable/unstable binary opposites but to say that bodies are never wholly fixed within categories even when they appear to be. Beyond the subversive importance of recognizing the rich potential of ephemera as evidence, in the context of Fiji's shifting yet tightly strung biopolitical arrangements, surface representations and material evidence cannot easily be trusted as readable texts of Fiji's politically lived realities. Instead, felt intensities expressed in, and surrounding, meke became evidence of political frictions, exposing the directionality of a multitude of Fijian desires for the future.⁵¹ In this book, these expressions converge with questions of cultural heritage, governance, agency, identity, migration, and social relations and obligations to form the focus of my analysis.

Models for Engagement: Addressing Epistemic Violence

Prior to going to Fiji, Fijian pastor Dr. Netani Gucake invited me to come to his service at the Foursquare Church of Fiji in Vancouver's suburb of Surrey. I had been interviewing his Fiji-born daughter, Lavonne Gucake Donu, about a Christian-themed meke she created for one of their church fundraising events. Her father was the pastor of one of the three Fijian churches in the Vancouver area, all of which were Pentecostal and mostly attended by Fiji Canadians of iTaukei descent. Unlike the Fijian Methodists who have migrated to Canada over the last few decades and who want to preserve and share their culture, traditions, and heritage, with which they still strongly identify, many Fijian Pentecostal migrants are ready to reject the past in search of "better" futures.

Getting to the church was an indicator of the social and economic marginalization of Canada's newcomers. I traveled for several hours to arrive at the location of the church, positioned so remotely in relation to Vancouver. My ability to travel there by choice, and not out of economic necessity, was a reminder of my privileged freedom to travel and move through space. When I arrived, Gucake Donu generously guided me to the room where the service was taking place. Inside there was beautiful live singing and music being played and lots of dancing out the words from the participants of the service. Fijians and some Caucasian Canadians, who had married into the Fijian community, comprised the group. There were no Fijians of Indian descent, which was not a surprise considering that many of them are Hindu. Yet this gathering was a reminder that the racial and religious tensions felt in Fiji continue to exist in diaspora. The group sang and danced for forty-five minutes in English and Fijian before any words were spoken. Even when the speaking began, music continued to punctuate the service for the next hour and a half.

Aware of my family's relationship to Fiji and my research on meke, Pastor Gucake and his wife, Diana, asked me to share the motivations for my research project during the service. I was at the beginning of my process, so I explained that my project, initiated after my mother passed away, was intended to honor her relationship to Anna Qumia, the Fijian nanny and domestic laborer my grandparents employed. I described how my mother's recollection of Fiji was an important part of how she came to identify herself, and her loving memories of Qumia gave her comfort, strength, and the ability to survive many hardships. The participants of the service seemed to feel the magnitude of this sentiment. It moved many to ask how they could help. Their generosity was overwhelming. At the same time, these feelings of care, support, and connection were not indicative of sameness. Instead they challenged me to consider the moral uncertainties and deep divisions embedded in my past and activated by my performative testimony.

Although feelings and sensations of intensity were relationally generated, I was about to learn how those who were present did not feel them in the same way, making affect political and forever changing the dynamics of my research and writing. During the service, Pastor Gucake explained to those present that I had shared with him photos of Fiji taken by my grandfather. Among the photos were pictures of Fiji's Vatukoula gold mine, a mine my grandfather inspected during his time living in Fiji in the 1930s and 1940s. Pastor Gucake explained that his grandfather, who cared for him as a child, died in the 1950s when the chimneystack in one of the images collapsed on him. As he shared this experience, he subtly, yet powerfully, shed light on the physical impact of colonialism while actively and effectively changing the dynamics of our relations. Despite these unexpected memories, Pastor Gucake was willing to continue our conversation. These feelings formed a part of the relational pact that emerged during the church service through intensities that were transmitted between our moving, expressing bodies—bodies implicated in formations of power.

Throughout my research and writing, I have been highly attuned to the politics of being a white Canadian settler and granddaughter of British colonial Fiji's inspector of mines and mining engineer writing about iTaukei Fijian traditions. The ethics and politics of my conducting research among iTaukei Fijians is rife with potential problems and even a kind of "epistemic violence," as dance scholar Adria Imada has put it.[52] To address this potential violence, I drew from dance, performance, and Pacific Indigenous studies to inform my primary modes for engagement: reciprocity, long-term and long-distance relations, movement exchange, ephemera as archive, and autoethnography. Yet my attempts to mitigate the potential violence through my choices and modes of engagement were always fraught. Throughout this book, I openly address the privilege and power dynamics that emerged during my research and writing.

As a non-Indigenous researcher, it was important for me to observe not only the ethical protocols of my university but also the Indigenous protocols of conducting research in Fiji, of which gifting is central. As mentioned earlier, the transmission of meke is itself explicitly related to Fijian practices of gift exchange, making it all the more important that I pay close attention to gifting protocols. Nabobo-Baba has argued that gifting is a long-standing way of knowing in Fiji, and while the form of a gift might change, the principle remains that of enhancing relations among Fijians.[53] Relations between people revolve around gifting, and respectful research in Fiji needs to account for the importance of reciprocity as a protocol of relationships, knowledge acquisition, and respect for the support and resources given to researchers.[54]

While recognizing that gift exchange is an important Fijian model for engagement, my problematic relationship to the project also skewed my approach to reciprocity. The research for this book began with the naïve intention of trying to make a gift of return. Out of respect for my mother's loving memories of Fiji and her Fijian nanny, Anna Qumia, which she shared with me as she raised me, I wanted to give something back to honor those memories and feelings. Despite these intentions, my personal relationship to the topic created some powerful blind spots and challenges. When I asked myself, "To whom do I give?," I realized how much had been hidden from view. What was Qumia's experience of being a nanny for an Australian family working for the British colonial administration? What were the economic and political dimensions of Qumia's caregiving? In what ways did colonial forces shape my mother's memories and love, and my own romanticization of them? It took the writing of this book to realize how notions of giving *and* giving back are heavily loaded with ethical complexity.

As a child, I did not question the stories about how the Fijian war clubs, the masi (patterned bark cloth), the tanoa (kava) bowl, the lali (slit drum),[55] and the tabua (whale tooth of high ceremonial value in Fiji) were given to my grandfather. The tabua itself, designed to circulate as a ceremonial gift of exchange, now sits in its own glass box in the home of a relative. These "gifts" were, in some ways, reduced to passive things and taken—if only out of circulation—for private viewing. As a child, it made perfect sense to me that, since these items were "given" to my grandfather, these objects now belonged to his children and grandchildren. Although I never met him, they served as indicators that he must have been a good person, who made some kind of noteworthy geological contribution to Fiji. It wasn't until I had begun my fieldwork that I began to understand that these items were indicative of a much larger issue of incommensurability between Indigenous Fijian and Euro-colonial perspectives about gift exchange. As Nabobo-Baba has pointed out: "Differences between the epistemologies of indigenous Fijians and colonialists had (and have) the potential to create serious misunderstandings. For example, as a result of the Fijian process of "gifting"—a process that meant different things to the acquisitive white man and the native—a lot of land was removed from native landowners and recorded as belonging to new settlers (colonizers)."[56] While I am not suggesting all Fijian gift exchange is the same, I also began to recognize the active long-term, long-distance social potential of these material objects—they were not simply nominal things that could be owned as personal private property.

The "gifts" I grew up with were not only in the form of material culture; they also existed as ephemeral affects in my mother's memories of Fiji and Qumia that, for specific reasons, formed a deep sense of her identity. To be clear, I believe my mother remembered and expressed her early childhood experiences of Fiji as particularly important and meaningful in relation to the painful life experiences that followed. For example, as a young woman, my mother was also the direct recipient of a British colonial legacy of gendered abuse when she became a victim of Australia's institutionalized forced adoption practices—the removal of babies from unwed mothers for adoption without their consent and against their will to prevent so-called racial decay.[57] Despite those who attempted to strip her of her identity and all that was meaningful to her during her placement in a home for unwed mothers, she used her childhood memories of Fiji to maintain a sense of inner strength and identity. Her fiercely anti-colonial perspective that developed from these experiences regularly made its way into our everyday lives and formed my understanding of British colonialism. As my mother's child, I resist undermining her memories and sentimental connections to Qumia. Still, performance ethnographer Dwight Conquergood, quoting Tzvetan Todorov, urged researchers to consider, "Can we really love someone if we know little or nothing of his identity, if we see, in place of that identity, a projection of ourselves or ideals? . . . Doesn't one culture risk trying to transform the other in its own name, and therefore risk subjugating it as well? How much is such love worth?"[58]

My mother would have known very little about Qumia, and I know even less. Taking the naïve stance of returning a gift of love would prevent me from questioning the social formations in which my family came to know Qumia. Even worse, my eagerness to respect and honor Qumia ran the risk of romanticizing her and even reproducing colonial subjugation by reifying and reducing her to the love in my mother's memories.[59] Love was proving to be a feeling of intensity full of power as well as potential neocolonial violence.[60] As someone whose intentions are intertwined with my family's colonial time in Fiji, I needed to be sensitive and reflexive about the processes and effects of gift exchange.

In addition to engaging with reciprocity, I also paid close attention to negotiations of power and privilege over time and space through multisited research. The majority of the multisited research for this book occurred over the course of two years (between 2011 and 2012) and is primarily the result of ethnographic fieldwork and archival research in Victoria and Vancouver, Canada, and Viti Levu, Fiji.[61] In the summer of 2015, I also spent time reconnecting with Fiji's Oceania Dance Theatre during their residency at University of Hawai'i at Mānoa—after Fiji's highly contested 2014 democratic election. My choice to focus on performances of meke in multiple sites helped me to gain a clearer sense of how and why Fijians were performing meke in differing ways and in resonance with local and national politics in Fiji and diaspora. In addition, the long-term connections spanned a crucial period of change in Fiji and enabled me to see the effects of these changes translocally. For example, my follow-up interviews with Oceania Dance Theatre dancers and Fijians living in Fiji's Hawaiian diaspora revealed that some Methodist Fijians had left Fiji because they believed Bainimarama's government was undermining their once privileged status and belonging. In Hawai'i, I was also invited to learn and observe two of the meke I analyze in this book. The meke, said to be enriched with Fijian mana, were believed to have generated mana translocally when performed in Hawai'i. Thus, my engagement with meke and its practitioners in multiple geographic sites revealed local and translocal expressions and stagings of meke as well as meke as a means to renegotiate identity. But it also brought attention to the privileges and barriers to global movements and migrations, including my own, and who gets to move, where, when, and how.

Connecting with Fijians in diaspora enabled a level of freedom for my interlocutors to speak about Fiji's politically contentious issues. Interviewing Fijians outside of Fiji was particularly important in the context of Fiji during military rule. Prior to arriving in Fiji, I had been warned of reporters being tortured and journalists refused entry into the country, all part of an official policy of censorship that ended six months prior to my arrival in Fiji.[62] The stories and whispers of caution and danger I heard from iTaukei in Canada (once my recording devices were turned off) became an important part of my rationale for not asking directly political questions in Fiji. Instead, I paid close attention to the tensions, anxieties, and regulated registers of feeling in and around meke—at the crossroads of multiple politico-religious pressures. Researching meke in multiple sites and over time provided crucial context and perspective to the shifts in Fijian identification evident in Fiji and Canada.

Proceeding from the importance of contact across time and space, throughout my research and writing I have continued to maintain connections with my Fijian and Oceanian friends and research contacts by sending copies of transcribed interviews, conference papers, chapters, and summaries of my research findings. My long-term, long-distance connections align with Indigenous scholar Linda Tuhiwai Smith's principle of reciprocity and feedback that comes with sharing knowledge and reporting back to the people and communities involved.[63] Such modes of reciprocity and exchange are important, as they regulate the balance of power by ensuring equal access to the knowledge that was collectively produced. While such reporting back also has the effect of extending the time and space of social relations and obligations, there were times during my research when I recognized my own impetus to bring closure, to control, and to shorten the obligations. In addressing these moments, I am critically reflexive about the ways in which they reveal uneven power being generated and negotiated within modes of cultural knowledge exchange. Building on the philosophical and political work of Epeli Hau'ofa, Vilsoni Hereniko, and others who have demonstrated the precolonial travel and exchange between Oceanic peoples, the Pacific Islands map I include covers a vast ocean area connecting islands within its frame (figure I.3). I further extend the frame to demonstrate contemporary travel and exchange between North Pacific and South Pacific Indigenous peoples living in Vancouver and on Vancouver Island, Canada.

Exchanging knowledge through movement was another productive, yet fraught, model for engagement. My knowledge and understanding of meke came through a critical analysis of the movement-based experiences and memories of my interlocutors in conjunction with those of my own. Rather than positioning myself statically within the research to observe, or read, culture as though it were a text, quoting Donna Haraway, I needed a "view from a body."[64] I had to be moving to understand the issues involving meke. Following the approaches of performance and dance ethnographers Deidre Sklar, Sally Ness, Priya Srinivasan, and Cindy Garcia, I learned meke in Fiji, Canada, and Hawai'i as a way to generate interview questions about the sociopolitical tensions evident within meke.[65] Doing so helped me to understand the differences in form that have developed from one locale to another from a dancer's point of view. While I would not necessarily feel the same sensations as others, by having a similar physical language of communication I was able to ask dancers about what they were feeling as

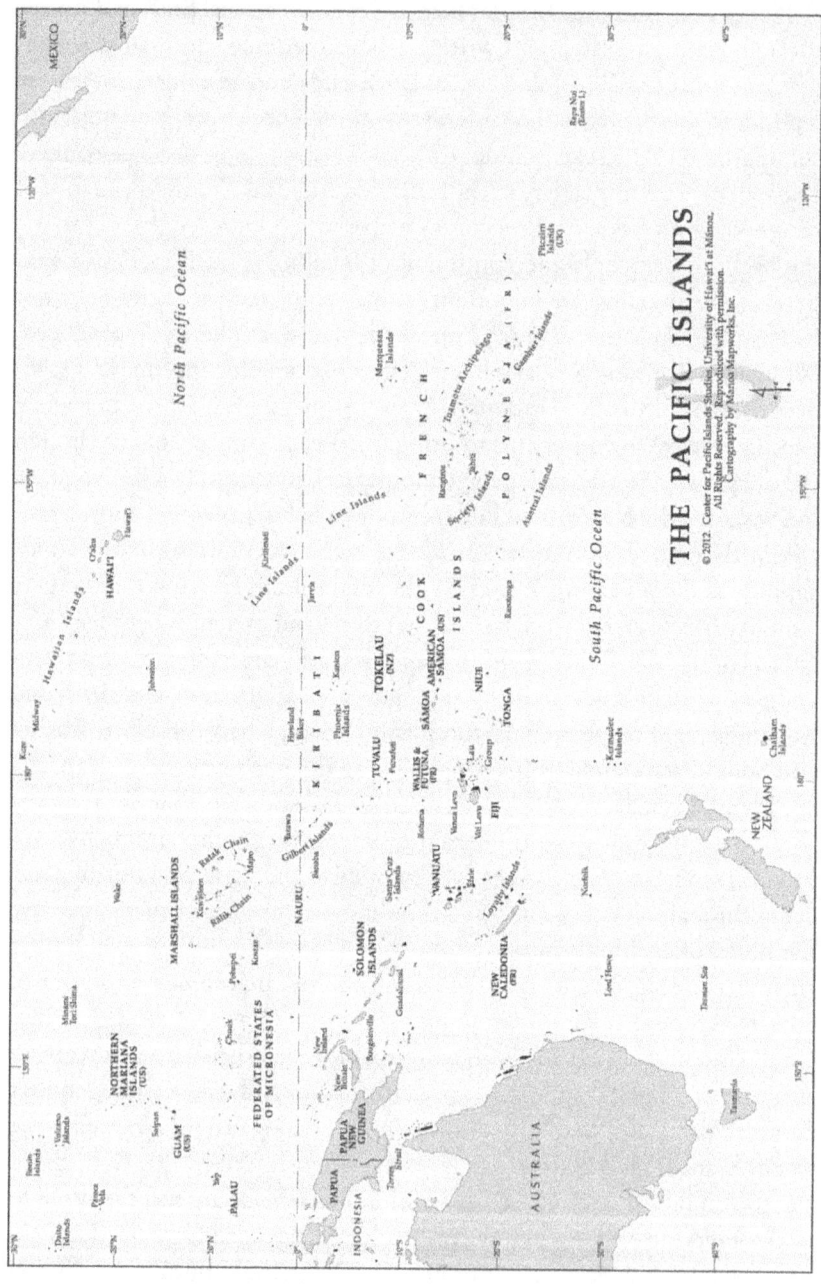

Figure I.3. Map of the Pacific. Courtesy of the Center for Pacific Islands Studies at the University of Hawai'i at Mānoa and Manoa Mapworks, Inc.

they moved through space-time and have them explain through a combination of words and movements. As a result, I interviewed the dancers and moved with them as a way to get at the felt and sensed experiences that were of key importance. Through such exchanges, I developed an understanding of the ways in which contemporary interpretations of meke movements are believed to dedicate a pathway between human bodies, the land, and spirit. In my endeavors to physically learn meke, including a meke created specifically for me to bring back to Canada, my own feelings of restriction and awkwardness also gave me insights into the current imposing politics of multiracial inclusion in Fiji and the feelings, sensations, and movements that have become associated with varying essentialized notions of Fijianness in Fiji and Canada.

A dance colleague warned that my focus on movement-based experiences and expressions may feed into a view that non-Western peoples and dances are more passionate, uncrafted, wild, and connected to their bodies than Westerners, who are more rational and objective. This is an important concern that links back to the early twentieth-century writing of German musicologist Curt Sachs (1937), who formulated a dancing body that passively reflected culture through universal and unevolved primal states of ecstasy and transcendence in dance.[66] I hope to dispel such a primitivizing reading of meke by demonstrating that movement-based feeling and sensing through space and time is not separate from thinking. In Fiji, the sensing body is also viewed as integral to Indigenous concepts of learning and knowledge production in Fiji.[67] There is no hierarchy of perception and reflection. As anthropologist Virginia Dominguez put it, "To maintain a bifurcated view of who should and who should not [show affection in scholarship] is to diminish us all and to make everyone's work suspect."[68] Additionally, experiences and expressions are not necessarily wild and subjective emotional outbursts but include the everyday ways in which bodies relate to one another. As a scholar from the West, I am not a rational, objective observer. As I hope to demonstrate through my reflexive writing, I am invested in understanding meke as a powerful, multisensory form of experience and expression.

Just as the ephemeral feelings and sensations that emerged from interviews and physically learning meke gave me important clues and insights into the recent restructuring of meke in Fiji and its diaspora, ephemera in the archives also gave me important information about the restructuring of the form in relation to British colonial governance. Inspired by Muñoz's work "Ephemera as Evidence," my earliest entry into this research began with the small scraps of paper, found scattered among my deceased mother's material belongings, on which my mother had written down her memories of being a child in Fiji. Somewhere between ephemera and material evidence, these were the "glimmers, residues, and specks of things" that did not fit squarely into official archives.[69] Enduring scraps of feeling became the clues for my grandparents' more authoritative collections (including formal and informal documents: letters, personal memoirs, colonial documents and reports, news clippings, and photos) and Fiji's National Archives. But because colonial circumstances also formed the ephemeral intensities and scraps of feeling, I studied these sources as always rife with potential problems.

I combined my embodied experiences and these unofficial scraps with the colonial, curated, and sanctioned evidence I uncovered in established archives to form, in Diana Taylor's terms, a repertoire and, as Ann Cvetkovich put it, an archive of feeling.[70] This framework enabled me to see the colonial anxieties and tensions shaping and reshaping colonial order. While at the National Archives of Fiji, I gained access to files from the "Colonial Secretary's Office" (CSO). Rather than ignore national anxieties that emerged in and around the archive, I pursued these felt intensities and found them to be important indicators of change. While anxieties made themselves apparent in the CSO files through word usage as well as the extent of dialogue and documentation surrounding particular issues of governance, traces of feeling in my family archive became important clues when searching through the CSO files. With this in mind, I moved back and forth between official and unofficial archival documents, following intensities and absences of feeling, to examine meke in relation to the changing rubrics of British colonial rule.

At the archives I was also given access to pre- and postindependence photographs of meke. With the generous permission of the archives, I have included a number of these photographs of bodies in motion throughout the book. Several images were taken during the 1940s, when my family lived in Fiji. These images (except for one family photo) were found at the archives amid hundreds of uncategorized photos with extremely limited information. Their treatment suggests the photos have been considered relatively less important than the well-organized, text-based colonial documents. Yet they provoke many valuable questions: Who took the photos? Who is performing? Who created the meke, and for what purpose? Who were the intended audiences for these meke and the photos? Did the subjects of the photos know they were being photographed? Were the photos official or unofficial documents? Most of these questions are left unanswered. For example, the 1945 image of meke ni yaqona (figure I.4)—a ritual that affirms specific social and political relations—being performed in Bau provides no context about why the highly meaningful ceremony was being performed. Recognizing the limits of my knowledge of these photos, I sometimes use the images in explicative ways, and sometimes I discuss the images explicitly for the information they contain and the critical questions they pose. I have also included images from individual collections to inform my discussion of contemporary meke.

Because my family's colonial history in Fiji during the 1930s and 1940s has partially shaped this book, I found it productive to focus on CSO files and photos that span this period in conjunction with my more recent correspondences with Fiji's government. The 1930s and 1940s time frame is significant because it represents a period of increased colonial anxieties about countercolonial Indigenous movements; the introduction of the 1944 Fijian Affairs Bill that was intended to train chiefs and people "in orderly, sound and progressive local government"; as well as post–World War II

Figure I.4. Yaqona ceremony, Bau, 1945. Courtesy of National Archives of Fiji.

interests in strengthening the Fijian economy through various means, including the marketing of Fijian culture for tourism.[71] I use documents of the past as well as my email correspondences with different levels of government to unravel why meke in its varying forms, as cultural heritage, entertainment, and a source of efficacy, provides a fertile ground for exposing recent post-2006-military-coup shifts in how Fijians identify with Fiji and "Fijianness."

As a countercolonial critique of objectivist research methods, I have chosen to use an autoethnographic approach that aligns with the works of recent dance and performance scholars.[72] With this in mind, this book is a response to early ethnographic writing about Fijian custom from missionaries, sociologists, ethnographers, and anthropologists. Often these sources maintain a distance between expert observer and observed, leaving out the voices and perspectives of those who are the focus of the research and perpetuating white power and authority. While these sources contain rich and detailed descriptions of meke and Fijian custom, I use them with caution remembering that they were often, wittingly or not, a product of Western colonial and missionary intentions to expand and to control populations around the globe. Such early accounts produced text-based knowledge that the West viewed as objectively neutral and universal while repressing other ways of knowing. As Conquergood has argued, viewing the world as an accessible, observable, and readable text ignores the "finely nuanced meaning that is embodied, tacit, intoned, gestured, improvised, coexperienced, covert—all the more meaningful because of its refusal to be spelled out."[73] I go beyond viewing the body as either a readable text or phenomenological being, to continue the important work of breaking down binaries of self-other, insider-outsider, and mind-body. Like Larasati, who drew inspiration from Edward Said, I include a critical self-awareness in my writing that gives me the paradoxical position of insider and outsider.[74] I approached this autoethnography as a rigorous form of embodied reflexivity—to reflect not only on my own body in relation to meke and to those with whom I was in dialogue but also on how the research is represented—in an ethics of responsive reciprocity that goes far beyond the writing.

The troubled nature of my relationship to this project informs my reflexive, autoethnographic approach to experiences and expressions of identity and inclusion and exclusion in and around meke. Because of my privilege and access, I aimed to remain vigilant and cognizant about assessing the dynamics informing how encounters unfolded. For example, in Fiji my colonial family history resulted in a myriad of unexpected responses to my presence that, at times, seemed to support new forms of state-imposed governance. While I expected the whiteness of my skin to trigger negative responses linked with a memory of colonialism, I often felt privileged in specific ways that enabled a status of inclusion.[75] Why did my colonial family history result in such levels of inclusion? Perhaps my inclusion might be seen as part of larger global processes of exceptionalism granted to white Westerners, like my grandparents, who were privileged with the mobility to travel across borders with a sense of safety and security. Alternatively, my inclusion may have mirrored the government's strategy to improve equality through widening citizenship in Fiji as a way to ally themselves with Western democratic trade partners. Perhaps understanding my inclusion also required a deeper historical context about the way Britain was "invited" to colonize Fiji. Although less common, I sometimes encountered resistance to my presence that might be more indicative of the anger and frustration felt toward white foreigners. In reflecting on my encounters, I seek to expose colonial legacies of privilege as opposed to perpetuating them.

Initially, I wrote my field notes in the present tense to bring the reader into the multiple layers of my kinesthetic encounters and to complicate the fixing of the body and its knowledge in the past, as has been the trend in representational approaches to writing about dance. Debates about the ethnographic present continue, and there are strong arguments for using it within dance studies, anthropology, and performance studies.[76] Yet this particular interdisciplinary research and writing is also in reflexive dialogue with Pacific studies and Indigenous communities from Oceania. Writing in the ethnographic present posed a greater risk of immobilizing through a sense of ahistorical timelessness and fixing people in time and place from my own heavily loaded perspective. As a result, through past-tense reflexive writing I acknowledge how past experiences form my partial knowledge and continue to shape the embodied, indeterminate present.

～

The book is organized to demonstrate how meke takes part in a complex web of relations that is full of restrictions and agency in each of the modes of expression I examine. In chapter 1, "Meke in a Changing Imperial World," files on crime housed at the National Archives of Fiji reveal cases of the British colonial government criminalizing meke as a form of witchcraft for expressing countercolonial sentiment. These files lead to contrasting family photographs and memoirs that demonstrate colonial notions of gender, culture, and heritage emerging from vivid sensorial images of watching meke. The chapter presents evidence of disturbing and offensive racial stereotypes from the archives of the colonial secretary's office as well as my own family archive to suggest that colonial governance in the 1930s and 1940s sought to regulate the movements of iTaukei bodies as a way to control a population that resisted through its spiritual practices, which sometimes included meke.

The next two chapters share a focus on the stagings of meke within national discourses of diversity-based inclusion. Chapter 2, "Governing Meke," builds on the history provided in chapter 1 by looking at the impact of colonialism on contemporary governance and its relationship to meke. Throughout, I consider my correspondences with multiple levels of government in Fiji in order to examine the role meke, especially war meke, plays in shifting relations of state power, authority, and economics coinciding with Fiji's most recent 2006 coup. In addition to meke's political and economic dimensions in Fiji, chapter 3, "Meke in Multicultural Canada," investigates how issues of inclusion and objectification impact meke in Fiji's Canadian diaspora. I analyze examples of meke and Oceanic dance for the ways in which they demonstrate distinguishing features between and within British Columbia's Fijian diasporas in their entanglements within Canadian multiculturalism.

In contrast to exploring the local and national stagings of Fijianness, the next three chapters address ambiguity in meke expressions of spiritual and political agency and authority. Chapter 4, "Spiriting Meke," examines how religion cloaks politics in Fiji in ways that impact meke, sometimes resulting in outright rejection of the form. By looking at competing religious perspectives, this chapter shows how spirit performed in meke generates a tension that makes sensing toward uncertain feelings and intensities ambiguously resistive of colonial legacies. Some Fijians reject meke, others see meke as "devilish," and others create meke with spiritual agency and authority. Deepening this examination of spirit, chapter 5 analyzes resistive processes for generating spirit and mana through sonic, rhythmic, and movement-based transmissions. Focusing on the creation and pedagogical processes of a meke, called *Mekhe ni Loloma* (to sing-dance about the gift of love), that was gifted to me, this chapter pursues an in-depth analysis of the ambivalence of this postcolonial/postcoup meke and the nuanced ways in which mana resists the objectification of culture through a politics of inclusion on Indigenous terms.[77] The final chapter, "Performing

Indeterminacy," builds on the previous chapters by scrutinizing the politics of inclusion and the legacy of colonialism revealed when Logaivau invited me to perform *Mekhe ni Loloma* in Fiji. As a Euro-Canadian citizen with a family history of settlement in both Canada and Fiji, my performance of this meke revealed multifarious power dynamics and layered problematics. I thus conclude the book with an exploration of dialogical performance ethnography in all its complexities and pitfalls.

Ultimately, *Dancing Sprit, Love, and War* demonstrates that within the context of almost one hundred years of colonial governance, meke continues to be a space for the emergence of Fijian culture and identity. For contemporary meke performers, meke does not exist separately from the bodies who create it and perform it. Within shifting political and religious contexts, gendered categories of inclusion and exclusion are reformulated through expressions in meke, which are not neutral or equal exchanges but rooted in material realities with consequences that shape lives and future relations. Meke operates in resonance with narratives of nation in Fiji and Canada—sustaining, suspending, and potentially disrupting narratives that seek to produce a particular type of recognizable and knowable Fijian citizen. Experiences and expressions in and around meke take part in governing Fiji's shifting and contradictory biopolitical terrain, which stands at a crossroads, with an uncertain future—all part of a larger ecology generating new relations of power.

CHAPTER 1

Meke in a Changing Imperial World

THIS CHAPTER EXPLORES MEKE as a site for British colonial constructions and negotiations of identity, power, and authority in Fiji during the early twentieth century. How did colonials construct distinctions in power and control through meke and larger movement-based migrations in the British colony? And why was meke an important part of these constructions and negotiations?

To explore these questions, I examine mid-nineteenth-century Wesleyan Methodist missionary accounts of Fijian meke (during a period of mass conversion to Christianity) to set the stage for analyzing colonial descriptions and representations of meke in the official and unofficial colonial documents and photographs of the early twentieth century. In particular, the chapter draws from 1930s and 1940s reports and correspondences of the Colonial Secretary's Office (CSO) housed in the National Archives of Fiji (NAF). The CSO was responsible for the administration of British colonial Fiji, and as a result, the CSO files are records of the challenges and deliberations behind decisions related to governance in Fiji. This was a time when countercolonial feelings were reportedly resurging and when several powerful daunivucus emerged in particular areas of Fiji through expressions of ancestor worship.[1] It was also a time of revitalizing an indirect, hierarchical, and race-based form of governance as well as post–World War II economic reconstruction. The CSO records show how colonial administrators drew from the ethnographic details of mid-nineteenth-century missionary accounts to construct Fijian practices statically within the past and as a threat to British civilizing motives through notions of "disorder," involving so-called devil worship, sorcery, and witchcraft (all punishable through corporal punishment), to regulate non-Christian meke expressions of ritual authority. Next, I look at how colonizers simultaneously constructed and reified Christianized meke traditions as sanctioned and legitimate within a social evolutionary framework. Scholars who attempted to salvage Fijian cultural traditions supported this construction as a function of ideal Fijian society. I use these sources in conjunction with a memoir written by my grandmother, Tess White, to examine simultaneous and contradictory colonial perceptions of meke in relation to Christian colonial power and authority, sometimes constructed through boundaries of race, class, gender, and sexuality. Ultimately, these sources show how colonizers strove to regulate meke in order to form boundaries of identity, authority, and control in ways that would distinguish the British colonizers (believed to be racially superior) and the larger social Other (including Fijians and settlers).[2] In addition, this presumed hierarchy formed the basis of the stated colonial mission to civilize, create good governance and order, and develop trade and industry (founded on private ownership) in Fiji.

Colonial records, as expressions of governance, reveal confusion and anxiety about how to define and construct boundaries in ways that would maintain colonial control and hierarchical order. As anthropologist Ann Laura Stoler has put it, "Archives are not simply accounts of actions or records of what people thought happened. They are records of uncertainty and doubt in how people imagined they could and might make the rubrics of rule correspond to a changing imperial world."[3] Documents and photographs involving meke as well as my grandmother's memoir exemplify the ways in which anxieties as well as other affective intensities are heavily implicated in the changing rubrics of power and make themselves apparent by word choices as well as the extent of dialogue and documentation surrounding particular issues of rule. These archival sources also provide glimpses into the cracks, fissures, and dissension that enabled other identifications to seep through imposed colonial boundaries around "civilized" comportment.

Rather than treating these historical records as unmediated and "outside the framing of the archival impetus . . . and political manipulation," I situate these sources as evidence of imperial motives and maneuvers to gain and maintain power and control.[4] In this "scenario" (to use Diana Taylor's term), I show how my own history, research, and writing are mediated by legacies of imperialism by putting my family within the frame. While none of these sources account for the ways in which Fijians themselves perceived the missionaries and colonizers, I hope to mitigate that by analyzing Fijian accounts of the past and present as well as histories produced by meke themselves in the chapters that follow.

Civilizing Missions

The British imperial motives to civilize Fijians taint mid-nineteenth-century Wesleyan missionary and late nineteenth-century colonial processes that pressured and shaped meke as a pre-Christian form of spiritual and ritual authority within changing rubrics of rule.[5] These sources do not come from a homogeneous group of Europeans. Some missionaries wrote to increase knowledge and understanding for evangelical purposes, while others were narrow-minded iconoclasts who wrote accounts full of hellfire to dismantle non-Christian ways of life. Nevertheless, while these differing missionary approaches were not directly concerned with building the British Empire, missionaries were participants in a civilizing mission rooted in social evolutionary theories of hierarchy based on biology.

According to mid-nineteenth-century Wesleyan Methodist missionary sources, meke as a pre-Christian spiritual and ritual practice involved the worship of kalou vu, or ancestor gods and goddesses, and kalou-yalo, or deified spirits of once powerful men.[6] Rev. Thomas Williams, who lived in Fiji from 1840 to 1853, wrote detailed descriptions of how the act of creating the meke chant and movements forged a strong link between a daunivucu and the ancestor spirits. To create meke, the daunivucu would communicate with the ancestor spirits by drinking yaqona.[7] Yaqona brought the daunivucu into a trance or dream state, and then the movements and chants flowed from the spirit world through the body of the daunivucu.[8]

Methodist missionaries in Fiji were motivated to expel such non-Christian spiritual practices and beliefs. While not all missionaries had the same approach, some were particularly hostile. Rev. Joseph Waterhouse, who was a missionary in Fiji from 1849 to 1863 and published descriptions of Fijian custom, provides a strong example of this destructive approach. He wrote in 1852:

> At the metropolis of Rangi-rangi there is a large stone which is said to be the mother of Dengei, the great god of Fiji. Whilst on our march I noticed a stone . . . dressed with a liku; and upon inquiry was informed that it was a female GOD! An unsculptured stone—a goddess! A basaltic rock an object of human worship!! . . . No persuasion could induce one of the natives to

touch it, and some of them seemed horror-stricken when I lifted up my foot, and bade adieu to her majesty by giving her a hearty and contemptible kick.[9]

Such actions were intended to destroy the value of non-Christian kalou worship, especially with regard to female kalou vu.

Alongside this vicious approach to Indigenous spirituality, a major shift to kalou worship and its role in enriching meke through ritual expression came from the adaptation of such concepts into the Bible. According to anthropologist Matt Tomlinson, in the late 1830s, the missionaries started to translate the Bible into Fijian, and by the late 1840s to mid-1850s, thousands of copies of biblical sermons and hymns and the entire New Testament and Bible itself were translated into the now-dominant Fijian Bauan dialect.[10] Of particular relevance is the way missionaries translated the Bible. The Wesleyans in Fiji took an approach to translating the Bible that replaced local spirits with the "one true" Christian God and translated other spirits, specifically tevoro and timoni, into "devils" and "demons."[11] This made missionaries the sole agents of the most powerful and all-encompassing spirit. It also meant the ancestor gods could still exist as less powerful and demonized spirits. The efforts of missionaries turned kalou worship into devil worship on paper and in the affective experiences of daily life and enabled Christianity to interweave its way into meke.

The accounts of Williams and Waterhouse, which were written for a Western audience and are often gruesome and violent, became key sources for 1930s colonial understandings of kalou ritual practices, including meke, as tied to heathenism, war, and cannibalism. For example, despite their wide range of purpose and meaning, Williams and Waterhouse often described meke in association with preparing for war, celebrating war victories, or recording stories of war. Williams generalized a vague and exoticizing account of the "fiendish war-dance" followed by "the indecent dance of the women," which are described in relation to postwar protocols of preparing bodies of enemies for the oven.[12] In another account by Williams of a meke performed for entertainment, "the dancers . . . all bear clubs or spears, perform a series of marchings, steppings, halts, and various evolutions, and a stranger would rather suppose them to be engaged in a military review than in a dance. As the performance approaches the close, the speed quickens, and the actions steadily increase in violence, accompanied by a heavy tramping on the ground, until the excited dancers, almost out of breath, shout, at the top of their voices, 'Wa-oo!' and the dance is ended."[13] Describing dancers' expressions as a kind of violence, Williams frames the meke as a source of danger, fear, and intimidation for his Western audience.[14]

In early recorded descriptions of meke, Williams and Royal Naval officer John Erskine used sexually exoticizing and shaming rhetoric that, as I will soon show, was also used in the 1930s CSO files to inform colonial ideas and regulations of meke.[15] For example, similar to Williams vague account of "the indecent dance of women," Erskine wrote about women performing war meke called dele or wate in 1853, describing these meke as being part of the ritual of kalou worship that occurred after a battle and in the process of, or preparation for, cannibalistic acts.[16] In a wate, women allegedly mocked and shamed captured dead enemies after a battle.[17] Erskine recounted the robust physicality of the women in this dance as sexually "lewd," likely because the women were wearing liku (a grass fringe wrapped around the pelvis).[18] In reference to such women's dances, Williams suggested that while some meke were becoming Christianized, others, such as the supposedly indecent nocturnal dances, were no longer being performed because of missionary influences.[19] Although the ancestor spirits were once a source of strength and healing for many Fijians, missionaries transformed them into a basis for considerable concern, misfortune, and shame, especially with regard to women's bodies.

Widespread war in the mid-nineteenth century accelerated the ways in which Christianity became entwined in Fijian custom. In 1854, after the large-scale and long-term war between the ruling chiefs of Bau and Rewa, mass conversion to Christianity occurred, which, perhaps as a political tool, became the one "true" religion of Fiji.[20] According to anthropologist and Fiji scholar Marshall Sahlins, the common people and less prominent chiefs waited on the conversion of more prominent chiefs. Ratu Seru Cakobau, who, as preeminent warring chief of Bau, was under attack by Rewa and struggling with internal revolt, converted to "the true God" and quickly changed the terms of battle.[21] Cakobau won the war and, according to Sahlins, "the old religion then gave birth to the new."[22] Thus, for over a hundred years, Methodist Christianity became "the religion of Thakombau."[23] In Sahlins's dialectical terms, missionary presence and war mediated the long-term mythological manifestations of Bauan experience, which ultimately shifted the social order.[24] After he won the long war, commoners and less preeminent chiefs were obligated to serve Cakobau as the Paramount Chief of the Bau confederacy and convert to Christianity.[25] Once

Cakobau accepted the Wesleyan Church, the vanua (the customs, beliefs, and values of Fijians) became rapidly interwoven with the church, allowing Christian worship to exist alongside practices and protocols, such as meke, involving chiefly authority and the worship of kalou.[26]

Cakobau's rise in power and authority alongside a rapid increase in European settlement were pivotal to the establishment and organization of British colonial governance. Historian Deryck Scarr wrote extensively about the period preceding annexation and clarified the complexities of Fiji's request to be ceded to Britain.[27] It was in a climate of intensive settlement of Europeans, who arrived in the late 1860s in the hundreds, and ensuing racism and lawlessness that British commissioners virtually forced an offer of cession out of Fijians.[28] While some European settlers, such as John Bates Thurston, became leaders in early precession forms of government for a "mixed" population and to protect Fijians from settler abuse, the result was open revolt from other settlers, who abhorred the idea of "superior" Anglo-Saxons being subservient to "the inferior race."[29] According to Scarr, annexation became unavoidable within the conditions of anarchy that unfolded in Fiji due to the systematic undermining of governance by British nationals and European settlers.[30] Once the British were convinced that Fijians accepted Cakobau as king of Fiji, Britain agreed to cede Fiji. But Thurston insisted on adding certain conditions to safeguard Fijians customs, beliefs, and values from colonial rule.[31]

British colonial measures to protect Fijians also shaped and regulated Fijian beliefs and practices along hierarchical principles that, as I will soon show, impacted meke. Within the 1874 Instrument of Cession, Britain declared its intention to promote civilization, Christianity, order, good government, and trade and industry in Fiji for European and iTaukei populations.[32] The British method for accomplishing its intentions was to work with Bauan and Methodist hegemony in ordering the life conditions of Fijians through a method of indirect rule—a racially specific form of governance established by Fiji's first colonial governor, Sir Arthur Hamilton Gordon, in the late 1870s. Gordon established indirect rule by the Native Administration and the Native Regulation Board, which worked in tandem with Indigenous leaders. In addition to the governing role of the British, Indigenous leaders were given an administrative role in governing Fijian society through the Great Council of Chiefs. Yet in her work on ritual politics in the late nineteenth century, anthropologist Martha Kaplan demonstrates that the colonial administration did not recognize the political-ritual authority of the iTaukei, people of the land.[33] Instead, as a projection of its own hierarchical principles of governance, the colonial administration only recognized the authority of the chiefs and expanded the sphere of communal responsibility under chiefly control.[34] Drawing upon the preexisting networks established by white settlers, traders, and missionaries, Gordon initiated indirect rule to consolidate administrative control over Fiji and achieved consolidation by centralizing Bau as a model of Fijian society.[35] Thus, governance formed at the intersection of chiefly, Methodist, and British power with cultural, social, and linguistic hegemony promoted using the matanitu, or confederacy, of Bau.[36]

In the period after Fiji's 1874 annexation, social evolutionary ideas emerging in anthropology informed the actions and perspectives of Fiji's missionaries and colonial administrators toward traditions such as meke. In their policies and practices, missionaries and colonial administrators implemented theories of social change that followed a unilineal trajectory through developmental stages toward so-called modernity.[37] While the British classified themselves as civilized, they catalogued Fijians as primitive, using chiefs, communalism, and subsistence economies as evidence in support of their assessment.[38] Within this perspective, colonizers linked traditions with the past, savagery, and primitive society, while linking modernity with the future, progress, and civilization. Missionaries and colonial administrators used social evolutionary theory in different ways to advance their own agendas, with the latter seeking to preserve and safeguard Fijian society in a modern "traditional" domain, while ridding it of the attributes deemed disruptive to British ideas of civilization.[39]

Colonial Choreographies of "Disorder": Unlawful Meke

In the 1930s, rising colonial fears about "disorderly" non-Christian spiritual beliefs and ritual practices involving meke that countered the "good" and ordered moral hierarchy of British governance served to initiate new policies and regulations.[40] While colonial administrators did not accept the power and legitimacy of ancestral and land spirit worship, they were concerned about iTaukei Fijians claiming power, influence, and economic control outside the colonial system of indirect rule. Two CSO Correspondence Files written between 1934 and 1937 (when my family moved to Fiji) deal explicitly with cases of meke in relation to understanding and criminalizing non-Christian Indigenous spiritual practices.[41] Within the files are correspondences involving three cases of meke that were negatively constructed as illegitimate and unlawful: a case of "devil dances," a ritual process used to create meke, and a criminal case involving eleven Fijians who were learning meke. In each case colonial administrators refer to "section 64," a legal instrument developed by the Native Regulation Board to suppress non-Christian spiritual beliefs and practices.[42] These correspondences demonstrate how, through section 64, some colonial administrators aimed to codify non-Christian meke traditions and customs negatively in order to eradicate them and, in turn, suppress the agency and ritual authority of the people of the land.

Within the CSO correspondences on crime and draunikau, colonial administrators used vague and ahistorical terms repeatedly to describe ancestor worship, including sorcery, devil worship, and witchcraft, in attempting to figure out how to control these practices under section 64. To legitimize the use of these terms, one report cited the mid-nineteenth-century account of Reverend Williams (made eighty years prior) to make the case that "Kalou-rere," "Luveniwai," and "Draunikau" could be described as witchcraft, whose practitioners "are dreaded by all classes, and, by destroying mutual confidence, shake the security and comfort of society."[43] Colonial administrators used such negative and countercolonial constructions of non-Christian kalou rites and rituals throughout the many pages of the files. Yet questions continued to emerge throughout the correspondences about the lack of clarity in section 64 in defining the various forms of draunikau, luveniwai, and kalourere, offering no understanding of what these forms of ritual practice meant to Fijians. The document states: "Any person who practices, or who assists in the practice of, the acts known in the Fijian language as draunikau or luveniwai, or kalourere, or any other similar practice, with whatsoever object, shall on conviction thereof by a provincial court, be liable to be imprisoned for any period not exceeding six months and, in the case of a male, to receive a number of lashes [with Cat o' Nine Tails or cane] not exceeding twelve at one time nor twenty-four in the aggregate."[44] These questions became more pressing and anxiety producing throughout the correspondences owing to the perceived spread of witchcraft across Fiji.

In January 1937, Native Administration district commissioner for Kadavu, A. J. Armstrong, reported on his concerns about a renewal and spread of witchcraft across many parts of Fiji and a "cult" of eighty adherents in Kadavu (an island south of Viti Levu) who were engaging in "free intercourse" and "devil dances." He reported that Fijians made ritual presentations (in the form of feasts taken into the sea) to the shark god Dakuwaqa (an ancestral god who gives meke) and presented yaqona to the gods of Kauvadra.[45] In addition, he wrote, "Women take part in these practices and between the sexes there is free intercourse—all yaqona plants and food plantations, are regarded as common property."[46] Here, Armstrong expressed his concerns that Fijian women were overtly sexual beings, that food and yaqona crops were communal property, and perhaps most insidious for Armstrong, that Fijian women were engaging "freely" in intercourse that was not under the private control of men. His opinions on appropriate and inappropriate expressions of gender, sexuality, and property ownership form the basis of his argument about the need for colonial intervention.

Condemning men and women dancing together became the basis for establishing colonial boundaries of power and distinction. Armstrong reported, "There is an island near Mataso village which is an old time place of worship. When the moon is bright devil dances are said to be done by both sexes in the nude."[47] Like Erskine's earlier description of "lewd" dances, the mention of nudity here was likely related to dancers wearing liku and not the ankle length sulu. But since the British aimed to maintain clear boundaries of class, race, and sexuality between themselves and Fijians, exoticizing and sexualizing the dances and dancers rhetorically demonstrated the necessity to civilize the Other.

Controlling Fijian bodies and behaviors was a way of maintaining colonial domination in the context of colonial fears about potential countercolonial, and antiwhite, sentiment. Through his correspondences, Armstrong was trying to influence colonial policies and regulations regarding the practice of so-called witchcraft. He was not only advocating for the end of any outward signs of ancestral worship, he was also constructing colonial boundaries around the bundled domains of sexuality, gender, race, private ownership, and physical comportment. The ultimate danger was to allow these rituals of kalourere, draunikau, and luveniwai to undermine the Christian civilizing mission and the development of trade and industry (including agriculture) within a market economy based on private ownership.

Understanding the ways in which colonial administrators understood the worship of luveniwai, a practice closely connected to meke, sets the stage for the criminalization of meke.[48] Colonial sources defined luveniwai as the kalou worship of stillbirth and miscarriage, a rite of invulnerability, a meke composition process involving the possession of veli (little gods or forest fairies), and as "spirits of remedy," "children of water," and "intercourse with water-spirits."⁴⁹ Although these definitions indicate a wide range of rites that likely differed depending on time and place, Armstrong authoritatively presented his opinion on the basis of the details he alleged were explained to him by a Fijian. Armstrong described these details in a report to the colonial secretary on April 12, 1937, written just three months before my grandparents moved to Fiji. In his letter, Armstrong sought to provide some clarity around the widespread resurgence of so-called sorcery, including luveniwai, in Fiji. According to his letter,

> Worship takes place in a group and not individually and the place of worship tends to be in the forest or an isolated rocky point. These places are kept very clean, and planted with flowers. . . . On the appointed time of worship luveniwai have the power of making songs and dances, and its followers must abide by tabu (including no adultery, thieving or anything that would detract from his work). If the follower does not abide by these conditions required by the luveniwai, he, his wife or his children could be penalized by death. This form of ancestor spirit worship is considered dangerous because of the deaths resulting from a disregard of the conditions of tabu that the luveniwai must observe. On the appointed time of worship the followers gather at the appointed place, and the yaqona is made.⁵⁰ When it is ready, the leader goes into a trance and forwith the luveniwai speaks stating the names of each spirit accompanying him from which the followers are to name the ones they want respectively, and the nature of the task they wish to do. . . . If a wound is inflicted, they are not yet visited, and if they are immune from wounds inflicted by these weapons, then they are truly visited.

Armstrong seemingly ignored all the implicit self-control and restriction involved in protocols such as tabu when he added the following information about those who practice luveniwai rites and rituals:

> Their appearances:—They are a very untidy, unkempt and dirty crowd, who seem to shun water, and on their skins are to be found scales (yaqona scales) and often suffer from scabies. Their characteristics:—A lazy crowd and do not plant food. They sleep late into the day, because of their yaqona drinking. . . . 1) They steal, 2) They are adulterers, 3) They are very fond of taking other people's property without permission, 4) They kill their fellow men, 5) They instigate dissention [sic], 6) They scorn to talk to anyone not a member of their society, 7) They appear arrogant, 8) They despise religion or

church, 9) They disrespect the orders of the Government. . . . [The practice of luveniwai] is also responsible for the migration of the Kadavu people into other provinces by intimidation.[51]

This passage about the role of luveniwai in the creation of meke outlines many of Armstrong's prejudices in relation to maintaining colonial order. Fijians of nonchiefly status making ritual connections to spirit gods through protocols (for example, presentation of tabua and yaqona and observing tabu) was an example of claiming ritual authority outside the realm of indirect systems of government rule. While Armstrong does not seem concerned with the ritual efficacy of such kalou rituals (to create and perform a meaningful meke, to impact the well-being of others, or to carry out a task), his description of those who practice luveniwai exposes underlying fears about being in control of a population that is constructed as resisting that control through intimidation, bodily comportment, appearance, a disregard for private ownership, antigovernment sentiment, and non-Christian Indigenous spiritual practices. Armstrong viewed these behaviors as a threat to the security and comfort of society.

Another 1937 case of practicing luveniwai, referred to as sorcery, resulted in the arrest of eleven young men who learned meke in Savusavu district, Vanua Levu (the large island north of Viti Levu), and provides an example of colonial attempts to control luveniwai worship under Native Regulation 64. Colonial administrators referred to the young men, from a town called Korotasere in Natewa Bay, as followers of luveniwai in the documentation of the case. The defendants were young men belonging to a club that involved boxing, developing agriculture, and learning meke. The charge of sorcery arose in connection with meke. Colonial administrators perceived the group to be demonstrating the desire to break away from the colonial control of the communal system and local authority and "carry out an agricultural scheme of their own."[52] This sparked fears that these meke practitioners were part of a renewed countercolonial Apolosi movement that promoted economic agency of the iTaukei people.[53] As a result, the meke was a source of great concern for colonizers and chiefs trying to maintain control.[54] The young men were charged with sorcery, and the court found all the defendants guilty, sentencing them to imprisonment (two men were sentenced for four months and nine men were sentenced for two months). In a letter to the secretary for native affairs on March 8, 1937, the district commissioner of Savusavu explained that the Fijians of the district "believe very strongly in the efficacy of the practices known as "luveniwai," "kalourere," and "draunikau."[55] In other words, these Fijians believed that when the spirit gods did their bidding, they could immediately achieve creation, invulnerability, or healing and/or destruction. The commissioner expressed his concern that these Fijians, as nonchiefly people of the land, were practicing ritual authority outside the domain of sanctioned systems of indirect governance. Ultimately, despite so-called evidence of heathenism, there was an appeal to the charges of luveniwai; the appeal was upheld and the case dismissed.

In a follow-up letter to the colonial secretary regarding the meke case, written June 3, 1937, the acting secretary for native affairs wrote that he visited the town, Korotasere in Natewa Bay, "where these heathen practices had been indulged in, and spoke seriously, and at considerable length to the people there regarding the evils of these practices." Remarkably, he went on to add that he was not aware of any recognized definitions of luveniwai, kalourere, or draunikau, but the lack of definition could benefit colonial authorities: "The wording of the Native Regulation No. 64 . . . is all very ambiguous, and I have always considered that it was purposely made so, in order that District Commissioners might have a wide discretion so that all practices might be stamped out."[56] The vagueness of Native Regulation 64 eventually led to the drafting of a new "Witchcraft Ordinance" based on similar reports and ordinances on witchcraft in Tanganyika and Kenya. Yet even this new Witchcraft Ordinance perpetuated broad and vague definitions of witchcraft, while promoting corporal punishment to stamp out resurgences of counter colonial sentiment.[57]

Charging Fijians with sorcery for creating and/or practicing meke was part of a bigger fear about challenges to colonial authority and a return of the Apolosi movement and earlier immortality and invulnerability movements that early colonizers imagined as a return to heathen practices, including cannibalism.[58] In attempting to secure a future for colonial Fiji, as good and civilized, the colonial response to ancestral and land spirit worship was to prosecute those practicing a wide range of activities deemed heathen and sentence them to imprisonment, hard labor, and the lash in the hopes of dissuading others from showing dissent.

Good and Lawful Meke

Alongside administrative concerns about non-Christian iTaukei rituals and practices in the 1930s, colonial administrators were also eagerly anticipating meke that they constructed positively within a Christian frame to support chiefly authority, social function, and cultural entertainment for the Western observer. This contradictory treatment of various forms of meke is indicative of larger constructions of order through so-called scientific descriptions of Fijian custom. Specifically, a social evolutionary framework, which, as mentioned, began weaving its way into church and state in the 1870s and continued into the 1940s, supported this positive construction of good and lawful tradition.

In the early twentieth century, historians, anthropologists, and linguists used social evolutionary ideas to inform their work of salvaging pre-Christian Fijian customs and beliefs from Western missionary influences through authoritative, rigorous, detailed, and thorough documentation using a functionalist lens.[59] Scholars used this lens to provide an account that promoted the protection of the traditional workings of Fijian society. In their efforts to support positive constructions of Fijian traditions, these scholars recorded meke about kalou vu, as the original founders of Fiji, to help Westerners understand how traditions ordered Fijian culture and society.[60] In so doing, they demonstrated the role of meke in preserving culturally specific knowledge of migration and settlement in Fiji that linked human and nonhuman bodies to the land and sea and, by extension, the material items that come from the land and sea.[61] For example, in 1941 linguist Arthur Capell and colonial administrator R. H. Lester published the documentation of a meke about Fiji's most prominent origin story that recounts the god-chief Degei, who, some say, ruled the birthplace of the first Fijians.[62] Fijians worshipped Degei as ancestor, spirit, and man, but he could also appear in the form of a snake. Through the migration, settlement, and the founding of their own chiefdoms, many ancestors emerged over time as secondary deities.[63] For example, C. J. Morey recorded a meke in the early 1930s about the power of the Shark God Dakuwaqa—a secondary deity, who manifested in ocean swells and unsettled a chief's canoe before the chief reached his destination in the Fijian Lau group of islands and killed the chief at sea.[64] Morey's documentation shows the role of meke in sharing cultural knowledge about how to live in respectful relationship to the land and sea. Thus, these scholars could successfully preserve Fijian culture and heritage by demonstrating its role in the functioning of an ideal Fijian society.

Early twentieth-century scientific writing, wittingly or not, also supported British imperialism. As arbiters of authenticity, historians, linguists, and anthropologists became authorities on the Fijian traditions they researched, thereby shifting cultural authority and agency from Fijians to research enclaves such as museums and archives. Colonial administrators used these authoritative accounts to inform their views on developing and implementing regulations and policies (for example, in the CSO deliberations on the new "Witchcraft Ordinance"). Perspectives entangled, however, as colonial administrators and scholars traveled in the same elite circles and their roles sometimes intermixed, as was the case for R. H. Lester.[65]

The following account by Fiji historian G. C. Henderson draws from his scientific, functionalist, and authoritative approach to historical evidence to comment on a meke he witnessed in 1929 with the acting governor and a group of government officials. He wrote:

> On the island of Lakemba we watched a meke that lasted for fifty minutes celebrating the death of a chief in the olden time. The performers kept up their singing for about half the time while their arms, legs, heads and fingers were kept continually in motion. We all watched carefully to detect, if possible, one false movement on the part of any one individual in that company of seventy men and women; but we saw none. The impression left on my mind there . . . was that in grace and regularity of movement, sense of time and rhythm, the native dancers of Fiji have nothing to learn from civilized people. The Fijians still love their meke.
>
> The records of the missionaries in the middle of last century fail to convey any adequate impression of the part played by the meke in sustaining the joyousness of the people, and making the wheels of government run smoothly. The missionaries looked upon it with no favorable eye: it excited lustful feeling, and sometimes ended in scenes of debauchery. Instead of preserving it, and trying to purge it gradually of its grosser elements, they adopted the usual policy of suppression. Thomas Williams in his book on Fiji and the Fijians defends the missionaries for this. . . . It does not appear that he or any other missionary realized how much was due to the meke for infusing a spirit of goodwill into many of the more disagreeable duties of a Fijian's life.[66]

Henderson's account of meke countered concurrent colonial concerns about the potentially dangerous and disordering threat of non-Christian ritual authority, including meke, by demonstrating how meke was a source of order, good governance, and entertainment for the Western observer. His scientific data produced the perfect model and ideal for all Fijian society, stabilizing the value of meke for the colony within the context of colonial order.

Family Frames

While colonial administrators and scholars actively constructed boundaries of identity and social order through meke, such boundaries were also being constructed and governed within Eurocolonial domestic space. My own family archives of photos, memoirs, and official colonial documents show how colonials formed boundaries of identity along specific notions of "civilized" comportment. These documents also expose colonial constructions of meke as good and lawful cultural entertainment and an object of the Western gaze.

My family took part in implementing British order, governance, and industry in Fiji. Soon after the discovery of gold, my grandfather and grandmother came to Fiji from Australia. H. M. Colonial Service (under the Colonial Office, London) appointed Frank Thomas Matthews White as government mining engineer—the senior Colonial Mines Service appointment in Fiji and the Western Pacific administration—to undertake the official administration of the new mining industry. My grandfather assumed duty on July 16, 1937, at the age of 27. Soon promoted to inspector of mines and mining engineer, he was a Fiji civil servant whose work duties included the establishment of a mining board (as advisor and then chairman), the drafting of new mining and allied legislation for the Colony of Fiji, technical administration of the mines section (of Lands, Mines and Surveys Department), geological investigations, mineral technology, and conducting original research on pozzolana mineral aggregates (which have the properties of cement). His total time in Fiji was eight years and two months.[67] During that time my mother was born, and except for a one-year period during World War II and the Coral Sea battle (when my grandmother and my mother stayed in New Zealand), she lived in Fiji until she was four years old. According to family records, they employed the domestic labor of Valeriana Qumia for the duration of their stay. My grandparent's hiring of domestic labor was part of the emerging colonialist and classist relations between growing numbers of British mining experts and their families and iTaukei.

Family accounts of Qumia's bodily movements and comportment have a haunting vitality in my family's memoirs and photographs, revealing the inequitable relations established by colonial authority via hierarchical and race-based distinctions. Despite her importance in these accounts, I know very little about Qumia. From her marriage and death certificates, Qumia appears to have led a unique life. She was born in Veivatuloa, Namosi. Her koro dina, or paternal village, was Vutia-Muanaicake in the district of Rewa. According to her marriage certificate, on December 2, 1944, at the age of twenty-two, she married a soldier from Vutia, Rewa. The certificate lists "domestic duties" as her occupation. Judging by my family records, Qumia married while still employed by my grandparents.[68] Although I do not know the exact dates of her employment with my grandparents, from these certificates I know that she was fifteen when my grandparents moved to Fiji, nineteen when my mother was born, and approximately twenty-three when they left. Her death certificate states that she died of cancer on April 17, 1985, at sixty-three and that her place of death was at the Home of Compassion in Tamavua. Spending her last years in the Home of Compassion indicates that she was Catholic and that she was somewhat separated from village living.

The image of Qumia wearing a black, ankle-length dress and holding my mother is indicative of the complexity of the intimacies at work in the domestic space of Eurocolonial relations with Fijians (figure 1.1). The photo is part of a series of formal bourgeois family portraits. The inclusion of Qumia in this series places her domestic service within the intimacy of colonial family relations. But the expression of formality in the way she stands facing the camera, holding my mother with one arm—almost at a distance—also hints at the boundaries of inclusion. The photos are in clear contrast to my mother's written memories of sitting in Qumia's lap under a frangipani tree and rubbing noses and the relaxed photo taken over two decades later, when my mother visited Qumia before relocating to Canada (figure 1.2). The photo tells a different story of relations formalized and shaped by Eurocolonial expectations of domestic service. The image preserved by my family is not cozy and intimate but carefully controlled and staged to uphold distinctions. The upright, sterile embrace indicates borders being maintained around racial, national, and class hierarchy and control over Qumia's prescribed bodily comportment and care. As Stoler has observed in her own research on colonial iconography in the Dutch Indies, photos such as this one are a reminder of the framing of life in the colony and the ease of colonial life made possible by servants "who labor offstage."[69]

To the extent that my grandmother's memories of living in Fiji featured Qumia, Qumia appears to have been at the crux of my grandmother's gauge on a changing imperial world. While I cannot confirm Qumia's experience of working for my grandparents, the following memoir, titled "South Sea Island Memories," written by my grandmother, indicates that the power dynamics between colonial elite women and Indigenous women

Figure 1.1. Anna Qumia with Hilary White Nunn, Suva, Fiji, circa 1943. Photograph by Frank T. M. White.

Figure 1.2. Anna Qumia with Hilary White Nunn, Suva, Fiji, circa 1968. Photograph by Frank T. M. White.

were complex relational negotiations. Written from a colonial perspective, my grandmother's memoir contains disturbing and offensive racial stereotypes. Her tone of authority, control, and romanticized proximity to Qumia creates an impression of specific dynamics of power and exoticism. In the memoir she describes Qumia as striking, gleaming, offering her service, a friend, helpmate, good humored, polite, leaving in a huff and a lurch, drifting about, and never in a hurry. While the memoir suggests a perception of comradery, her recollections of friendship, loyalty, and affection were unlikely mutual. As Stoler found in her many interviews with Indonesians who worked for Dutch colonials as domestic servants, these individuals did not recount the sentimental memories held so dear by colonial families.[70] To show how Eurocolonial domestic space framed my grandmother's and Qumia's relationship within a disparate array of fraught, unwanted, sought-after, and troubled affections, I offer an extended passage of the memoir here.

"South Sea Island Memories"

I remember Valeriana well as she stood there looking in through the open doorway; from the top of her upswept dark frizzy hair to her bare brown feet, she made a striking picture; she wore a short-sleeved, low-cut white blouse and an ankle-length sulu or wrap-over skirt of red and white cotton material, tucked in at the waist; there was a red hibiscus flower tucked into her hair above her ear, and her gleaming smile showed a row of strong white teeth. She had come to offer her services as household help.

My husband had accepted an appointment in the Fiji Islands, and we had just moved into our bungalow, which was set on a rise among green lawns, wet with constant rains, and overlooking a palm-lined road which wound its way into the township of Suva.

In the humid tropical heat, I knew I would need plenty of help with the work of the house, and I was glad to engage Valeriana—or Anna, for short. I explained that I should like her to "live-in" and keep me company when my husband's work took him away to other islands of the group.

Anna furnished her room in true Fijian style, her bed being a pile of woven grass mats with coloured wool fringes, and her pillow-slip of white linen was richly embroidered with many colours. The first night we were left alone in the house, I felt a little uneasy, remembering that her ancestors had been cannibals not so very long ago, but as time went on, I was very glad to have her company, and over the years she proved to be a friend and helpmate who saw me through many troubled times; it is true that she left me in a huff now and then, but she always came back.

Anna saved up enough money from her small wage to buy a hand-propelled sewing-machine, and in her off-duty hours, would sit cross-legged before it, making her dresses; she made up colourful cottons in European style, but always to the ankle, or worn over a full-length sulu, as Fijian custom demanded. But she looked really spectacular in her meke costume, when she dressed uniformly with a row of dusky belles to perform a native dance for some ceremonial occasion; she wore skirts of tapa-cloth, made from the bark of the paper-mulberry tree, the skirts being arranged in tiers and gathered into the waist; over a simple white blouse she wore garlands of leaves and flowers about her neck and wrists, and a red hibiscus tucked into the side of her hair; hibiscus were plentiful, coming in shades of red, pink, gold and white, and flowering daily on every garden hedge.

From time to time, we were onlookers at a meke; I well remember the aroma of crushed greenery and coconut oil worn by the participants and the drumming rhythm which accompanied their movements; after watching the warrior's fiery dance, with much stomping of the feet and chopping of the air with war-clubs, the girls' dance, with movements of hands and arms only, seemed very sedate and ladylike.

Anna drifted about her work in the house; there was never any need to hurry in the islands, and the climate was enervating; she would sit on the doorstep each morning, arranging hibiscus blooms on the ends of *sasas*, those long thin stems stripped from the centre of the palm-leaf; bunched together into a large vase, the sasas spread out with the weight of the flowers and filled the corners of the house with a riot of colour. Sometimes, Marianna would call from the road-way, "Anna! Valli! Eh, Psst!" Sometimes, Penianna or Vanianna would bring their plates for dinner, great piles of dalo, the staple root vegetable of the Islanders, with a little something tasty on the side—kai, vivili, or other shell-fish being very popular, and they would sit on the kitchen floor, exchanging local gossip.

We had heard that Fijian servants never stay very long; that they don't really have to work; with such lush tropical growth throughout the Islands, there was plenty of food for the picking; there were oranges, bananas and coconuts growing wild, fish in the sea and wild pig in the hills; but if they wished to enjoy the pleasures of life in the township, they were required to have some regular employment. Anna left me in the lurch one day, but after a few days in her koro or village, thought better of it and came back.

As she entered the dining room to lay the table for dinner, I was putting the finishing touches to a small pair of blue bootees;

"Will it be a boy or a girl," I mused.

"It'll be a girl," she replied emphatically.

And sure enough, it was, as we were soon to find out.

"I said it would be a girl." Stated Anna.

"And what made you so sure?" I enquired.

"I drau-ni-kau'd it," she replied good-humoradly.

"Drau-ni-kau" means "the pointing of the leaf," and when the leaf is pointed one can cast a spell for good or evil. One can even will a person to die—*and die he will*; in recent years, however, an enlightened chief held out against it, and although already pining away, roused himself and recovered, thus disproving the age-old power of the "drau-ni-kau."

Whether our daughter was the result of the "drau-ni-kau" or not, she was a delight to us all. Sometimes, we would have an evening out at the local cinema, leaving Anna to mind the baby and, incidentally, to have a few friends in for some "wireless-listening," for which they all thanked us very politely, on our return.

Life ran smoothly and peacefully in our island home until Hitler began stirring up trouble in Europe; there were repercussions throughout the world, and anger spread among us all. One evening, on returning from the cinema, we heard some gruesome sounds emanating from the radio, and found the girls seated before it with rapt attention; Anna was joining in with the horrifying sounds of Ugh! Grrr! And something that sounded like the crunching of bones! It was the weekly all-Fijian broadcast, which was usually fairly humorous, but this sounded far from funny.

"They're boiling that Hitler in Oil!" she informed us; and if Hitler had been around, I think she'd have been only too happy to stoke the fire and stir the pot!

The war dragged on and the Turanga (head of the house) became involved in local military preparedness; he was away from home when Anna left me again; then, Pearl Harbour exploded! A second enemy was headed for our shores. Mothers and babies were hastily evacuated in a New Zealand troopship, which had brought soldiers to the defense of Fiji. The ship zigzagged all the way to Auckland, dodging an enemy submarine, which had been following us from Suva Harbour.

We arrived safely, however, and spent a fairly peaceful year looking after our babies. In the meantime, terrible things were happening at sea, and what followed is history; it was the Coral Sea Battle which cleared our part of the Pacific, and, after a year or so, families were permitted to return to their Island homes.

We returned in a ship carrying military personnel, reminding us that the world war was not yet over. But the seas were calm and we reached Suva without mishap. The Turanga was there to meet us, and as we drove through the palm-lined streets to our home on the hill, I reflected that we should have to make new arrangements for nursery help. The old home looked much the same, set among the exotic tropical plants, the vivid crotons, variegated coleus and flowering Hibiscus.

And indoors, Hibiscus radiated from their jars; I wondered who had put them there. As we settled into our armchairs, my husband said, "I've got a surprise for you."

I looked up as I heard the rattle of a tea-tray, and saw above it the smiling face of—*Valeriana!*[71]

My grandmother was part of a "civilizing" colonial presence aimed at maintaining colonial order. In a colonial space of Euro-domestic structure, her memoir is, as Nicholas Thomas writes, "expressive and constitutive of colonial relationships."[72] It reveals the colonial stereotypes of Fijians as cannibals, which caused her to feel uneasy, as well as happy, peaceful, and lazy. Yet the tone of control over Qumia through her romanticized nostalgia is exacerbated when Qumia is rendered virtually mute by the memoir, save for the grunts, groans, gossip, and her "good humored" expressions. The stereotypes, along with other language used in her memoir, draws on tropes, images, and racialized phenotypic descriptions ("frizzy hair," "bare brown feet," "low-cut blouse," "strong white teeth") to construct a naturalized and physiological separation between "cannibalistic," exotic Fijian "savages" and "reasonable" and "civilized" British subjects.

The memoir also indicates shifts and pressures related to Indigenous spiritual practices in 1930s and 1940s Fiji. My grandmother recounted an interaction with Qumia involving the Indigenous spiritual and ritual practice of draunikau.[73] Qumia claimed to have had an effect on the sex of my mother through draunikau—a practice that some colonial administrators understood to be tantamount to devil worship, sorcery, and black magic, at least in part owing to colonial fears of disruptions to colonial order. These negative connotations to draunikau seem to contradict my grandmother's light-hearted and dismissive account of Qumia's prediction of my mother's birth.

My grandmother's description of meke, observed between eight and sixteen years after Henderson's, also supports the notion that meke were good and lawful so long as they outwardly acknowledged acceptance of Christianity and colonial authority. Aside from her brief mention of a ceremonial aspect in a meke involving Qumia, these meke did not worry her but met with her colonial approval as a kind of cultural enactment and entertainment. In her admiring account as an "onlooker," these meke nevertheless supported existing power structures by distinguishing who was "colonial" (observing) and who was "native" (being observed)—a division also exemplified in photographs of meke from the late 1940s from the National Archives of Fiji, including an image of men's meke performed at Nasova for a colonial audience in 1948 (figure 1.3) and an image of women's meke in Beqa from 1949 (figure 1.4). The photograph of the women's meke (figure 1.4) shows a line of dancers in motion, with Fijians in the foreground, sitting and watching the performers, and a man dressed in all-white garments observing and walking between the Fijian observers and performers. While I am unable to confirm who the man was or why he was attending the meke, to cut into the space between Fijian performers and observers in such a way signals a sense of privilege and freedom to move without regard for the positions and perspectives of the Fijians present. But his stance also declares a power and authority to observe and even inspect the dancing. Wittingly or not, the photographer captured a sense of entitlement and authority in motion. In contrast to the earlier 1930s concerns with "devil dances" being condemned by A. G. Armstrong that were done at night, outside the gaze of colonial authority, these meke done in spaces made available to observing colonial eyes affirmed for people like my grandmother that the British were in control of the colony.

In the meke my grandmother describes, binary gendered expressions were indicators of civilized comportment. Expressions of gender seemed acceptable to her as a vivid set of rhythms and movements that denoted men as fiery warriors, who moved robustly, and ladylike women, who moved sedately. In her memoir, the link between men and warriors recalls earlier missionary accounts of meke in connection to heathenism and war as well as the ahistorical use of those accounts in the CSO files to regulate meke. Yet her account demonstrates a different construction. Rather than sensing any threat from these warriors, my grandmother perceived them as exciting and just exotic enough to be entertaining. While Armstrong's reports of allegedly sexually free and robust dancing women were a gendered construction

Figure 1.3. Men's meke wau, Nasova, 1948. Courtesy of National Archives of Fiji.

Figure 1.4. Women's meke, Beqa, 1949. Courtesy of National Archives of Fiji.

of disorder—a sign that colonialism was failing to civilize and control its population—my grandmother's descriptions are a reminder that her perceptions of ladylike and sedate movements were equally a colonial construction, an indicator of European gendered ideals. Photos of meke from the 1940s confirm a tendency to separate bodies in alignment with a male/female gender binary. (See, for example, figure 1.5 of a women's vakamalolo at Nasova, 1948—the same event as the all-male meke wau in figure 1.3; figures 1.6, 1.7, and 1.8 in Beqa, 1948; and figures 1.9 and 1.10 in Nanukuloa, 1944, which are all illustrative of this gendered binary in meke performing events.) Regardless of the actual motivations to generate a binary gendered division through the separate performances of men and women at these events, my grandmother's approval of such meke was also an approval of

Figure 1.5. Women's vakamalolo, Nasova, 1948. Courtesy of National Archives of Fiji.

Figure 1.6. Men's meke wau, Beqa, 1948. Courtesy of National Archives of Fiji.

Figure 1.7. Men's meke wau, Beqa, 1948. Courtesy of National Archives of Fiji.

Figure 1.8. Women's meke iri, Beqa, 1948. Courtesy of National Archives of Fiji.

Figure 1.9. Men's meke iri, Nanukuloa, 1944. Courtesy of National Archives of Fiji.

Figure 1.10. Women's meke iri, Nanukuloa, 1944. Courtesy of National Archives of Fiji.

men and women performing separately what, to her, were timeless gender-specific gestures.

Prior to my grandmother's description of Qumia's meke costume, with tiers of masi (a traditional bark cloth made by women) (see figure 1.8), my grandmother described Qumia sewing ankle-length sulus (wrapped skirt) that "custom demanded." The custom of wearing ankle-length sulus was an outward indicator of accepting Christianity and the government. The photo of women performing meke in Beqa in the late 1940s (figure 1.11), after my grandparents had left Fiji, shows women wearing an ankle-length sulu with tiers of masi over top. Missionaries and British colonizers understood the sulu to imply civilized behavior and comportment in contrast to the "nudity" Armstrong condemned in Kadavu.

Figure 1.11. Women's seasea meke, Beqa, 1949. Courtesy of National Archives of Fiji.

The colonial construction of meke as good and lawful cultural entertainment, and an object of the Western gaze, paved the way for meke as a tourist attraction and object for sale and consumption. While in 1937 young men in Savusavu district who were attempting to develop their own economic power and control were criminalized for their involvement in meke—framed as "sorcery"—flashing forward to 1963, the negative construct gave way to a colonially sanctioned construct of cultural entertainment for tourists. The photo of Western tourists watching young boys in Savusavu district perform meke (figure 1.12) is a haunting reminder of the colonial impact on that region. The tourist gaze perpetuates colonial constructions of civilized subject versus primitive Other in this photo by dividing the "white" observers from the "nonwhite" performers. These tourists, who are presumably privileged, with the time and money to vacation in the tropics, are consuming Fijian culture and heritage as entertainment and an object of the past. Yet while the tourists captured their experiences with their cameras, they were also being photographed. This

Figure 1.12. Tourists watching meke (children), Savusavu, 1963. Courtesy of National Archives of Fiji.

image enables us to see the tourists in relation to the young boys doing meke—it captures the divisions while forcing us to think about the process of boundary making in relational terms. Through this image, the equation flips and it is no longer "white" observing "nonwhite" performer—a reading supported by the gaze of the Fijians sitting on the hillside, who are also observing the tourist scene.

Movements and Migrations: Indirect Resistance to Indirect Rule

While meke movements were a site for colonial anxieties about order and control, so were larger movements and migrations of Fijians in space. How did colonial populations respond to the larger movements and migrations of Fijians in relation to colonial ones? The following official colonial reports and documents show how leading up to and during World War II colonials expressed concerns about increased numbers of Fijians in urban centers and moving about the countryside. Colonials predicted negative social and economic ramifications if such uncontrolled movements and migrations were allowed to continue, and measures were put in place to increase surveillance and control. Just as colonial controls and regulations of meke were predicated on constructions of Fijians as ahistorically primitive, so too were colonial controls and regulations of larger iTaukei movements and migrations.

Governor Gordon established the Native Administration and indirect rule in the late 1870s as a highly structured hierarchy spanning from the village council to the Council of Chiefs.[74] But by the late 1930s and early 1940s, this system was losing its hold on Fijians, who were no longer demonstrating subservience to community and communal life and demonstrating respect for chiefs as well as Europeans. Colonial administrators used paternalistic language to justify increased controls over iTaukei movements and migrations, which had larger economic implications for the colony, as the following suggests. In a report to the colonial secretary and secretary for Native Affairs, the district commissioner for Savusavu district in 1937 wrote:

> Natives are moving about the Province more freely than ever before and are beginning to demand payment for work hitherto performed communally. . . . The Young Fijian is undoubtedly asking for his freedom but it is for a freedom to do nothing at all and to be released from all discipline.

> The idea of any permanent work or settling on the land is his last thought, and should he be granted his freedom at this stage it will mean the loss of every control over him together with the loss of over fifty years of pioneer work.[75]

The commissioner's concern about Fijians demanding payment for what would otherwise have been referred to as "communal" work poses immediate questions about the economic workings of indirect rule. Fijians demanding payment for labor that was otherwise "given" would have been a major threat to the economic benefits the colony reaped under the banner of communal work within indirect rule. This document also exemplifies a colonial manifestation of the civilizing mission, articulated in the Deed of Cession, to be in control of Fijian bodies and keep them where they can be observed—even if indirectly. The quotation, which appears directly after a reporting of the criminal case of meke involving luveniwai, indicates colonizers' concerns with Fijian movements and migrations hindering British governance, economics, and "every control" over Fijian bodies.[76] The "freely" moving body had an agency that the government wanted to suppress through denying the freedom to participate in non-Christian meke as well as self-determination to move throughout the country.

When Fijians, such as Qumia, moved away from their villages, their behavior (now outside the purview of village chiefs) formed a source of growing anxiety for urban Europeans, who continued to paternalistically frame Fijians as instinctive, tribal, primitive, and less culturally evolved than Europeans. As R. H. Lester stated in "Effects of War on Fijian Society," an address to the Suva Rotary Club during World War II:

> Some people have expressed concern at the behaviour of certain Fijians quartered in Suva. The rowdy behavior was in an artificial atmosphere away from their social organisations and from a discipline and authority which they understand. There is nothing in Suva to take the place of tribal authority, which is instinctively obeyed. This also applied to the young women, the sound of whose shrill voices and uncontrolled laughter in the streets mar the stillness of Suva nights. . . . Hundreds of young people and children have been sent back to their villages in recent months. I think it will be generally agreed that their absence has made the night less hideous. Other pessimists prophesy trouble when the troops return from the front. "Wait until the 1st Battalion gets back," some say.[77]

Although Lester believed these concerns to be groundless, others viewed this urban migration as a threat to colonial control.

To address colonial concerns about post–World War II Fijian behavior and demographics, the colonial administration reorganized and revitalized the Native Administration during the mid-1940s on the basis of its original hierarchical principles. In 1944 an influential paramount chief from Bau, Ratu Sir Lala Sukuna, instituted the Fijian Affairs Bill—a neotraditional plan to revitalize indirect rule, intended to keep Fijians in the village (as well as draw Fijians back into their villages) and within the controlled purview of village councils and the Council of Chiefs as well as improve the material conditions of village living.[78] According to Ratu Sukuna, who perpetuated British social evolutionary language in his speech, the 1944 bill sought to "train chiefs and people in orderly, sound, and progressive local government better to fit them eventually for the give and take of democratic institution."[79]

With pressures to express oneself and move in alignment with British Christian colonial governance and indirect rule, my family archives draw attention to how Qumia moved: in meke and in and out of her village and Eurocolonial structures. While those in positions of power and authority asserted control over movement and mobility through the revitalization of race-based and hierarchical boundaries of identity, Qumia moved in ways that appear to have countered, to a degree, such distinctions established through indirect rule. For example, my grandmother's memories of Qumia coming and going are sprinkled throughout her memoir. Sometimes Qumia left "in a huff," sometimes she left "in a lurch." It is clear at least to my grandmother that Qumia traveled between their Eurocolonial home and her koro, or village, repeatedly. Qumia managed to slip in and out of the "indirect" colonial gaze by moving between Eurocolonial structure and village. By being Catholic, Qumia also slipped outside the Methodist gaze that formed part of the colonial hegemonic order. And she slipped out of my grandmother's Euro-domestic gaze by returning to her village.

Although her employment with my grandparents may have afforded Qumia some reprieve from the immobility of "indirect rule," my grandparents had the agency to travel freely, a reminder of how the colonial government constructed and maintained boundaries of privilege by allowing some to move across borders while restricting the movements of others. For example, my grandmother experienced a different sense of mobility than Qumia when it came to World War II, during times of danger. She wrote, after the attack on Pearl Harbor, "Mothers and babies were hastily evacuated." After a peaceful year of "looking after our babies . . . [while] terrible things were happening at sea . . . , families were permitted to return to their Island homes." These attacks on islands of the South Pacific were part of a larger attack on the British imperial presence in Southeast Asia. Yet while Qumia remained in Fiji at a time when Fiji, as a British colony, was in danger of attack, British colonial wives and children were kept from harm's way. This is not to say that colonial mobility rendered Qumia immobile. Instead, it is a reminder that colonial governance in Fiji continually strove to control Fijians while privileged colonials could travel to safety.

Conclusion

Recalling Stoler's insight that records of uncertainty and doubt speak to how people make regulations that correspond to a changing world, I suggest that Fiji's mid-1930s to mid-1940s colonial administration sought to maintain their authority and economic position in uncertain times via regulatory methods that supported chiefly authority while striving to eradicate "sorcery," "witchcraft," and "devil worship" and hindering the movements of Fijians.[80] Colonial governance brought into force new hierarchical formations of power that heavily favored some traditions interwoven with Christianity over other non-Christian ones, involving ritual authority and transcorporeal relations—blurring divides in gender and between the living and the spirits of ancestors and the land. These colonial shifts generated new forms of power and distinction around colonial boundaries of identity (from less civilized heathenism to more civilized Christian liberalism).

As the following chapter will show, these colonial constructions continue to haunt meke and governance in Fiji. For example, prior to his 2006 coup, Prime Minister Bainimarama used negative constructions of the past, developed by missionaries and British colonials, to create reactions built on fear to animate and enflesh his vision for Fiji's future of multiracial harmony. In a public speech prior to his 2006 coup, Bainimarama linked ethnonationalism with a depiction of Fiji's past as two-dimensionally lawless and cannibalistic, making multiracial harmony an appropriate reaction and solution to the supposedly dangerous and threatening past.[81] Bainimarama's rhetoric made radical leaps across time and imaginaries to produce a new kind of multiracial Fijian citizen and a democratic and harmonious Fiji. Yet as the next chapter will show, expressive bodies performing meke generate a more complex understanding of Fiji's shifting political realities.

CHAPTER 2

Governing Meke

Choreographing Pasts, Expressing Futures

Hundreds of bodies moved together in rhythmic unison, with sharp, bound, muscular movements accenting the rhythms of the music. Wielding weapons, the bodies formed clear patterns. Voices called and shouted out across space, bodies responded. In choreography of martial might, iTaukei warriors demonstrated their strength to Fijians, Fiji's guests, and the rest of the world in a military parade—a contemporary war meke, or bole—a challenge to war. The military kicked off the 2012 Fiji Day, an event that once commemorated cession to Britain but now celebrated Fijian independence. The military's bole did not coalesce diverse individuals across axes of difference; rather, the male and female performers moved as one, representing conformity and sameness, in formations that moved linearly across the raralevu—the open field in Albert Park—Suva's modern-day village square. Their synchronized movements emphasized conformity, making the bole look like one preeminent, iTaukei body in motion. The military's expressive and martial strength offered a haunting and nostalgic homage to Fiji's warring past, effectively perpetuating iTaukei military power and governance in the present. In the context of military rule, the choreography asserted that, despite external political pressures and economic sanctions, Fijians are collectively strong, powerful, and mighty in body, mind, and spirit.

Yet the Fiji Day parade's central chant—"Celebrating a United Fiji"—was ambiguous. Though the words conveyed a particular ideological vision, like many meke, the movements did not always offer a literal translation of the text. While the military's leader, Bainimarama, espoused multiracialism in his own verse, the movements of bodies on the national stage expressed something else—an iTaukei military power and authority supporting Bainimarama's "cleanup" and reform of Fiji. The parade, viewed as a contemporary bole, gave insight into the indirect meanings that were generating a national spirit and energy for the viewer-participants. The amalgamation of events offered much more than a representation of culture and heritage: it was a performance that generated relations of power and authority.

∽

Given Fiji's 2006 military coup, which was made in the name of multiculturalism, "'good governance,' anti-racism, and anti-corruption," what is the value of looking at a national Fiji Day military parade, during military rule, as a war meke?[1] What might such a perspective reveal about how competing identifications with Fiji and Fijianness, evoked by the military parade as well as other Fiji Day festivities, coexist or inform one another? This chapter explores the shifting ways in which Fijians identify themselves in and around meke for the national stage and discusses the political and religious forces that impact, frame, or restrict meke in multiple ways and contexts. Since Fiji's independence in 1970, top-down governance favored the constitutional rights and privileges of iTaukei over Fijians of Indian descent. Nevertheless, after this most recent coup, shifts in power diminished top-down hierarchies in favor of horizontal formations. In this fluctuating terrain, differing narratives of the past compete for Fiji's future.

This chapter is a response to the open space created by my engagement with various levels of government during Fiji's military dictatorship. The details of this process say a great deal about Fiji's current political climate and the dominant ideas of power that feed into this ecology, bringing particular questions to the foreground. How did power operate in post–2006 coup Fiji? And what were the body politics governing Fiji's citizens and regulating that power? How was meke, including larger choreographic renderings of nation such as the military parade, part of that arrangement? What were Fijians (the leaders, government officials, and citizens) reaching toward? Perhaps just as importantly, why were some so willing to support my research on meke and others more anxious?

After a brief overview of Fiji's past coups d'état, I evaluate encounters with three levels of Fijian government, each with its own stake in Fiji's future. While the iTaukei Institute of Language and Culture aims to safeguard Fiji's iTaukei culture and heritage against erasure and loss in order to support a future that protects chiefly authority and Christian iTaukei land security, Fiji's Ministry of Education espouses narratives of the past as inequitable, fractured, and belligerent in order to advocate for a future of multiracial harmony whereby "all" citizens of Fiji have equal constitutional rights regardless of descent.[2] Finally, I discuss three meke performances for the national stage in relation to Fijian governance as a way of analyzing thick feelings of indeterminacy created by Bainimarama's military takeover. These meke—war meke for the festival of Pacific Arts, war meke at the Fijian Cultural Center in the Arts Village of Pacific Harbour, and meke for Fiji Day—unsettle and reify governing discourses and produce unstable and contradictory expressions of Fijian belonging. In the space of uncertainty created by the most recent coup, new bodies emerge at once governed by and governing through these three layers of discourse about past, present, and future.

This chapter thus moves between personal ethnographic experience and broader analysis to explore the narratives espoused at each level of government in relation to dancing for, about, and on Fiji's national stage. By exploring postindependence meke for the national stage and my experiences communicating with Fijian governing institutions, I show how meke embodies shifting relations of power, citizenship, and identity.

Coups d'état Context

Coups d'état leaders before Bainimarama asserted links between chiefly authority, iTaukei preeminence, and rights to land ownership as God given against challenges to that power. The year 1987 marked a turning point in Fiji's political relations, when the first-ever elected multiracial Fiji Labor Party (a coalition of Fijians of Indian and iTaukei descent headed by an iTaukei commoner, Timoci Bavadra) challenged chiefly and iTaukei preeminence.[3] One month after the election, the iTaukei "ethno-nationalist" Lieutenant Colonel of the Royal Fiji Military Forces Sitiveni Rabuka staged the first of his two coups that year to restore power to chiefly authority. Rabuka gave the Great Council of Chiefs—a constitutional system of power and authority installed by the British colonial administration in 1876 to enable a system of indirect rule in collaboration with the Methodist Church—authority to sanction a new constitution.[4] The 1990 constitution reaffirmed the idea that chiefs had a divine, God-given claim to sovereign power and granted laws and rights that denied the same rights to Fijians of Indian descent.[5] Rabuka's coup asserted Christian iTaukei sovereignty as a physiological basis of belonging, or biopolitical arrangement, with God.[6] Not surprisingly, the Methodist Church and the Great Council of Chiefs supported Rabuka's ethno-nationalist objectives. These two powerful and influential institutions continued to govern iTaukei and protect their "God-given rights" to the land. Because of rising tensions between iTaukei and Fijians of Indian descent who wanted equality, the military coups in 1987 led to increased racism aimed at Fijians of Indian descent, destruction of their property, and massive migration to a number of diasporas including Canada.[7]

In 1999 iTaukei preeminence was again challenged when a Fijian of Indian descent, Mahendra Chaudhry, won a democratic election to become prime minister of Fiji. The chiefs opposed his position as leader of Fiji. And one year after he was elected, ethno-nationals George Speight and Ilisoni Ligairi staged a coup.[8] After the 2000 coup, Laisenia Qarase became Fiji's prime minister, promoting policies that would favor Indigenous Fijians until Commodore Frank Bainimarama's 2006 military coup.

The coup of 2006 brought a narrative of multiracialism that, on the surface, appears to reach toward a future of ethnic and racial tolerance, unity, and harmony through a rejection of a dangerous past. In a speech prior to the 2006 coup, Bainimarama argued that leniency of the Qarase government toward perpetrators of the 2000 coup had sanctioned a disrespect for the law that had resulted in increased incidents of rape, homicide, and desecration of Hindu temples, and he expressed anxiety that such policies could take Fiji back to its cannibal past.[9] Bainimarama issued an ultimatum for the government to bring the proponents of the 2000 coup to justice and remove political barriers to economic equality based on race.[10] When his demands were not met, he took control of the government in the capacity of executive authority, rationalizing his military takeover to media by saying Prime Minister Qarase was corrupt and responsible for inflaming tensions between ethnic communities.[11] Bainimarama used an account of the past as dangerous (owing to its systemic racism) and threatening (by invoking cannibalism in his audience's imaginations) to justify imposing state power over Fiji's citizens in order to direct all Fijians toward a future uncharted territory of multiracial harmony and unity.

During the time that I attended the 2012 Fiji Day celebrations, Fiji's unelected prime minister, Bainimarama, ruled by decree. He had abolished the Great Council of Chiefs, suspended Fiji's constitution, and instituted official censorship. His measures resulted in mass exodus of judges, reporters, and editors. He ruled as unelected prime minister for eight years until, in 2014, he renounced his military role and called for an election, which he entered as the head of a brand-new political party called Fiji First. He then created a new constitution without vote or consensus and won the "democratic" election. He secured his legitimate position as prime minister of Fiji when he strategically named his military successor, Mosese Tikoitoga, who had proven himself loyal to Bainimarama at the time of his appointment as military commander.

Ruminating on "Ethnicity": iTaukei Institute

A few months before traveling to Fiji to conduct fieldwork, iTaukei Fijians I consulted with in Canada told me on two separate occasions that there were reasons to be concerned about the safety and protection of my family, myself, and my research while in Fiji. They explained that under the military dictatorship of Prime Minister Bainimarama, journalists had been tortured in military barracks and deported in addition to other human rights abuses.[12] Even in Canada they felt they needed to censor their criticism of the Fijian government for fear of endangering their relatives and friends in Fiji. They suggested I do the same. Their stories and whispers of caution and danger were part of the larger narratives pushing and pulling at the relations between Fiji's citizens and state sovereignty.

Despite the warnings, I followed the advice of Fijian scholar Dr. Apo Aporosa and met with Dr. Sekove Bigitibau, former director of the iTaukei Institute of Language and Culture, which operates under the Ministry of iTaukei Affairs. During our meeting, he called the current director of the iTaukei Institute to organize an immediate meeting with me. When arriving at the institute for the first time, I showed up with three-quarter-length pants (thinking I was sufficiently observing the cultural norm of covering the knees) and was instructed to put on an ankle length sulu.[13] They had extras at the front desk. I put on the sulu and went up the elevator with my family.[14] I met with the director and his assistant, who were kind and interested in my project.

They asked me questions about my research, and I explained my rationale and interest in the politics of identity in relation to meke. Despite my ethics and motivations, I still feared that my candor might endanger my family and work. To my surprise, they were very supportive. They immediately suggested I connect with the Ministry of Education, sending them an email, adding, "Mrs. Kelly's work is of interest to the Ministry of iTaukei Affairs."[15]

After communicating their endorsement, however, the institute immediately indicated their political agenda when my correspondent handed me a document to review titled *Implementation of the 2003 UNESCO Convention in the Pacific with Special Emphasis on Multinational Nominations*. The document outlines Fiji's objectives, as a multiracial nation, for the safeguarding of Indigenous intangible cultural heritage (ICH) such as traditional songs and dances.[16] With Fiji's tumultuous history in mind, reading the term "multiracial" used in an unproblematic way spread discomfort and confusion all over my body. Not fully understanding why or how the document was deploying the term, I tried to move beyond the distracting pull it had on me so that I could continue to engage with the important words my interlocutor was sharing with me about meke.

His words evidenced the magnitude, power, and influence of the increasingly dominant charismatic and evangelical narrative of Fiji's "devilish" Indigenous traditions. He cautiously challenged the governing influence of this rhetoric when he told me that he did not think that Fiji's non-Christian Indigenous spiritual practices were entirely without some positive aspects. His comment came out as a cautious query; perhaps he felt safe to utter his dissenting thoughts in the presence of an outsider. After all, I was still caught up in figuring out why Indigenous Fijians were not choosing to embrace their non-Christian spiritual practices like so many other Indigenous populations around the globe who celebrate Indigenous spirituality as a way to push back against histories of imposed silence and erasure by Christian missionaries and colonizers. He spoke cautiously, carefully testing the boundaries of what he could safely say.

With that decentering utterance, I suddenly realized where the center of power was. My contact created a small crack or fissure in the current dominating account evangelicals and charismatics espouse of Fiji's so-called devilish past. Perhaps sensing my relief at his critical perspective, he went on to say what many I spoke to would not dare to, that he drinks yaqona to go into a trance state to create his meke choreographies—an act that many of the evangelical churchgoers I spoke to in Fiji and Canada considered tantamount to devil worship. iTaukei consider a yaqona-induced trance state part of Fiji's non-Christian spiritual approach to meke composition. This approach allows the land spirits or ancestor gods to enter the body of the daunivucu in order to impart the meke movements and chant. His cautious remarks burrowed into my mind, forcing me to ask, Why was he challenging this dominant narrative within the context of our conversation? And why was he challenging the narrative so cautiously? He clarified the answers to my questions when he told me that he comes from a village that no longer exists. He explained that when Fiji's main roads were first being built, the colonial administration considered his village inaccessible because it was too far inland and moved his entire village to the roadside for "accessibility." As a result of his family history, he was particularly concerned with safeguarding Fiji's traditional beliefs and practices so that they do not become erased like his village. Later I discovered that the governing influence of the evangelical and charismatic churches was not my consultant's only concern. The institute was also fighting for the protection of Indigenous knowledge in the face of recent post–2006 coup discourses of multiracialism.

The conversation I narrate above begins to clarify how meke is central to the ways in which some Fijians and Fijian government institutions reify and unsettle competing national discourses. In the context of Bainimarama's multiracialism, which, at least on the surface, espouses racial harmony and national unity, the safeguarding and protecting of iTaukei preeminence through its intangible cultural heritage, of which meke is key, is precarious at best. Bainimarama has disabled social systems (supported by intangible cultural heritage) that he believes allow racism and inequities to flourish. The Great Council of Chiefs is one of the systems that Bainimarama has dismantled, weakening their political leverage and, by extension, the chiefly system and its privileges in the constitution. An institution like the iTaukei Institute, which answered to the Great Council of Chiefs via the Ministry of iTaukei Affairs but also answers to the Bainimarama administration, is in an uncertain political position; there is no way to achieve the objectives of one without working against the objectives of the other.

Despite Bainimarama's post–2006 coup goals of moving beyond past modes of governance that used traditional practices and protocols to secure chiefly authority, my discussions with my consultant at the iTaukei Institute clarified how the institute aimed primarily to safeguard and protect the iTaukei culture and heritage that the government sought to overcome. Those at the institute lamented the loss of customs and traditions such as meke. They viewed culture and heritage as being under threat from Westernizing forces, the suppression of traditions from church and state, and increased pressures to produce art and culture that expressed multiracialism.

Within this complex political situation, meke was being pulled in at least three directions: by charismatics and evangelicals who rejected meke; by those who wanted meke to mix with the cultural traditions of other ethnocultural groups; and by those who wanted to protect meke as cultural heritage as a way of preserving and promoting iTaukei preeminence.[17]

Given my overt intent to research tensions and anxieties around notions of ethnicity and identity in performances of meke, why was the iTaukei Institute so supportive of my project? Though meanings for and boundaries of ethnicity are created and re-created in relation to specific past and present political, economic, and social contexts, I believe the institute saw my research as a potential source of safeguarding meke and iTaukei Fijian cultural heritage within a context of more fixed understandings of ethnicity.[18] During my time in Fiji, those at the institute had safeguarding meke on their minds because in 2010 Fiji ratified UNESCO's 2003 Convention for the Safeguarding of Intangible Cultural Heritage and made the iTaukei Institute an authority on the project.[19]

To understand the potentially fraught workings of UNESCO safeguarding in Fiji requires some historical context about the UNESCO support for intangible cultural heritage in the Pacific subregion. After decades of meetings and researching how best to support and sustain living traditions and their practitioners, in 2001 UNESCO established the ICH Lists, from which expert panels could declare "Masterpieces of Oral and Intangible Heritage of Humanity." With the development of UNESCO's ICH Masterpiece program, state parties could create an inventory of their own intangible cultural heritage by defining, identifying, and listing the cultural assets of their territory.[20] It is within this context that in 2003 UNESCO declared Tongan lakalaka a masterpiece. Lakalaka, a song-dance illustrative of text, fit the parameters of the program perfectly: it is not simply a historic piece that gets repeated but a distinctive performance practice with over one hundred years of being constantly re-created, actively composed, and performed; and lakalaka is an important component of Tongan cultural identity.[21] Although named an explicitly Tongan masterpiece, the lakalaka is also performed in Fiji in the Lau group of islands, where important Tongan influences continue to be present. This example illustrates that intangible cultural heritage does not fit squarely within nation-state geographies, drawing attention to a major shortcoming of the UNESCO Masterpiece program. The cultural possessions of a territory, as cultural studies scholar Rosemary Coombe has observed, have become linked to possessive individualism, whereby certain objects and cultural heritage have become tantamount to essentialized group identities.[22] Culture is reified as national property and the nation becomes "a property-owning 'collective individual.'"[23] Furthermore, listing intangible cultural heritage, as a form of safeguarding a cultural possession, recalls missionary and colonial histories of modernization and civilizing projects, for which museums have preserved what was wiped out.[24]

Within the framework of UNESCO's more updated 2003 Convention for the Safeguarding of Intangible Cultural Heritage, which aims to provide greater support for communities and practitioners in local cultural recreation, meke is a perfect fit. It is within this updated UNESCO context that the iTaukei Institute was keen for me to explore meke as a candidate for one of UNESCO's two lists: "Representative List of the Intangible Cultural Heritage of Humanity" (geared toward increasing cultural heritage awareness) and "List of Intangible Cultural Heritage in Need of Urgent Safeguarding" (geared toward cultural heritage in urgent need of measures to stay alive).

On the surface, safeguarding Indigenous song-dance seems like an ethically sound project, but the ethics and politics are far more complex, particularly when applying UNESCO's definitions of intangible cultural heritage and safeguarding to Fiji. Intangible cultural heritage is defined as: "practices, representations, expressions, knowledge, skills, as well as the instruments, objects, artifacts and cultural spaces associated therewith. It is manifested in the domains of oral traditions and expressions, performing arts, social practices, rituals and festive events, knowledge and practices relating to nature and the universe as well as traditional craftsmanship, which embrace almost every element concerning the cultural development of humanity."[25] Safeguarding is referred to as "comprehensive measures aimed at ensuring the viability of intangible cultural heritage, including the identification, documentation, research, preservation, protection, promotion, enhancement, transmission, as well as the revitalization of various aspects of such heritage."[26] According to UNESCO, intangible cultural heritage is crucial for understanding and promoting cultural diversity and continuous development.[27] Although the UNESCO document promotes an international level of safeguarding against the threat of disappearance and transformation of "living" intangible cultural heritage, at the local level, these objectives risk fixing meke in time and place. Safeguarding may result in negating cultural heritage transformations and migrations as relevant aspects of cultural diversity and development.

On the one hand, there is great value in a project that promotes research, understanding, sharing, and protection of intangible iTaukei knowledge. Meke, as a living mode of expression, contains vast amounts of knowledge about historical events, past and present spiritual and religious practices, ways of living off the land, and an aesthetics of social interaction and is part of making sense of the world. Bodily movements through space (such as shifts of weight, rhythm, and relations with bodies) are, as dance studies scholar Jacqueline Shea Murphy has suggested, philosophical, spiritual, and political negotiations in Indigenous dance whereby the dancing is itself a powerful tool in generating agency, self-determination, and resilience.[28] Given the political and religious pressures particular to Fiji, however, the ethics of applying these universal objectives of safeguarding to Fiji are potentially problematic.

In Fiji's report to the UNESCO Convention on Intangible Cultural Heritage, past director of the iTaukei Institute Sekove Degei Bigitibau explained why safeguarding was urgently necessary, inadvertently producing a haunting reminder of Fiji's Christian-colonial legacy of safeguarding through indirect rule: "Indigenous Fijian customs, language, dances, traditional etiquette, etc. are oral and preservation rests pivotally on continual usage and observance. However, given the onset of a dominant global culture, with the combined influence of a conducive cosmopolitan livelihood, an apathetic youthful population, and emphasis on economic development, has placed intangible heritage in a precariously desperate position, continually being threatened, and exploited."[29] What is not so obvious here is that Bigitibau took an explicitly Methodist stance when he explained that traditions and customs of the past involving the vanua (with the chief at the center) require family roles and responsibilities to be passed on from generation to generation as "God given heritage."[30] Bigitibau also reinforced the importance of the Methodist Church in safeguarding culture in his 2007 thesis in which he argued that new churches are a threat to "intrinsic Fijian identity" and a threat to Methodist values and beliefs tied to custom and tradition.[31] Bigitibau espoused Fiji's intangible cultural heritage as belonging to Indigenous Fijians, whose pasts are tied to the Methodist Church and the land, and in need of international safeguarding from current political power shifts. But the safeguarding objectives that support Fijian identity as a synthesis of the colonially imposed, chiefly Methodist authority conflict with the objectives of iTaukei who reject traditions and chiefly authority in order to reach for democratic participation, equal opportunities for leadership, and individual economic prosperity.

In efforts to protect "intrinsic" links to the land and traditions as "God given," the act of safeguarding intangible cultural heritage might also reify a long-term political, economic, social, and religious divide between Fijians of iTaukei descent and Fijians of Indian descent. In reality, the convention fulfills a particular ethnonational conservative agenda in Fiji aimed at keeping power and land in the hands of iTaukei. To exemplify this, according to Bigitibau, loss of land and changes to land tenure are major threats to Fiji's intangible cultural heritage because land is integral to such cultural heritage in Fiji.[32] For Bigitibau, intangible cultural heritage in Fiji belongs to iTaukei whose land ownership, and all that comes from the land (including customs and traditions), is a gift from God. In this equation, challenges to land ownership are heathen acts since they intervene in God's divine plan for iTaukei. Thus, the guiding principle behind UNESCO's convention might (unintentionally) bolster iTaukei national conservative and Methodist values aimed at maintaining ethnic preeminence to sustain the status quo.[33]

Ruminating on "Ethnicity": Ministry of Education

My correspondents at the iTaukei Institute emphasized the importance of education in the process of protection, preservation, and revitalization of Indigenous cultural knowledge and suggested I discuss my research with the Ministry of Education. The institute initiated the dialogue by sending an email explaining their support for my research: "Her research is close to the heart of our department and ministry. . . . The country, especially the iTaukei population, has a lot to benefit from her research, which is why this Ministry [iTaukei Affairs] supports her research."[34] While the institute had no concern with my research ethics protocol, the Ministry of Education's permanent secretary responded with reservations about my use of the term "ethnicity" and asked me to "ruminate" on my use of the term. The ministry wrote: "We further advise that our Permanent Secretary holds some reservations on the use of 'ethnicity' in your topic. This is in line with connotations that impact negatively and denote racial affiliations as propagated in our mandate. However, seeing the importance of the subject and its closeness to the heart of the iTaukei Institute as alluded below, I leave you to articulate the issue [with the Institute]."[35]

When I received the email, I was sure that I had hit a nerve. I was worried that my research might not appeal to conservative Fijian nationals in positions of power, and I was concerned about the safety and security of the materials I had gathered and wanted still to gather. I was also confused by their reservations about the term "ethnicity." It was not clear what the Ministry of Education had reservations about. In a country that espouses an official discourse of "race" and "multiracialism," why was the term "ethnicity" so distressing? In my own usage of the term, I problematized essentialized notions of ethnicity and was examining how meke plays a role in the generation and renegotiation of ethnic identification. Nowhere in my writing was "ethnicity" an essential biological fact. Perhaps that was the problem. Perhaps the idea of biological difference was key to a discourse of multiracialism. Despite my best efforts, I could not figure out what the ministry's policies were with regard to notions of "race" in relation to "ethnicity." But the email became an important source for understanding political hostilities and hierarchies within the government and how Fijians were maneuvering around them.

~

Analyzing the concerns and sentiments exchanged through these emails in the above field note clarifies the directionality of multiple levels of governance in Fiji. The correspondence indicates tensions between the two different government bodies and their desires for different futures for Fiji. The iTaukei Institute safeguards the past by mapping and preserving Indigenous knowledge for a future of chiefly authority and iTaukei rights and privileges against transformation and loss due to globalization, Western influences, and land loss. In opposition to this, the Ministry of Education is trying to move beyond ethnicity, which they view as a divisive tool and source of conservative nationalism, toward multiracial harmony and national unity. Understanding the different objectives required a deeper look at what is at stake in the use of terms such as "ethnicity" and "race" in Fiji. My usage of the term "ethnicity" triggered a negative response with the Ministry of Education because they saw my research as either a dangerous reignition of rivalries that the current government was working to move beyond or a dangerous challenge to naturalized markers of race.

Thus, these emails comprise "sites of unease" that bring to life political tensions and divergences: who has power and in which ways.[36] For Stoler, the archive reveals governance through affective interchanges intended to educate on the correct responses, desires, and sentiments being expressed.[37] Governance in these emails does not appear uniform and unidirectional but is part of a negotiation between the two government bodies with competing objectives. For example, consider the sentiment that my research is "close to the hearts of the iTaukei Institute." The sentiment expressed indicates the felt dimensions of what is at stake. Although the ministry is careful to respond quickly and with a careful repetition of the words "at the heart of the institute" to show respect for what matters to the institute, it is clear where the power ultimately resides. In the current Bainimarama administration, the Ministry of Education is one step closer than the institute to nation-state sovereign power and one step closer to Bainimarama's objectives of permanently reducing the power and authority of the Great Council of Chiefs and the Methodist Church (organizations with which the iTaukei Institute aligns).

During the time I was in Fiji in 2012, there was a tendency to associate ethnicity with a set of static traditional cultural practices rooted in the past, biology, and geographic region. This approach to ethnicity is in line with anthropologist Marcus Banks's view that "in the modern world ethnicity is indissolubly linked to nationalism and race, to ideas about normative political systems and relations, and to ideas about descent and blood."[38] In other words, some in Fiji are linking ethnicity to race and biology (through the blood) but also linking ethnicity (as biology) to cultural practices, including traditions that are viewed as possessions. Inequitable rights and privileges based on static notions of ethnicity in Fiji rely on a division between Fijians of Indian descent and iTaukei, who are, as Bigitibau has put it, "intrinsically" connected to the land.[39]

If the Ministry of Education is concerned about perpetuating divisions and tensions between ethnicities, why do they use the language of multiracialism? The term "race" in Fiji connotes biological descent and has been used in past census statistics to sustain Fiji's constitutional inequalities in terms of voting power and land ownership.[40] The current official discourse of multiracialism, however, gives equal space to Fijian citizens regardless of descent. As a postcolonial national rhetoric with prior limited success in Fiji, multiracialism aims to generate tolerance of the different cultures, religions, ethnicities, languages, and traditions that exist in Fiji's diversely populated society.[41] The emails force attention on the political process of identification differentiation in relation to a changing constitution that is supposed to control for such differences.

Ruminating on "Ethnicity": National Stagings and What Can a Body Do?

My experiences with the iTaukei Institute and the Ministry of Education exposed much about the directionality of governance in Fiji and inform how I view meke as implicated in the shifting and uncertain territory opened up by Bainimarama's military governance. Making sense of this disorienting terrain, I ask, What can a body do?[42] And what can a body expressing meke do? In the following three examples, I explore how meke expressions unsettle and reify the predominant and competing narratives Fijians and Fiji's governing bodies espoused. These performances—which include "Teivovo" presented at the Festival of the Pacific Arts in the Solomon Islands, a performance of meke at the Fijian Cultural Center, and Fiji Day performances of a military parade, meke, and meke fusions—sometimes challenged categories and boundaries of identity and sometimes generated a securing, yet emergent, locus of identification.

Teivovo: Festival of Pacific Arts

Until recently, Fiji used traditional dance to represent itself at the Festival of Pacific Arts (which shifts its location throughout Oceania every four years) in four distinct groups categorized as Fijian, Indian, Rotuman, and Chinese.[43] As Pacific scholar and filmmaker Vilsoni Hereniko has pointed out, despite living together for more than 125 years, dancers of varying descent were not allowed to perform each other's dances.[44] Instead, this format protected dance traditions and national identifications against appropriation, firmly entrenching the idea that culture belonged to specific groups from specific places and loss of that ownership over that culture was tantamount to loss of identity.

Fiji's past presentations at the festival also contributed to a postindependence idea of nation that protected iTaukei preeminence and sovereign rights to land. The Festival of Pacific Arts, which opened in 1972 (two years after Fijian independence), developed in a climate of wanting to revive and protect Indigenous arts and culture of the Pacific that had been impacted by years of colonization and to develop a sense of postindependence national belonging based on past practices. The following early objectives of the Festival of Pacific Arts, quoted from a 1972 festival brochure, make evident the importance for newly independent nations of reestablishing past practices: "We hope this Festival will . . . serve to re-establish much that is in danger of being lost.... Perhaps it may also enable a recapturing of some of the old chants and dances, as they were when they were originally created and in the form the peoples of the Pacific enjoyed them long ago."[45] For festival organizers and goers, however, it was not sufficient for *any body* to recapture the chants and dances. Rather, these past practices needed to be recaptured by bodies that represented and confirmed Indigenous national belonging.

Today the work of the Oceania Center for Art, Culture and Pacific Studies at the University of the South Pacific in Suva, Fiji, challenges the idea that political bodies are secure sites for expression and communication by blurring divisive categories of identification and fusing traditions with contemporary artistic forms. The expressions of artists at the Oceania Center are examples of what a body can do within a post–2006 coup, shifting biopolitical terrain. Although many of the members of the Oceania Dance Theatre at the Oceania Center seemed to support Fiji's shift toward multiracialism (which relies on a model of racialized bodies living harmoniously side by side rather than together), it would be more accurate to describe them as favoring a notion of interculturalism that allows for dominant and nondominant cultures and identities to interact and transform.[46] Dancers at the Oceania Center shared an overall desire to dissolve rigid categories of culture and identity (which is part of what attracted them to the center in the first place). They also revealed a shift toward a new kind of horizontal governance of self and other. Even with an appearance of stability, the dancers were always in a process of emergence and transformation through their movements through space and time in relation to other bodies and formations of power.

In their production of *Drua: The Wave of Fire*, performed in Suva at University of the South Pacific and then at the Festival of Pacific Arts in the Solomon Islands (2012), the Oceania Center demonstrated varying identifications with a national and broader Oceanic body politic. The stated underlying goal of the production was to realize the philosophical and political goals of the center's founder and prior director, Epeli Hau'ofa, and his temporary successor, Vilsoni Hereniko.[47] They aimed to revive a precolonial tradition of interculturalism in the South Pacific and demonstrate how current traditions are built on knowledge sharing across Oceania. The production blurred the colonially imposed divisions between Micronesia, Melanesia, and Polynesia and used traditional dances, including meke, to tell the story of drua (double-hulled canoe) and drua culture shaped collectively by Kiribati, Samoa, Tonga, and Fiji prior to Western contact.[48]

Furthermore, the production challenged racial categories at the festival by using a cast of Fijians of mixed descent, including Indian descent. This was the first year the University of the South Pacific (a regional university) sent the Oceania Center to perform at the Festival of Pacific Arts.[49] Although the cast came from Fiji and performed in the same major festival sites as all the other island nations represented at the festival, the Oceania Center (the only entity at the festival not representing an island nation) maintained their identity as a multicultural/multiethnic group by performing under the banner of University of the South Pacific.[50] In this regard, Hereniko was able to achieve his objective of breaking out of the restrictive and conservative nationalist politics that have kept national dances distinct at the festival and in Fiji as well as acknowledge a more pan-Oceanic identity.[51] As a measure of their success and a more open-minded attitude at the festival, festival organizers invited the Oceania Center to perform at the following festival in Guam (2016).[52] Yet by using primarily traditional dance to tell a story from the past, the production also appealed to the safeguarding objectives of viewers in Fiji and at the Festival of Pacific Arts who are politically invested in reviving and protecting the culture and heritage of Indigenous peoples across the Pacific for the future.

Although the production was not technically representing Fiji alone, it centralized Fiji in its narrative through its use of meke and "Teivovo," a precolonial Bauan bole, or war challenge.[53] Since 1939 Fiji's national rugby team has used Teivovo to challenge and intimidate their opponents and to heighten the team's energy for the game.[54] Fijians I consulted spoke about the Teivovo as aggressive and masculine owing to the expressive physical force of the challenge. In the face of increasing evangelical and charismatic rejections of meke, especially in cases where meke content is linked to past acts of war and kalou worship, it is particularly significant that OCACPS used Teivovo in its production. In its unifying lyrics and movements, Teivovo asserts a Fijian national identity linked to the notion of iTaukei warriors connected to the land.[55]

According to Manoa Rasigatale, who reconstructed and transformed the Teivovo for the rugby team, the meaning of the form is complex.[56] It refers to a stage in the planting and harvesting of yams. Rasigatale explained that to clear the land, iTaukei burn it to prepare for planting. Once burned, the plants can then be uprooted. When they are uprooted and the roots turned toward the sun, they die. That is what the challengers are calling out to their opponents; their opponents will be uprooted and die, giving all the power to the challengers. In the Teivovo the knowledge of war is intimately connected to the knowledge of how to survive off the land.

It is generally the case that each area of Fiji has its own unique meke, but when Teivovo is performed as a unifying symbol of Fiji it symbolically breaks from that regionalism. Master Damiano Logaivau, the daunivucu for *Drua*, explained that the directors of the production asked him to include an element in his meke that would be recognizable to all Fijians.[57] Although not following the movements of the rugby team's version entirely, Logaivau incorporated many of the same movements and lyrics at the beginning of his war meke with the idea that, through recognition, the Teivovo could generate shared Fijian pride.

In the Teivovo for *Drua*, dancers indicate their readiness and challenge for battle by a stance that features a deep bend at the knee and hip with an upright torso (figure 2.1). Pelvises all face to one side with upper torsos rotating to face the opponent. Elbows are high and the meke war clubs (i-wau-ni-meke) are pulled tight beside their heads, ready to swing.[58] The

Figure 2.1. "Teivovo," dress rehearsal for *Drua: The Wave of Fire*, Japan-Pacific ICT Theatre, University of the South Pacific, Suva, June 3, 2012. Video still by Aaron Kelly.

dancers cry out, "Tei vovo Tei vovo," meaning the opponent will be plucked and planted upside down causing the opponents' roots to dry in the air.[59] As the dancers cry out they simultaneously pound the ground with alternating feet. They repeat the cry and begin to advance forward while staying low. They cry, "Rai tu mai rai tu mai," meaning, "Look at me we have the same aims—you want victory and so do I." They continue to advance forward pounding the ground harder and more energetically. They shout, "O au na viriviri ni kemu bai," meaning, "I will be your barricade, a wall you cannot tear down." They make a final advance forward with greater speed and force calling out, "ie! ie! ie!," ultimately finishing the dance with a soaring jump, their arms and clubs swinging above their heads. According to Logaivau, they end the challenge this way to increase the energy, excitement, and fear.

At first glance, Teivovo seems like a "technology of power" in Foucault's sense, a technique used to "actualize" bodies and categorize them as "natural" iTaukei warriors who represent a national body politic for all to emulate. Despite these regulatory aspects, however, *Drua* complicated the idea of homogenous nation by challenging rigid boundaries of race and gender. In *Drua*, dancers of varying backgrounds and gendered identifications performed, undermining connections between iTaukei sovereignty and hypermasculinity. Indeed, some of the cis-gendered men self-identified as "feminine." And although the inclusion of Teivovo was intended to generate a unifying Fijian spirit, in my interviews it was clear that the directors, Logaivau, and the cast celebrated the diversity of Fijians and respected the ways in which descent, customs, and practices interconnect across Fiji. In Logaivau's Teivovo, the dancers did not look like iTaukei warriors from the past: some had metal piercings and some were of Indian descent. In all these ways, Logaivau and the cast resisted categorical identities imposed by the state.

Logaivau also challenged the Teivovo's Bauan unifying force. Midcentury Bauan war meke, as depicted in images from the mid-1940s (figures 2.2, 2.3), typically emphasized synchronicity through rigid linear formations.[60] In contrast, Logaivau's contemporary meke used his own three-dimensional choreographic formations that he said "represent life."

After dancers finished the Teivovo, they continued to move together but in ways that were more vigorous. Dancers swung their clubs and used the momentum to move their torsos, with full range of motion. In their jumps and runs, dancers began to change formations and new fan dancers joined.

Figure 2.2. Meke ceremony, Bau, 1945. Courtesy of National Archives of Fiji.

Figure 2.3. Meke wau, Bau, 1945. Courtesy of National Archives of Fiji.

The dancers started to move in individual ways and in circular formations that closed in and expanded out into space. According to Logaivau, the formations and movements of his meke were meant to represent diversity in the way people live and move through life, rather than making it look like one body moving. Through his choreographic choices, Logaivau subtly challenged Fiji's past Bauan preeminence and aligned his meke with a shift toward racial equality and respect for difference.

For the most part, the Teivovo dancers shared Logaivau's views and rejected rigid cultural and racial boundaries that maintain the status quo. For example, when I asked dancer Peni (pseudonym) what he thought about the 2010 government decree to use the term "iTaukei" and "Fijian" in reference to citizenship, he explained that the term "iTaukei" made him feel uncomfortable because it created "divisiveness to differentiate."[61] Even though he is iTaukei, Peni preferred to call himself "Fijian."[62] His views on meke extended from his position on the decree. He explained that meke can be done by anyone. "It is not something we have to hold onto, but share it; it has benefits for everyone. It should not just be for natives."[63] Like Logaivau, Peni wanted to do away with racializing categories. Instead, Peni reached toward a future for Fiji and meke generated by the desire for intercultural inclusion in the expressions of Fijian art, culture, and heritage. Peni's perspective generated a space of maneuverability where new identifications gravitating around issues of race, ethnicity, culture, and nation could emerge.

Many of the dancers at the Oceania Center said they did not like performing meke because of its restrictive protocols. For this group of artists, meke was too restrictive as an expressive outlet. According to dancer Etueni Tagivakatini, "Meke makes me feel stuck because if I do something wrong, I am not really a Fijian. I don't want to feel that. So, in order not to feel that, I don't want to do it [meke]. It is a lot of pressure."[64] Thus, for some of the dancers I interviewed meke can demand that one fit into a particular mold and move within set boundaries and prescribed behaviors. They spoke of wishing for future meke that, if fused with contemporary dance, might become more relevant to them and to a contemporary Fiji.[65]

Despite their desire to transcend boundaries, bodies performing Teivovo also generate categories of identity. For example, to find ways of embodying the aggressively masculine antediluvian warrior, almost all the dancers, regardless of descent and gender presentation, imagined male Bauan iTaukei warriors of the past. Many imagined chief and warlord Ratu Seru Cakobau (1815–83), known for his aggressiveness and success in war, in order to fit their bodies and expressions into a representation of what they believed war meke should look and feel like. By performing this aggressive masculinity, they were in some ways generating secured bodies—bodies based on past significations.

Some of the dancers also suggested that the rhythms and accents of their movements were biologically innate. Three dancers I interviewed—Sadi Velaidan, Boro (pseudonym), and Peni—raised the issue of a "naturalized" iTaukei identity in meke. They explained that the accents and rhythms particular to meke, such as heads tipping sideways to punctuate the rhythms of the feet and torso, are automatic for iTaukei. In other words, they are not learned but essential to the iTaukei body. In contradiction to their desires to blur boundaries of identity, they said meke will not come naturally if a dancer is not connected to land through descent and not truly iTaukei.

Velaidan, who is a young Fijian man of Indian descent, relished in the expression of masculine warrior strength he associated with iTaukei, particularly "the specific accents of the head movements, the sharpness, the strength and the power of the meke actions."[66] Despite being commended by the other dancers on the strength of his expressions, Velaidan does not think meke accents and rhythms come naturally to him because he is of Indian descent. He tells me he studied the accents from his iTaukei friend Boro to become proficient in them.

Boro, however, dislikes meke because even though he believes it comes naturally to him, he refers to himself as "feminine" in his gender presentation. Performing what he terms "the violence" of meke does not fit comfortably with his sense of self. Boro finds it difficult to include himself within the restrictive boundaries of what it means to be iTaukei. Yet instilled in him is the notion that the ability to accent the rhythms and movements in a certain way is "natural," biological, and, quoting Boro, "runs through the blood."[67]

In contrast to Boro, Peni was drawn to Teivovo because, as he put it, "the movements look tough. When you see men doing it, you feel like you want to be part of it. As men, you have this strength and sometimes you really want to show that strength."[68] Peni spoke about this masculine strength entering his body when he heard the chanting and the rhythms of meke, reinforcing an inborn, or essential, Fijiness:

> Like vakarau! for Fijians on the battlefields during hard times,[69] Fijians are not hiding they are moving. Let's take it! It is the Fijian way, it just comes,

and we are born with it—not to hide but get ready, face it head on. That is how I feel. It strongly connects to how I identify as Fijian. In the old Fijian stories of war when soldiers say stop, they [the Fijians] say we move forward, don't stop. It's the feelings of it in the meke. You don't feel afraid of anything.[70]

Peni connects the experience of performing Teivovo with Fijian wars fought fearlessly by warriors in the past and to a readiness and fearlessness for his own future.

Part of what Peni is keen to express through his masculinity, readiness, and strength are binary sex and gender divisions as well as compulsive heterosexuality. "One good thing about religion," he told me, "is gay rights, they are trying to stop it. There is nothing in the Bible saying that it is okay to be gay. We don't discriminate, we love them, but it wasn't God's plan and so you have to help them to see the right path. It wasn't God's plan for men to be with men." Peni's experiences and expressions of virile masculinity in the Teivovo align with conservative Christian views in Fiji that normalize heterosexuality as "good" behavior.[71] Peni, who refers to himself as a disciple, is part of the explosion of new charismatic and evangelical churches in Fiji that attempt to forge a direct link with God. For evangelicals, God is always watching, thus one must govern one's own behavior based on "God's plan," and help others become "good" Christians. In this sense, meke can play a role in evangelical Christianity's policing of gender and sexuality.

Recognizable markers of iTaukei, such as rhythms and accents expressed in meke, form the external signs upon which bodies can be governed and categorized. And as Erin Manning has written, "Systems of governance rely on these signs to compartmentalize the bodies in their midst."[72] In the Teivovo, dancers generate seemingly stable bodies that fit into normative ideas about the male iTaukei body.

Although the iTaukei members of the Teivovo cast aim to embody the correct rhythms and accents that they believe are innate, their movements are also contradictory with regard to the external signs of race and gender. Velaidan's and Boro's feelings of discomfort with recognizable markers of iTaukei, such as aggressive masculinity, demonstrate that not all bodies fulfill these norms and expectations. Peni's movements and energy are driven by his religious and political alignments and his desires for a new Fiji that blurs boundaries of race, culture, and ethnicity while securing boundaries of sex, gender, and sexuality. Thus, it is possible that meke performances can simultaneously bolster traditional narratives while also enabling the emergence of new identities that unsettle naturalized boundaries of race and gender.

Whereas Boro's experiences and expressions in meke are governed by fears of strict heteronormativity and hierarchy, Peni's experiences of meke are, to a degree, self- and relationally governing. Peni gets the energy he needs to perform the Teivovo from using techniques he learned while volunteering for the Reproductive and Family Health Association of Fiji. He explained that the family planning NGO taught him how to find his inner strength through "positive feelings." Rather than seeing structural inequities such as racism, sexism, and homophobia as being the source of inequity, Peni expressed that personal hardships will cease to exist with a better attitude through self-imposed and nonhierarchical directions of governance. Together, the dancers at the Oceania Center performing Teivovo show that secured bodies are just as processual, relational, and uncertain as bodies that do not fit rigid boundaries, categories, and images.

Fijian Cultural Center

At the Fijian Cultural Center, meke also unsettles and reifies Fijian identity but does so by safeguarding and preserving the past in selective ways to protect future national belonging and ownership over Fijian culture as iTaukei. The Cultural Center opened in 1978, eight years after Fiji became independent, and was still in the early stages of organizing itself as a nation-state and in need of narratives to help cohere its population around common goals and allegiances. The Cultural Center also partook in the shaping of a national identity. Judging from the photographs of meke taken at its opening (figure 2.4), the Cultural Center generated a narrative of Fiji's past that contributed a sense of Fijian nationhood based on iTaukei belonging. Manoa Rasigatale, who, as mentioned earlier, is responsible for the reconstruction of Teivovo as a war challenge, directed and staged the initial performances.[73] He encouraged iTaukei not to be ashamed of the past but to learn the views and practices of the ancestors and to revive them. Rasigatale drew from pre-Christian Indigenous practices, including meke, to inform a national discourse enshrined by patriotic warriors.

At the center in 2012, the past continued to be safeguarded, even reenacted, through performances of meke and firewalking under new pressures of uncertainty. My experiences at the center led me through a nostalgic tour of the past: it began with a tour of a bure (a traditional house for men) and a bure kalou and koro (pre-Christian religious building and village), after which I, along with local visitors and international tourists, enjoyed a performance of meke woven into a dramatized story (which visually replicated photographs of the center's opening celebration). An emcee, one of the center's original performers who had worked at the center for over thirty years, translated the story, which was scripted in the nationally recognized Bauan dialect. The performances I observed during my visits throughout July of 2012 began with a firewalking demonstration.[74] The emcee explained that the ability to walk on fire without being burned is an inherited practice performed by the Indigenous Sawau people of Beqa and that an ancestor spirit or land spirit god (who came in the form of an eel) gave the Sawau people the gift of power over fire.[75] While it is not my intention to question or discredit this belief, which from an outsider perspective seems powerfully enabling, I also recognize that the firewalking is part of a larger performance that presents masculine iTaukei bodies as having extraordinary strength and power owing to their past spiritual connections to the land—

Figure 2.4. Fiji Dance Group performing at the opening of Fijian Cultural Center in Pacific Harbour, 1978. Courtesy of National Archives of Fiji.

a notion ironically unsettled by a 1978 image of a Fijian woman who is firewalking on Laucala Island (figure 2.5).[76] Next, the performers staged a race to open coconuts and the winner took the prize—one of the women of the village. Finally, a dramatized conflict led to a Teivovo and a battle. The emcee situated these scenarios in the context of pre-Christian worship of ancestor and land spirits, techniques of human sacrifice, and cannibalism.[77] The Cultural Center thus oriented itself not toward Fiji in the present but an iTaukei past solely ordered by hierarchies of chiefdoms and the worship of kalou vu, or ancestor gods.

The Cultural Center, as a postindependence nation-building phenomenon, is one technology of power and governance disseminating knowledge to Fijians and an international audience of what iTaukei bodies are and should be. My observations of these presentations and the audiences they attract as well as interviews conducted with the emcee suggest that the Cultural Center's stagings of the past are aimed at both tourists and Fijians. The first performance I attended had an audience that seemed to be made

Figure 2.5. Women walking over hot stones during a firewalking ceremony, Laucala Island, 1978. Courtesy of National Archives of Fiji.

up of mostly tourists. The audience for the second show I attended was roughly eighty iTaukei children, who had taken the bus all the way from Ra province (about an eight-hour bus ride). This was one of the Cultural Center's many performances for Fiji's schoolchildren. With four decades of national influence, the center continues to generate a notion of iTaukei as descendants of powerful warriors and gods, crafting a sense of national identity rooted in pre-Christian iTaukei traditions and protocols, while ignoring the many other influences of Fijians of Indian, European, Chinese, Rotuman, Banaban, and Tongan descent on Fijian culture and heritage.

While the Cultural Center in the 1970s salvaged and protected Indigenous cultural heritage to secure a postindependence iTaukei (and not multiracial) nation, the Cultural Center in 2012 constructed the past as a time of extraordinary iTaukei strength and power, which contrasted with the evangelical and charismatic rejections of traditions and national shifts toward multiracialism. Protecting notions of Fiji's past as iTaukei is part of an ethnonational political investment in protecting chiefly authority, iTaukei rights to land, and constitutional preeminence against these new religious and constitutional threats.

Fiji Day

Although Fijians of Indian descent seemed optimistic about racial tensions improving, my own experiences of a military parade, meke, and meke fusions at Fiji Day suggested a lingering tension despite a discourse of multiracial harmony. The military parade, described in the opening of the chapter as a national war meke and a postindependence coups d'état challenge ritual, serves to illustrate the ambivalence of the Fiji Day celebrations. Like meke, the military parade is a living mode of expression. It contains historical knowledge and is a way of perceiving and living in the world. Bodily movements through space-time in relation to other bodies reveal philosophical, spiritual, and political negotiations between the remnants of past colonial culture and new Indigenous articulations of identity. The expressive force of the parade is also about agency, self-determination, and resilience.

The international community viewed the 2006 military takeover as a sign of Fijian turmoil. As with Fiji's previous coups, the economy slowed after the 2006 coup. Aid stopped from the United States (which is legally required to suspend aid in countries that have had a coup).[78] Bainimarama's failure to hold democratic elections in 2009 as promised also had a damaging effect on his legitimacy in the eyes of international bodies, and Fiji's economy suffered as a result. For example, Australia, New Zealand, and the European Union (the largest buyer of sugar from Fiji), who will only trade with and provide aid to democracies, imposed trade sanctions.[79] In addition, the Asian Development Bank and Pacific Islands Forum halted Fiji's development aid money, and Fiji was also suspended from the British Commonwealth.[80] The military parade's demonstration of strict control over bodies aimed to counter the international concerns about Fijian disorder.

Fiji Day's military parade staged an amalgam of British colonial and Fijian influences and challenged the world to see Fiji as ordered and in control. Signs of control resembled British colonial signifiers of authority. Unlike other meke, whereby bodies move deeply at the joints to accent the complex rhythms, these bodies appeared not to bend at all. They were rigid and upright, even as they moved forward in their march with rifles held tight. Faces indicated nothing. Heads remained fixed on top of spines. The bodies were like a canvas for the larger symbolism of national sovereignty at work. Combatants wore a mix of costumes, though a large number sported Fiji's military sulu: white with a zig-zag hem. The sulu, wrapped around the waist and hanging to just below the knees, was initially worn to show allegiance to the British colonial administration and to the Methodist Church. Today, iTaukei in Fiji who consider themselves Methodists continue to wear the sulu. White and red uniforms, rifles held tight to rigid bodies, hats on heads, a military band playing round and bouncy marching songs, and neutral faces (no smiles or frowns). Yet the success of this parade and the multiracial festivities that followed were not only about displaying order; they were also about appealing to neoliberal Western democratic trade partners. The parade and what followed were choreographed to secure inclusion in such global networks.

The parade also challenged British colonial legacies and Western democracies. Not only had Bainimarama broken the law and nominated himself as leader in 2006; he attacked systems of indirect and hierarchical governance set up by the British colonial administration. After the sharp, percussive canons and twenty-one-gun salute forced the rhythms of the nation-state into viewers' bodies, accelerating the intensity of the ritual, Fijian president Ratu Epeli Nailatikau stood in as a representative of a higher order (as a kind of chief-monarch hybrid) normally appointed by the Great Council of Chiefs. In March 2012, however, just months before the military parade, Bainimarama dismantled the Great Council of Chiefs by government decree, which was for the council an outrage, particularly because he was viewed as a commoner.[81] The parade, by the 99 percent iTaukei military, forced Fijians and the world to recognize the political authority of the iTaukei people, and not just those of chiefly status.[82]

Bainimarama also dismantled the power and authority of the Methodist Church, which has historically been closely tied to the Fijian state (see examples of this in Rabuka's 1987 leadership). President Ratu Epeli Nailatikau's address for Fiji Day warned against such an alliance. He said Fiji should "tread cautiously in its choices for the future" and that merging religion with state will result in racial and ethnic discrimination.[83] The separation of church and state is a major threat to the top-down way power and governance have been organized in Fiji and the many Fijians who are invested in maintaining ethno-national privilege. In some ways, his address was even more significant because of the way he delivered it. He appeared in person only long enough to say that he would not be giving his speech live—it would be televised that evening. Since "politics—like bodies—emerge out of frictions, accidents, disagreements, and interlockings,"[84] it is significant that he removed his Fiji Day body from his Fiji Day message and thereby dissolved the potential for public frictions, disagreements, and politics.

After a lengthy military parade, the dance and music programming was equally ambivalent, deployed as a method for instilling a sense of a united and multiracial Fijian identity and simultaneously a reminder of iTaukei preeminence. The program began with the Conservatorium of Music meke group Kabu ni Vanua. The Conservatorium is an urban Suva music school whose students perform meke as a way to pay their tuition costs. The school opened in June 2008 and has quickly earned a national and international reputation for its energetic, skillful performances of meke as well as for its respectful approach to traditional protocols.[85] Kabu ni Vanua began its performance with an excerpt of a synchronized and high-energy men's meke. The meke excerpt, from a vakamalolo titled *Rogo Saka na Wekaqu (Hear Ye O My People)*, started with the iTaukei men sitting in a row wearing long grass skirts with grass fringe around their ankles and upper arms. The central dancer called out to the chanters to begin. The dancers moved together as one. When the lali tempo sped up, the dancers' arms moved faster and sharper. Fingers shook, elbows lifted, jabbed, and pulled in angular ways. Torsos moved with the arms and curved forward, extended up, and twisted in every direction. The dancers expressed joy and quickly had the audience cheering. Next, iTaukei women performed a seasea (standing meke) called *Sa Lutu a Caucau Vanua* that refers to dew falling on the land (see chapter 4). Wearing masi skirts, grass fringe around their ankles, and white blouses, the meke began with the women entering from both sides of the space in straight lines. Their left legs led every advance forward toward the other line. With each step, on every beat, their right arms reached forward and their heads tipped. Arm movements were clear, direct, and exact. Once they joined in the middle, the women faced forward and quickly kicked their legs low and forward while leaning back. With every kick, they circled their arms, their palms momentarily joining in front of their torsos, bringing the audience to heightened levels of energy and joy.[86]

After Kabu ni Vanua's meke was a mixed program of tradition and fusion dances. A Rotuman group of six men, wearing red sarongs with skirts of long leaves on top, presented a traditional Rotuman song-dance called Tautoga with three sections: sua, tiap hi, and tiap forau.[87] With a deep, wide stance, the men shifted their weight side to side to the live singing voices and rhythms of wooden sticks hitting a pillow (in place of mats). Arms and wrists moved with the rhythms. Depending on the section, sometimes arms circled low with hands clasping in front, sometimes hands and arms moved in a pulling and gathering back motion. After each verse, the front line moved to the back. They repeated this shift in formation with every section. Next, the use of movements through space became more fluid with Fijiwood, a dance group comprised of Fijians of Indian descent who offered a fusion of Bollywood, hip hop, Tahitian, and even a little Macarena. Next was an all-male hip hop crew in jeans and T-shirts that switched places with a Samoan group of men and women wearing red sarongs who presented a dance battle that combined virtuosic head spins and fast pelvic and leg work. Finally, a dance group called Rako moved dynamically through space when they presented a contemporary mix of Rotuman, Raratongan, Tahitian, and Samoan dance.[88] After short breaks, during which the Fiji police band played, the dancing continued with a Tahitian group, followed by a Hawaiian/Tahitian number by a team called Mix and Match. This part of the program represented a wild celebration of diversity, multiracial harmony, and intercultural merging and hybridity.

Although Fiji Day performances provided a potent opportunity to dismantle firm boundaries of identity, with the exception of the interracial and intercultural fusion dances, viewers were reminded of secure boundaries between iTaukei and Fijians of non-iTaukei descent. Kabu ni Vanua's frequent reappearances throughout the day in traditional costumes (and meke) ultimately prioritized nostalgia for an iTaukei Fiji past. Such is the complex political ecology of the dancing for Fiji Day: fusions may indicate an opening for new relations and dance forms, but such performances occur alongside more traditional forms that emphasize the preeminence of iTaukei and "naturalized" categories of race.

In their performance for the national stage, Kabu ni Vanua generated a type of Fijianness rooted in chiefly authority and respect for traditions and protocols with which many iTaukei Methodist audience members would likely identify.[89] The director, Master Lai Veikoso, is motivated to safeguard meke out of respect for traditional protocols and customs within the bounds of Christian worship.[90] Veikoso explained some of the traditional protocols the school follows:

> We do a presentation of a whale's tooth—our ancestors say that it adds to the mana and more inspiration for the piece. Also, given that many of our students would have been commoners [if they still lived] in the village setting, the whale's tooth is to say, "We hope it is okay for you, as commoners, for us to dance that chiefly dance." It is a mark of respect and a way to seek forgiveness for making a mistake, and absolving us of ill will. Once we have learned the dance there is a premiere, called a sevu ni meke. He [the daunivucu] could invite a guest [such as] a prominent chief to be the guest of honor. After the meke has been presented, we take gifts (twenty-liter drums of kerosene and many yards of fabric) to the choreographer. It is about providing care for the daunivucu.

Although Veikoso is personally motivated to safeguard past practices and protocols, his group is also shaped by the Fiji government.

The Conservatorium of Music's Kabu ni Vanua offers a complex picture of the relationship between meke and governmental influence. In fact, the government often chose the Conservatorium's meke group to represent Fiji at international and national events for the Ministry of Tourism. During the time I was in Fiji, there was no government funding for individual artists, companies, or institutions through the Fiji Arts Council.[91] Because of the lack of arts funding from the government, artists turned to commercial lines of support and tourism to make money. According to Veikoso, although the primary focus of the school is classical music, it survives on the financial support from the Ministry of Industry, Trade, and Tourism and the Ministry of Foreign Affairs for their meke performance contracts.

The Conservatorium's reliance on the government for economic support, however, gives the ministries of Tourism and Foreign Affairs power to govern its approach to meke. For example, Tourism Fiji (responsible for the Fijian government's marketing and promotion of tourism) wants the dancers to look like iTaukei from the past. They ask the Conservatorium to send dancers with hair worn in a so-called traditional manner (not straightened or long and wavy, etc.).[92] Tourism is a major part of Fiji's economy, and the industry thrives on the idea that visitors should feel welcome and have a good time, while also experiencing exotic encounters with Fijians who provide a window to the past.[93] Veikoso explained that his group provides the Ministry of Tourism with what they request: a depiction of a unified, Indigenous Fiji (which Veikoso explained did not otherwise exist outside of his efforts) and high-energy, synchronized dancing that evokes inviting sentiments to match the ministry's catchphrase: "Fiji: Where Happiness Finds You."[94] In the context of Fiji during its military dictatorship, I borrow Pacific studies scholar Teresia Teaiwa's term to call this a case of "militourism": putting a friendly and welcoming face to Fiji's military dictatorship.[95]

Veikoso, who is of Bauan descent (from Tailevu), aims to generate a consolidating notion of iTaukei. Being Bauan, he explained, gives him an extra sense of authority because, as he put it, Bau is "the leading province in Fiji."[96] As mentioned in chapter 1, Bau achieved its "hegemonic ambitions" by the mid-nineteenth century through conquest and continues to generate a dominant universalizing force in Fiji.[97] In addition, he explained that he creates uniformity in his group by drawing from techniques he learned while touring with a United States folk dance group: wear uniforms, move with precision, dance from the heart. He encourages his dancers to express themselves but stay within the bounds of synchronicity so as not to allow individualism.

In addition to performing for tourists, Kabu ni Vanua has also performed internationally for the Ministry of Foreign Affairs as part of a promotional team for all the embassies and for the Melanesian Spearhead Group.[98] Some dancers explained that the group has also become a part of the prime minister's entourage, adding a traditional iTaukei element to the events he has promoted (such as the Fiji pavilion at Expo 2012 in Korea and the unveiling of Fiji Airways' new masi print logo on Fiji Day 2012). Although the prime minister was calling for a more inclusive use of the term "Fijian," he still chose to present himself with a meke group that generates a Christianized image of an iTaukei past. This creates a complex dichotomy. On the surface, his choice seems like an important way of giving voice to a previously colonized people. But in the context of Fiji's espoused multiracial inclusion, the use of traditional Indigenous dance with dancers that look like iTaukei from a time past, while evoking Christian sentiments, generates a haunting reminder of exclusion and political upheaval.

By providing an economic lifeline to the survival of the Conservatorium of Music, the government, through the Ministry of Tourism and the Ministry of Foreign Affairs, influences meke for the national stage. These government ministries, like the iTaukei Institute and the Ministry of Education, govern the bodies of performers to actualize or fix them in the face of changing formations of power to suit their own political trajectories. The performances of iTaukei preeminence in the military parade and the Conservatorium's meke performances sit uneasily next to Fiji Day's multiracial fusions, exemplifying how bodies both govern and are governed through nationally staged performances.

Conclusion

This chapter has shown how Fijian dance practitioners and institutions unsettle and reify three predominant national discourses. Each account unfolds from a version of the past in order to move toward a particular vision for Fiji's future. Sometimes these accounts safeguard the past for Fiji's future, and sometimes they construct and reject a version of the past for future salvation. Sometimes traditions are refashioned for multiracial futures through fusions of cultural dance forms that appear to affirm multiracial harmony. Such narratives implicate expressive bodies within these shifting terrains of power.

Within an uncertain space of social and political change, a space opened (however tenuous) for new relations of power, new directions of movement, and new bodies to emerge. Interestingly, meke experiences and expressions expose the ways in which power in Fiji appears to be changing from vertical—with a military dictator, pastor, or chief at the pinnacle—to horizontal, as transnational NGOs and evangelical churches pop up and take charge of development and self-help initiatives and performers explore new multiracial and intercultural fusions. In light of these changes, nationalist performances generate iTaukei security and preeminence amid a new unsecured multiracial Fijian body. But how do performances of meke in Fiji's Canadian diaspora generate power in relation to a vastly different demographic? And what happens to governance and identity in and around meke within Canadian national discourses of multicultural inclusion?

CHAPTER 3

Meke in Multicultural Canada

Throughout the 1980s, large sea vessels equipped for repairing trans-Pacific telecommunication cables, which lay across the ocean floor, traveled between Fiji and all the Pacific Rim countries and stopped in Esquimalt, British Columbia, to give their crews some rest. On one visit from the cable repair crew, my mother, who worked for the Intercultural Association in Victoria, managed to convince them to perform some meke for Victoria's Folkfest. Folkfest, a multicultural festival, showcased the multiple cultural traditions of diasporas living on Vancouver Island.

My childhood memory of the shipworkers' meke performance recalls certain qualities and features. Women wore long sulus with short-sleeved tops made of blue cotton patterned fabric. The men wore shorter black sulus with short-sleeved tops made with the same blue fabric. Although the women and men wore costumes that unified them, they did not dance together. The women sat in a group, separate from the men on stage, with upright torsos and legs bent and pulled to one side, not crossed. They moved their arms in simple, clear, geometric lines, and patterns. Then the standing men danced together as a cluster, using geometric arm and leg movements to move through space. The group provided their own vocal chant and lali rhythms. The men sang for the women, and the women sang for the men.

Although this was the first meke I ever watched, I had experienced Polynesian dance fusions on several occasions. I was six when I first saw Polynesian dance with fire blazing on both ends of a torch. Sefo Avaiki, who had recently come to Canada from Rotuma, circled a torch around and through his legs with fast rhythms and movements. His legs shook in his

Polynesian mixture of Samoan, Tahitian, and fire dancing. The torch spun and circled high and then dropped down between his deeply bent knees to accentuate his movements. He was wearing a sarong. His eyes followed the torch, and his face was beaming. He punctuated rhythms with his feet and knees. Blasts of heat and light streamed past. Avaiki, who became my mother's longtime friend, taught me with his danced expressions by igniting this fire in me—full of anticipatory energy, joy, respect, and strength.

Avaiki has put a lot of thought into how he transmits his cultural knowledge and identity to build community. Some thirty years after I first experienced his dancing, and at the start of my doctoral research, he invited me to a gathering of South Pacific peoples. At the gathering, he spoke about how he chooses to transmit his life knowledge by weaving together a history of colonial subjugation with Indigenous methods of moving past that subjugation through dance. In response to questions I asked about his dancing, he explained that he had learned to dance in a context of colonial power imbalances. He studied Rotuman traditional dancing and chanting in school from his elders by watching, listening, respecting, and harmonizing with those next to him. Rotuman elders centered their song-dances on the ancestors and the gods of Rotuma. Yet when he reached third grade, the school no longer allowed the students to speak Rotuman inside the school compound. The British colonized Rotuma, like Fiji. But Rotuma, which now forms part of the Republic of Fiji, is culturally distinct from Fiji and maintains more Polynesian cultural influences. Although he comes from chiefly status in Rotuma, he faced subjugation in relation to the British as well as in Fiji, where he is without title or status. He argued that despite the top-down and divisive colonial governance he experienced growing up, he has worked personally and professionally to move beyond that subjugation and to build sustainable social relations within the larger Oceanic community on Vancouver Island through teaching members of the community about Rotuman dance and culture.

In Canada, identifications with Fiji are diversely experienced and expressed through dance. Since my interest in Fijian dance emerged out of my own familial history within Fiji and its Canadian diaspora, my understanding of its nuances and complexities is partial and needs to be situated within my own upbringing as a white, European Canadian whose family has a colonial past. Growing up on Vancouver Island I was also reared on multicultural festivals and notions that celebrated ethnocultural difference in a country that made multiculturalism official in 1971. Although the official discourse tends to presume Fijian Canadians belong to a homogenous ethnocultural group, as I began my ethnographic fieldwork in Vancouver and on Vancouver Island, I realized there were aspects of Fiji's colonial history involving racialized political and religious hierarchies and tensions that were also being expressed through dance. Fijian Canadians, who have differing histories of dispossession, displacement, and marginalization, articulate identifications with Fiji in divergent ways that are, nevertheless, entangled with one another.[1] With this in mind, what does it mean to identify as Fijian in Canada? How are essentialist categories of identity, so dominant and divisive in Fiji's postindependence reality, transcended or sustained in relation to local Canadian notions of multiculturalism, as well as non-Indigenous and Indigenous peoples in Canada? Additionally, why has meke, as an expression and representation of Fijian identity, provoked anxieties for some Fijians living in Canada?

The image of telecommunication cables connecting Fiji with Canada and needing local adjustments and care is a reminder of the historical, yet constant, political, economic, and cultural interplay between Fiji and Canada. The cables of the British colonies evoke a history that connected the globe through uneven relations of power.[2] Today, the countries have very different economic realities, with Canada's average gross domestic product almost nine times that of Fiji's.[3] These translocal lines of communication are haunting vestiges of the past and yet they continue to generate new relations, interconnections, migrations, and identifications between and within Fiji and Canada. Haunting, felt affectively as frictions and unease, refers to a complex articulation that resembles colonial and postcolonial Indigenous and non-Indigenous racial tensions and pressures in Fiji while also striving toward social inclusion in multicultural Canada amid the country's efforts at reconciling colonial legacies of violence and abuse toward Indigenous peoples.[4] The cables remind me that dances traveling between these countries, which touch the Pacific, help shape a diasporic identity formation created by a "living, micro-cultural, micro-political system in motion."[5] Oceanic dance is a system in motion that crosses the Pacific, enables identifications to interconnect, migrate, and align with shifting circumstances. As dance scholar Carrie Noland has theorized, gestures that migrate from one site of performance to another become confronted with new responses that cause a shift in the gesture's meaning and the way it is experienced.[6]

In this chapter, I examine migratory song-dance expressions and representations of Fijian and, more broadly, Oceanian culture and identity in festivals and public performances meant to reach both Fijian Canadian and broader publics in the context of Canadian multicultural policy and discourse. To do this requires a brief look at multiculturalism in Canada and the demographics of Canada's Fijian diaspora. With this context in mind, I analyze four examples of Fijian cultural performance and language used by performers to talk about culture and identity. First, I discuss a meke presented at a Vancouver-based Pentecostal church fundraising event that sought out a wider Vancouver audience, only to reveal the prejudices of particular Christian congregations toward Fijian meke. These negative perceptions of Fijian tradition interestingly provoked the creation of new meke that supported Christian values. Next, I discuss the ethnically based tensions—between Fijians of Indian and iTaukei descent—provoked by meke performances at a Vancouver-based Fiji Day Festival and the absence of meke at a separately organized Fiji Day festival. Next, I discuss a meke performed at a Vancouver Island–based multicultural festival in order to consider how Fijian dancers have reimagined island boundaries to become "Oceanic Dance" within their new diasporic context. Last, I discuss the performance of a Māori haka recounted by members of Fiji's Vancouver Island–based diaspora. This example shows how pan-Oceanic expressions of venerable ancestral warriors, described as aggressively masculine, sustain and absorb difference. I analyze these festivals and performances for the ways in which they demonstrate distinguishing features between and within British Columbia's Fijian diasporas in their entanglements within Canadian multiculturalism. The participants and leaders I consulted within each context linked culture to essentialized and categorical notions of gender and ethnic identity and origin. At the same time, they also renegotiated essentialized identities to form new identifications, exchanges, social relations, and obligations with Indigenous and non-Indigenous peoples in multicultural Canada. These examples show how gender, ethnicity, power, and indigeneity intersect with stagings of multicultural, diasporic Fijianness in disparate ways.

Canadian Multiculturalism and Fiji's Canadian Diaspora

While Canada officially adopted a policy of multiculturalism in 1971, in 1988 the country embraced an official Multicultural Act to combat discriminatory barriers, recognize and empower its diverse citizens, and assist communities with cultural legitimacy activities.[7] Through policies of integration, multiculturalism encourages individuals and communities to identify with their "ethnic origins" while also identifying with a multicultural nation. Integration does not refer to intercultural merging, interaction, and transformation (except in the province of Quebec).[8] The notion is also different from Canada's earlier 1960s assimilation approach, whereby individuals relinquish their distinctive cultures.[9] Rather, Canadian multiculturalism refers to ethnically bound individuals and communities living harmoniously side by side, in a metaphorical mosaic.

Canadian multiculturalism starts with the premise that Canadian migrants arrive from an "origin" that is culturally and ethnically homogenous. This approach to categorizing people treats bodies as fixed by past signifiers and representations of racialized bodies and matches culture with categories of people. According to the act,

> whereas the Government of Canada recognizes the diversity of Canadians as regards race, national or ethnic origin, color and religion as a fundamental characteristic of Canadian society . . . ; [the] Multiculturalism Policy of Canada [aims to] recognize the existence of communities whose members share a common origin . . . ;[10] [and in the] implementation of the Multiculturalism Policy of Canada, assist ethnocultural minority communities to conduct activities with a view to overcoming any discriminatory barrier and, in particular, discrimination based on race or national or ethnic origin.[11]

As I will illustrate, it is not the case that particular cultures come with particular types of people. Such categorizations, as anthropologist Bonnie Urciuoli has put it, fail to recognize the "naming of groups and identities that have come into existence over centuries of economic and political relations, as these have played out colonially and globally."[12] Canadian multiculturalism, and some of the policies and practices that emerge from the 1988 Multiculturalism Act, are unable to address the more nuanced notions of culturally particular, gendered, intercultural, and variant experiences that have emerged from colonial economic and political histories in Fiji.

As a process of identity adjustment for Fijian Canadians, meke embodies the diverse sociopolitical, economic, and religious realities of migrating to Canada. Before I begin exploring the examples, it is important to note how Fijians in Canada identify themselves. While identity classification has changed in Fiji as part of the larger political shift toward multiracialism, many of the Fijians I have spoken with in Canada identify themselves more specifically in relation to Fiji's older classifications as being of Indian descent or of "native" descent. For example, I located Fijians in Vancouver through various community and media organizations (where I found Fijians of Indian descent) and Fijian Pentecostal churches in Vancouver (where I found Fijians mostly of iTaukei descent). Fijians of Indian and iTaukei descent come together to enjoy rugby, a ubiquitous sport in Fiji, but differ in terms of religious affiliations and their choice to participate in meke.[13] Distinctions exist between the iTaukei who consider themselves Methodist and iTaukei who align with Pentecostal churches. And further distinctions and tensions exist between the Fijian Pentecostal churches in Vancouver.

Fijians in Canada do not belong to an immutable culturally and ethnically cohesive group. The Fijian diaspora in Canada is multifarious, with individuals of varying backgrounds, including, but not limited to, Indian, American, Samoan, Rotuman, and Tongan. According to Canada's 2016 census, the size of the Fijian diaspora in Canada who were born in Fiji is approximately 24,665.[14] The same census tells me that within this group, the Fijian Canadian population born in Fiji is highest in British Columbia (mostly Vancouver), at 17,530, with the next-largest group in Alberta (mostly Edmonton), at 4,625, and the third-largest group in Ontario (mostly Toronto), at 2,300.[15] Most of this diaspora, however, is composed of Fijians of Indian descent, who live in and around Vancouver and have migrated there since the 1980s because of systemic racism in Fiji.[16] I focus here on how the dancing of Fijian Canadians reflects their heterogeneity and addresses the ongoing transformation of diverse political realities and ethical concerns related to various forms of "difference."

Vakamalolo (Sitting Meke) for a Fijian Pentecostal Church Fundraiser

Wearing masi print shirts with long, ankle-length brown skirts and plastic red hibiscus flowers behind their ears, the dancers of Irish, Indian, iTaukei, and Tongan descent sat with their legs crossed on the stage and pulsed a rhythm with their knees. Behind these women was a row of equally diverse men wearing T-shirts with long grass skirts. Together, these dancers aimed to connect with the earth as they pounded the stage with their hands. Then their fingers sprang upward from their mouths toward the sky to demonstrate they were not heathens worshipping Fiji's devils or demons but Christians. They folded their hands together to create the image of a Fijian fan and punctuated the rhythms of the music by pulling the tips of their hand-fans up with every downbeat. Their hand movements were not soft or fluid but sharp, geometric, and patterned. Their eyes watched their hands to give the movements life.[17] The phrasing of their movements and rhythms was also framed with cobo—a hand clap that has historical significance expressed through its rhythms, sounds, and motions. While dancing, they created accents with their heads softly but not fluidly and with ease, tipping side to side. Their movements and accents connected their feelings and their bodies to the past, to their Christian faith, and to a shared nostalgia for Fiji.

The movements were angular, quick, and performed with a feeling of commitment and preparedness. This commitment from the many dancers, who were moving as one, created a unifying sense of fearlessness, playfulness, confidence, and readiness. They moved their bodies forward to the ground and came back up strong; the movements expressed "let us go and not be weary or weak."[18] Their energy extended outward to the viewers to share a sense of generosity of spirit and cultivate joy, happiness, and peace.

The choreography, by Fiji-born Lavonne Gucake Donu, reflected creative choice as well as the choreographer's inspiration from God, her family, her training at the Fijian Adi Cakobau School (famous for educating young iTaukei women in Fijian traditions and chiefly protocols), and her dancers, who sat next to her on stage. Elements of her past informed her preference to weave together movements from across Oceania. Although her costumes and her movements connected what she was doing with the past, she mobilized this pastness in order to ignite new meaning and new memories. As a relatively recent immigrant, her dance-based feelings were generating a renegotiation of identity in Canada.[19]

∽

The above description introduces Lavonne Gucake Donu's vakamalolo meke, which she presented at a Vancouver-based Pentecostal church fundraising event in 2010, and illustrates how danced experiences and expressions migrate and connect Fiji with its Canadian diaspora through performances of Fijianness. Donu's meke combined traditional movements with new Christianized movements and music to present a distinctly Christian, Fijian Canadian identity.[20] In certain ways, the meke transcended essentialist notions of gender and ethnicity, so dominant and divisive in Fiji's postindependence reality, as Canadian men and women from varying backgrounds came together for Fiji and to raise money for cyclone disaster relief in Fijian villages. At the same time, Donu aligned this performance of meke with the expectations and conventions of Canadian multiculturalism, legitimating the Fijianness of this meke in Canada through homogenous and cohesive representations of contemporary Fijian iTaukei traditions.

Donu's meke made frequent use of cobo, a particular way of cup-clapping the hands. Cobo as a movement, sound, and rhythm relates to what research participants referred to as traditional iTaukei customs that have emerged out of rituals, such as meke ni yaqona (figure I.2), that were once part of the worship of ancestor spirit gods or kalou vu. Meke ni yaqona is a sacred ritual involving the presentation of yaqona, whereby participants ignite meaning in the movements, lyrics, cobo, and the gathering of people to witness the performance for a high chief, who is believed to embody the spirit of the ancestral gods.[21] In current performance of these customs, cobo's rhythm, movement, and depth of sound helps communicate a physiological feeling of vinaka vaka levu, defined here as deep gratitude and respect.[22] In light of its cultural and historical significance, cobo gives strength to meke, while also generating a feeling of iTaukei legitimacy. Cobo performed in the context of meke at the Vancouver church fundraiser put these feelings of gratitude in motion, activating and enacting a migration of spirit and affect to create a sense of Christian harmony. Simultaneously, cobo supported a notion of Fijianness in Canada that is distinctively iTaukei, maintaining certain categories of race, ethnicity, national belonging, and citizenship.

Donu's choreographic choices in other aspects of the meke also signaled iTaukei heritage. For example, by stretching two fingers out and clasping her other fingers, she created the image of a fan with her hands—an action she had watched elders perform in Fiji. In her words, "This fan movement has been done over and over again by previous generations."[23] This action thus provided her body with a translocal link to an iTaukei past, adding to her feelings of legitimacy and security.

In dynamic tension with these meaningful, historically weighted gestures, dancers' identities emerged as they performed a series of finger motions that sprang upward from their mouths while alternating hands. Donu explained that she did not learn these gestures from Fijian elders. Rather, the performers used these light, joyful, quick movements to embody the lyrics of the song, which mean "word of God," and to express their reverence to

God, distancing their dance from the pre-Christian, Fijian meke that the iTaukei performers in this group associate with "devil worship, cannibalism and war."[24] In contrast, when they pounded their fists on the ground to the lyrics "the word of God travels the earth," their movements referred to Fijian vanua (customs and traditions of the land) that link earth with God. Thus, while distancing themselves from pre-Christian religion in one movement, other actions reconfirmed notions of iTaukei's God-given rights to Fijian land, beliefs and tensions that clearly have migrated from Fiji to Canada through movement-based expressions. In their embodiment of Fijianness as traditionally iTaukei and Christian, they distinguished themselves from the Fijians in Canada who are Hindu.[25]

Donu's meke performance drew from a number of different countries of Oceania.[26] The group organizers used these movements to connect with wider Vancouver-based Christian communities hoping to undermine dominant and essentialist notions of ethnicity and identity. For example, Donu included a series of stacked and twisting fist motions that came from Wallis and Fatuna—where her mother is from. Donu recalled: "My mother did a dance movement growing up that involves the actions of picking the coconut, halving it, and then squeezing the juice out. But it has been suggested that it is also like the wringing out of the grog [yaqona] for the grog ceremony. When teaching Canadians who don't speak Fijian we called it the salt and pepper move. That was the easiest way for them to learn, by describing the actions in terms that Canadians would understand."[27] Movements like the "salt and pepper move" shift in meaning as they migrate and interact with dancers from a wide range of backgrounds. Dancers bring their own unique experiences to the choreography, and as cultural sensibilities and expressions interact and transform, the meke counters essentialist notions of culture and identity.

Nevertheless, the use of space also maintained and blurred certain boundaries between men and women. In Fiji, divisions between men and women (regardless of ethnicity) are embedded within Fijian culture and tradition and exacerbate gender inequities and male-dominated hierarchies.[28] This gender separation is reflected and produced in meke. Donu explained that while older traditional meke observed a separation of men and women, she chose to have men and women dance together. As a young Fijian immigrant, she was participating in a recent trend to mix women and men together in meke by arranging a long row of seated women in front of a long row of seated men.[29] Although women in Fiji once performed meke with their legs together and folded to the side (a practice likely linked with wearing the shorter liku skirt), long sulus covered these women's crossed legs.[30] Despite the interaction of men and women dancing together that aligns with progressive ideas about gender equity, toward the end of the dance, the men, who were wearing long grass skirts, jumped over the women and danced in front of them, completely concealing them as they finished the dance. In the end, the contemporary Canadian meke distinguished the women and the men by their formation, movement, and costumes, reverting to a more conservative Fijian binary separation of men and women that supports male privilege.

Terms like "multiculturalism" seem obvious and unproblematic, but when analyzed in relation to Fijian dance in Canada you see, as Urciuoli has put it, a range of possible "strategic deployments."[31] Through the performance of meke, meke practitioners such as Donu reach toward inclusion and recognition in Canada. In this regard, Fijian Canadians construct Fijianness in alignment with Canadian multiculturalism that treats culture as bound to homogeneous ethnic groups with a common origin. In this approach to ethnocultural groups, culture is not interconnected or melting together but living side by side in a harmonious mosaic.[32] Although in some ways Donu's meke demonstrated the Vancouver realities of cultures interacting and transforming, it also constructed a conservative gendered Fijianness for Canada's multicultural mosaic as traditional, iTaukei, and Christian.

Vancouver Fiji Day Festivals

Meke, in its presence and absence from Fijian Canadian community events, plays a role in renegotiating Fiji's past and present political and religious realities while negotiating new connections and relations in multicultural Canada. I illustrate this ambivalence by analyzing two Fiji Day festivals that occurred in the summer of 2011. Fiji Day, as a national celebration of Fiji, has shifted to reflect and produce evolving iterations of Fijian identity. In Canada, the two Fiji Day festivals were events that reflected and produced incongruent, yet entangled, Fijian Canadian identities through their programming. While I did not attend these festivals, I discuss the interactions with participants and organizers of these festivals and what these interactions say about the politics at play in these celebratory events. Together the festivals illustrate how Fiji's political tensions, resulting from the past British colonial system of indentured labor, take on a haunting quality as they continue to be affectively embodied in the Fijian community in Vancouver. Tensions increase further when Fijian Canadians compete for cultural legitimacy and a desire for inclusion, yearnings haunted by British colonial cultural typologies and hierarchies.

Before learning about the two competing Fiji Day festivals, it was already clear that relations between Fijian Canadians in Vancouver were fraught. In 2011 I was at the Fiji Cultural Center in Vancouver and sat down with a group of Fijian Canadians of Indo-Fijian descent.[33] They had invited me to share a meal with them, and we talked about life in Fiji versus life in Canada. At first, the members of this group seemed to have moved beyond Fiji's histories of colonial subjugation and postindependence racism. They indicated their love of Fiji and that the ethnically divisive politics of Fiji do not exist in Canada. One member said, "In Canada, everything is good, we are all just Fijians now." They explained that in Canada, there is no such thing as "native" Fijian or "Indo" Fijian; everyone is just "Fijian." I soon realized this was not the complete picture. After some members of the group left the Cultural Center, one of the remaining members looked me in the eye and told me how the two 1987 coups felt. With his fist slamming down hard on the table between us, he said, "They stabbed us in the back!"[34] This point of friction is indicative of colonial haunting: while initially expressing their desire to find new ways of identifying with Fiji in Canada, my interlocutors also expressed a resurgence of frustration and anxiety connected to Fiji's colonial and postcolonial history.

I quickly learned of another point of friction between Indian and iTaukei Fijian Canadians in Vancouver that resulted from the addition of a second Fiji Day festival, which I will refer to as FijiFest. The tensions became evident during my interview with the organizer of the first Fiji Day festival, hereafter referred to as Fiji Day Fest.[35] The primary organizer for Fiji Day Fest, who self-identifies as being of Indo-Fijian descent, explained that the festival aims to connect with multicultural communities in Vancouver. As evidence for his commitment to multiculturalism, he showed me 2009 and 2010 video footage of the festival. The footage started with an "international parade," which consisted of performers wearing a selection of traditional folk costumes of the world with country names worn as banners across their chests. The parade constructed multicultural harmony on the premise of static and distinct cultures from the past. After the parade, the footage showed mostly classical and contemporary Indian dance and music aimed at the primarily Indo-Fijian audience. In comparison, the iTaukei Fijian programming was minimal, reduced to a brief kava ceremony and a few meke dances performed by a Vancouver-based iTaukei Fijian Canadian group.

When I asked about this meke group, my interlocutor became noticeably tense. He explained that Fijian Canadians from this group had been criticizing his Fiji Day Fest, and they had since withdrawn from his festival and started their own FijiFest with primarily iTaukei Fijian programming. He told me explicitly not to talk to two iTaukei Fijian Canadian men about their withdrawal from performing meke at the Fiji Day Fest. The divisiveness evident from our conversation and the festival footage contradicted the earlier sentiment "we are all just Fijians in Canada" and indicated a much more complicated sentiment. It rubbed away at the image of Fijian Canadians living harmoniously, having left behind a difficult and complex political history in Fiji. Instead, stress and defensiveness surfaced as feelings rooted in memories of ethnic tensions in Fiji that continued to impact the Fijian diaspora in Vancouver.

I then interviewed members of the meke group who organized the most recently added annual FijiFest and learned of their competing desires for social inclusion in Canada. Members of the group told me they based the programming for their festivities on rugby and native Fijian music, including a popular musical group from Fiji that produces a mix of more traditionally native Fijian music and dance with popular Western music. Interestingly, they explained that they withdrew from the 2011 Fiji Day Fest because of a "scheduling conflict." What was clearly a source of noticeable discomfort for the Fiji Day Fest organizer was treated defensively as a nonissue for the organizers of FijiFest, indicating a politically complex and divided situation.

In response to my questions about the two Fiji Day festivals, members of the meke group indicated further divisions. They explained that mostly Fijian Canadians of Indian descent attended Fiji Day Fest because the organizers were of Indian descent. They argued that their festival attracted more "native" Fijians because "native" Fijians organized it. Both Fiji festivals were attempting to connect with wider Vancouver communities and wanting to express their love of Fiji; the two festivals, however, also perpetuated a divide, with one geared toward affirming Fijian Canadian identity as autochthonous to Fiji and the other geared toward affirming Fijian Canadian identity as Indo-Fijian.

Each festival group marginalized the other through a process of exclusion, as manifested in festival programming, in order to achieve inclusion in multicultural Canada as an ethnocultural group. Nevertheless, the tensions and unease that emerged from these coexisting festivals would not be felt if one Fiji festival were to exist without the other. The presence of tension between these festival groups indicates unsuccessful attempts at exclusion and erasure. Indeed, the festivals indicate that differing approaches to identifying as Fijian in Vancouver coexist, complicating the ethnocultural typology produced by Canadian multicultural policies and discourses. Despite these policies, which have the effect of separating people on the basis of categories of ethnic origin, these two festivals together—as expressions of Fijianness in Canada—produce a uniquely experienced but relational encounter, becoming part of an emergent, not pregiven, Fijian diasporic identity.

Meke Iri (Fan Song-Dance) at a Multicultural Festival

While Canadian multicultural policies and discourses exacerbated colonial and postcolonial race-based tensions in and around meke in Vancouver, on Vancouver Island, Fijians and others from the South Pacific align with the Canadian image of "mosaic" while also blurring typological discourse when they adopt an Oceanic ethnological origin, expressed in dance. As a result, Fijian dance among Fijians and other peoples of Oceania living on Vancouver Island provides a means to renegotiate identity in contradictory ways. To illustrate this ambivalence, I analyze a meke iri performed for a Vancouver Island–based multicultural festival in 2011. The performance, and the language used to describe it, shows how particular gendered cultural beliefs and practices relating to nationalism, religion, and tradition are at times actively sustained and, at other times, used to absorb Fijians into a broader local Oceanic community and a pan-Oceanic identity, especially when the dancing forms a means of North and South Pacific Indigenous cultural exchange.

The notion of Oceanic dance is itself in need of interrogation since it is contradictory: sometimes it operates to remove differences rooted in culture, tradition, nationalism, or religion and, at other times, it works to establish such differences as an ethnological term of classification. It operates in ways similar to multiculturalism by contributing to ethnic classifications and processes of identity formation. Yet in contrast to recent criticisms of multiculturalism as a concept that positions non-Western peoples as being passively swept into accepting Western values, modes of thinking, and aesthetics, I suggest that adopting the broader identity classification of Oceanic Dance is an agentive process of intercultural relations emanating from Vancouver Island's Pacific peoples.[36]

On September 3, 2011, Vancouver Island's Greek Fest presented dances of the world (including Greece, Poland, Ukraine, Oceania, Spain, and more) as a harmonious multicultural event.[37] At the festival, I observed a meke iri performance by Pearl of the South Pacific Polynesian Dance Group. The dance group's performance of meke situated Oceanic identity within this multicultural montage. Emphasis on the Oceanic aspects of the group's identity served to connect South Pacific Islanders to each other and to enable a connection to other Canadian diasporas on Vancouver Island.

The term "mosaic" has been used frequently in Canada to describe multiculturalism in official discourse. Statistics Canada, for example, used the word in a report titled "Canada's Ethnocultural Portrait: The Changing Mosaic" to interpret results of the 2001 census: the number of visible minorities in Canada is growing. And Canadians listed more than two hundred ethnic groups in answering the 2001 census question on ethnic ancestry, reflecting a varied, rich cultural mosaic as the nation started the new millennium.[38] The word "mosaic" creates a visual image of different ethnocultural identities/colors in their own spaces, retaining their separateness, while making a whole picture of Canada. Greek Fest is an example of a mosaic, with different groups representing a wide variety of nationalities and ethnicities. Nevertheless, looking more closely at the dances themselves shows how kinetically ambiguous these groups are. Ultimately, ethnocultural identities/colors do not stay within particular boundaries, even when they claim to.

Mua Va'a, who is the director, one of the key performers, and master of ceremonies for the Pearl of the South Pacific dance group at the festival, adopted a reified notion of culture that is supported by Canadian multiculturalism discourses. Va'a told me in a postperformance interview that the group's performances are a valuable part of Canadian multiculturalism.[39] He explained that his group provides a "taste of the cultures of the South Pacific" and a "sample of traditions" through the dances. In other words, he sought to share cultural understanding and generate an appreciation of Oceanic culture and heritage with his Canadian audiences by choosing to represent Pacific cultures in ways that demonstrate their distinctiveness.

Va'a's approach to teaching and performing Oceanic dance at the festival celebrated difference within strategic sameness. Va'a introduced the dances from distinctive islands and called out a greeting in each island's native language, emphasizing the contribution of each to the whole. He also offered exclamations of joy and welcome in Greek, Rarotongan (Cook Islands), and Fijian, "Opa! Kia orana! Bula, bula vinaka!" Such a strategic use of language both celebrated and maintained difference. The dance he presented, a Fijian meke iri performed by three Samoan men, similarly overlooked and sustained difference. The movements performed were recognizable meke iri actions: the men's torsos were upright with deeply bent legs; they punctuated the rhythms of the music by quickly and sharply pulling the tips of their Fijian fans up with every downbeat while moving the head and torso; and they pounded their feet on the ground (figure 3.1). Together, performers strove to evoke the venerable strength and power of Fiji's ancestral warriors through these rhythms and accents.

The assertive and vigorous masculinity performed in this meke exemplifies a migratory movement-based expression through which bodies are locally and translocally situated. Many iTaukei men I spoke to in Canada and Fiji told me that one's ability to accent meke rhythms and movements

Figure 3.1. Pearl of the South Pacific performing meke at Greek Fest, Victoria, BC, September 3, 2011. Video still by Aaron Kelly.

in a certain way is natural ("runs through the blood") and tied to ancestors who were powerful warriors. These so-called aggressively masculine accents and rhythms of meke movements have become recognizable signs that mark bodies as coherently organized by race, sex, gender, ethnicity, and Fiji's past. While bodies can never be reduced to such external signs, governance relies on such recognizable signs to categorize and control bodies. In the meke iri, dancers generated bodies that fit into gendered and racialized categories by performing the naturalized rhythms and accents that are explained to be innately part of the male iTaukei body. Linking this example back to the broader argument of this chapter, the meke iri reveals the ways in which some Fijian Canadians, and peoples of Oceania, at times deploy a sense of Fijian culture and identity in Canada as essential, stable, cohesive, and continuous. Yet the performers themselves were not Fijian, which calls into question the claim that these rhythms, movements, and accents are innately iTaukei.

The Fijian meke iri movements and accents performed at the festival also blurred difference. In dynamic tension with the aggressive masculine accents and rhythms were more fluid and playful movements described to me as "general Polynesian." They chose these gestures to align with a broader pan-Oceanic identity. General Polynesian movements refer to a contemporary and widely adopted style of movement that Hereniko has described as Rarotongan.[40] The Rarotongans brought the dance to Rotuma in the 1940s, and since then it has become influenced by Fijian, Samoan, Tahitian, Tongan, Maori, Fatunan, and Gilbertese dances.[41] Movements for the Rotuman version of the dance, called mak Rarotonga, for men involves moving "the knees in and out while standing slightly on tip-toe, and for the women to shake the hips from side to side, at the same time forming patterns with the hands and fingers."[42] This Rarotonga dance style is popular across the South Pacific because it is considered fast, sensuous, and fun and "allows for individual expression of feelings in a more explicit way—through the face, hands, hips and leg movements."[43] Rarotonga dance, as it has migrated to Vancouver Island, is part of what makes Va'a's meke Oceanic, to an extent blurring boundaries of ethnic difference among Pacific peoples. In this meke, cultures merge, interact, and transform, shaping cultural identity and belonging within multicultural spaces.

While the rituals and protocols surrounding meke are important to Fijians today in diaspora, certain elements of the rituals surrounding the creation, teaching, and performance of meke have shifted out of necessity, blurring boundaries of ethnocultural difference. For example, if someone wanted to perform a meke in Canada that was created in Fiji they would still need to approach the daunivucu who created it or the chief from the village the meke is from and make a proper request by following certain protocols.[44] Fijians living in diaspora, however, are not able to observe these protocols of respect online or over the phone. As a result, iTaukei choreograph new meke in diaspora with new movements, as was the case with Va'a's meke iri. According to Va'a, the resultant blurring of differences was a necessary part of making the dances accessible to a broader Canadian community on Vancouver Island as well as generating a feeling of connection to Fiji and Oceania.

The Oceanian dance group also absorbed Fijian cultural and traditional differences into a broader Oceanic identity through costumes. While in Fiji, several iTaukei explained to me that meke costumes activate feelings of inner strength and identity because they carry meaning associated with the customs of the Fijian land (the vanua). In Canada, however, costumes are difficult to obtain since the materials needed, such as masi and grass skirts, are not readily available. Instead, at Greek Fest the costumes for the meke iri were identical to an earlier Tahitian dance: colorful grass fringe hung from below the knees, blue knee-length sarongs, and black tank-top shirts. The costume signifiers of tradition and authenticity typically used in Fiji shifted in the Canadian context, perhaps out of necessity and/or by choice, to signify a more general Oceanic identity.

The meke iri was performed to "Meda Mai Ia" by Sekove Raikoro, a popular Christian song in Fiji at the time of the performance and also a popular choice for Fijians and others performing meke in Canada because of its accessibility and its blending of Fijian culture, Christianity, and Western influences. Va'a asserted that this upbeat music energized both dancers and the spectators, making it more accessible to Canadian audiences and enabling inclusion and cross-cultural community building.

Va'a was not alone in his strategic use of music. Another group of Fijians, Samoans, and Rotumans explained their use of a popular Fijian song titled "Raude" by Black Rose for their meke wesi (spear meke) at a separate event. "Raude" is a pre-Christian meke chant with added contemporary popular rhythms.[45] The members of the meke wesi group stated that by adding a Western contemporary rhythm to the traditional chant the music becomes less distinctively Fijian and enables more people to dance to it and identify with it. Drawing from the popular to establish a sense of kinship across previously encrusted racial and ethnic divides is not unique to Canada's Oceanian diaspora. According to Katerina Teaiwa, consumption of the popular is also a powerful tactic within New Zealand communities of Pacific peoples, while in New Zealand relations between Indigenous Pacific peoples are complexly situated "between migrant and Native" owing to their common connections to the sea, culture, and history.[46] In Canada, where Pacific peoples are situated within immigrant/diaspora relations with a largely non-Indigenous settler population, the use of popular Westernized Fijian music for meke in Canada provides an indicator of one strategy Fijians use to identify themselves in Canada to generate inclusion.

Aligning the dances of Oceania more closely with Western multicultural values and aesthetics, in terms of using flashy, ethnic costumes, Westernized music, and altering movement content to make it more exciting, the dances appeal to Westerners and hence become more profitable. Va'a does not support these tactics for the purpose of financial gain, however, and expressed concern that distinct dances and cultures of Oceania will become tokenized or assimilated into dominant North American values and aesthetics. He argued that such watering down of cultural practices for profit would thus lead to a loss of cultural identity for future generations of Oceanian descent born in Canada.

The Canadian Multicultural Program, which seeks to achieve the objectives of the Multiculturalism Act, aligns with Va'a's vision for preserving ethnocultural identity through cultural heritage activities in Canada. Va'a explained that teaching and performing traditional dances of the Pacific as opposed to just dancing casually can work to promote cultural heritage.[47] With this goal in mind, Va'a works to generate dance performances that are aesthetically appealing to Canadian audiences but include a knowledge-building component. For Va'a, minimizing certain differences for the marketing of Oceanic dance does not necessarily dilute ethnocultural identity. Instead, such accommodations enable sharing and generate appreciation from Vancouver Island audiences. Since the Multicultural Program has recently moved from within the Department of Immigration, Refugees and Citizenship to the Department of Canadian Heritage, Va'a can now access Canadian Heritage funds for cultural legitimacy activities within the scope of achieving the objectives of Canada's Multiculturalism Act.[48]

Through his complex negotiation of difference, Va'a generated a sense of Oceanic community, identity, and cultural inclusion at the Vancouver Island festival. In his final introduction to the last dance from Samoa, Va'a explained to the audience that his dancers were from Samoa, Fiji, Rotuma, and New Zealand and that they shared in common a love of culture, dance, and songs. He stated that the final dance in their festival program was performed with "our next generation [adults with their children]. We never stop learning [from each other about our cultures]. There are not many of us now but we keep growing as a community." His comments indicated that all members of his group were part of a community that identifies itself as peoples of the Pacific or Oceanian in composition. In addition to using dance performance as a way of building an Oceanian community, Va'a's efforts were, for him, a valuable part of contributing to an idea of his new home as a harmonious multicultural mosaic.

While such multicultural festivals have often focused largely on the cultural identification of newcomers, immigrants, and refugees within a largely non-Indigenous settler population, Va'a has also used the dance to widen Oceanian intercultural exchange between South Pacific and Canadian coastal Indigenous communities at the One Wave Gathering, a gathering of North and South Pacific Indigenous artists that the Pacific Peoples' Partnership has organized for the last decade. Pacific Peoples' Partnership is a Vancouver Island nonprofit organization that has for over forty years focused on bringing together North and South Pacific Indigenous voices in a network of knowledge exchange with the aim of supporting community development, social justice, sustainability, peace, and the environment.[49] The work of this organization supports relationships that, as Teaiwa has argued, "are as powerful as, if not more than, the state and other public institutions."[50] Va'a, who was president of Pacific Peoples' Partnership during the writing of this book, used dance as a form of cultural exchange to create relations that extend the notion of Oceania between the North and South hemispheric divide, bringing together historically colonized and divided groups.

Māori Haka for an "Island Night" Fundraiser

While meke performed as part of a larger Oceanic construct strategically sustains and blurs difference to generate a sense of inclusion and cultural exchange, a Māori haka also demonstrates a gendered process for becoming Oceanic in Canada within the context of long-term social relations and obligations. In this section, I discuss a haka performed in 2009 for a fundraising event. Many of the Fijian and South Pacific men I interviewed recalled this haka as a powerful relational experience with long-term, cross-cultural, community-building effects. These men, many of whom have been in Canada for at least twenty years, described the dance as a reclaiming and rebuilding of a pan-Oceanic identity based on precolonial relations spanning across the Pacific Ocean. While they described this experience as affirming Oceanian identity, they also constructed a somewhat essentialized, conservative link between male warriors and tradition, producing a cultural web of relations that legitimized their identities in Canada.

In 2009 many of my Fijian and South Pacific interlocutors on Vancouver Island participated in a haka for an "Island Night" event to raise funds for a high school girls' rugby team in Merritt, British Columbia. The event, organized by Avaiki, was initiated after the rugby team volunteered at his car wash to raise money for a mother whose children were tragically murdered. According to Avaiki, the enthusiasm surrounding the event was high because of the intentions behind it: the car wash fundraiser aimed to support a grieving mother, and the "Island Night" fundraiser subsequently thanked the girls' rugby team for their volunteerism. The event attracted South Pacific peoples from across British Columbia, who came and danced at the event. The final dance performance of the evening was a haka, and the participants included twenty to thirty men from different islands of the Pacific including Aotearoa, Niue, the Cook Islands, Samoa, Tonga, Fiji, and Rotuma. Avaiki described the haka as having "an amazing spirit, like we were going to bring the roof down."[51]

By doing a haka together, Fijians and other Pacific peoples dynamically negotiated the changing aspects of Oceanic identity entangled within Canadian culture. There were no static and uniform culturally authentic experiences, and yet the experience of dancing together created a feeling of vibrant intensity through their shared movements in time and space; the experience was shared but still unique from body to body. My interlocutors explained that even though the men all came from different places (each with their own history) dancing the haka together created a feeling of the South Pacific as a whole and did not signify one particular culture. Rather, they were generating a new sense of culture and identity in diaspora through movement-based experiences and expressions.

Avaiki stated: "In Canada, we have individual pride and a love of our Pacific Islands of origin and the dances that come from them. However, in Canada, we represent ourselves as a whole, not from separate island nations. It is the spirit we share—we are never away from the dance, we all dance for the same reasons: entertainment, to make everybody happy. . . . These things are very important to our people."⁵² Avaiki further explained that this shared Oceanic spirit came from the experience of living in Oceania: a history of identifying as warriors (described as expressing power, strength, and "aggression" in war dances), a love of the ocean (described as "our playground"), a communal sense of love and caring, and a sense of shared history vis-à-vis traditions of ocean navigation, shipbuilding, music, dance, food, and kava. Participants blurred island differences to connect through these similarities, and through the sharing of dance experiences, to generate a feeling of inclusion in Canada.

Language used to describe performing haka demonstrates that, in terms of generating a sense of identity as Oceanic on Vancouver Island, there was more going on than danced representations of South Pacific culture. Rather, dancing haka together was an expressive process of becoming cultural. In other words, in sharing the experience of doing haka, participants actualized, or brought into existence, an Oceanic identity with cultural meaning and significance. This haka enabled the living rhythms and pulses of Pacific culture to move and breathe as these Pacific peoples of Vancouver Island and across British Columbia themselves moved and breathed life into a shared Oceanic identity. As Avaiki put it, "With all of us, we have individual ties to where we come from but when we come together, as people of the South Pacific, it is a very different feeling. It's a feeling that we can't explain. It is common to us. . . . It's that we know our ancestors rowed and fished and played in our ancestral playground. And at one point it became a battleground, but now we group together."⁵³ This statement demonstrates how dance creates and re-creates relations between groups that were dismantled by missionaries and colonialism. Prior to the presence of missionaries and colonizers, travel and exchange between the Pacific islands was endemic, resulting in a culture of shared traditions.⁵⁴ According to Hereniko, however, missionaries discouraged long-distance voyaging between islands of the Pacific.⁵⁵ In addition, missionaries and Europeans brought diseases that decimated populations.⁵⁶ The loss of the manpower needed for the long-distance voyaging that enabled Oceanic culture to thrive was dismantled. Such Oceanic relations are powerful today as part of a strategic rendering of precolonial and pre-nation-state relations that span the Pacific. This is why, according to Pacific scholar Nicholas Thomas, the term "Oceania," connoting "a sea of islands with their inhabitants," is now preferred by scholars and peoples of the Pacific over the term "Pacific Islands," which connotes "small areas of land surfaces sitting atop submerged reefs or seamounts."⁵⁷ The shift aims to celebrate "the connections between peoples" instead of to "affirm particular peoples in a nationalist mode."⁵⁸ For historical reasons, identifying as "Oceanic" was politically important for community building among Pacific peoples on Vancouver Island.⁵⁹

The participants of the dance also generated a shared feeling through a gendered and nationalistic mode. They all knew how to do haka from playing and watching men's rugby, where it has become popularized and infused with a spirit of New Zealand nationalism.⁶⁰ In this case, that particular gendered nationalism widened to include all the South Pacific men participating in the haka. As a result, they were all able to get into the danced expression of what they termed aggressive—as an expression of an Oceanic ancestral warrior spirit.⁶¹ In addition to connecting through a spirit of nationalism, vigorous masculine strength, and South Pacific pride, they also connected through the shared experiences and memories of performing war dances, dances that have been culturally important across the Pacific Ocean for generations. According to Avaiki: "All South Pacific Islanders have war dances—it's a common thread. So, we can all come together to do haka as a group. We all know how to bring into our dancing a fighting spirit. And, we know how to transmit that aggression to create fear and intimidation in the spectator. War dances are aggressive. For most of us, this aggression is portrayed by war paint on faces, facial expressions, body language, and the strength of the arm movements. So, [performing a haka] was mainly representative of the whole South Pacific."⁶² This statement asserts how a shared pan-Oceanic warrior ancestry can create an intercultural experience. At the same time, generalizing the fighting spirit and taking it out of historical context may serve as a way of producing an essentializing, aggressive masculinity.⁶³

As an expression of Oceanic identity on Vancouver Island, my Fijian, Rotuman, and Samoan interlocutors described how the haka event countered the residues of divisive colonial attitudes while producing a sense of cultural identity and belonging through movements and sensations that articulated new intercultural experiences in Canada. The "Island Night" gift, and the haka in particular, generated mana in diaspora in the sense that it was effective at fostering a strong sense of community between peoples of the South Pacific and Merritt, British Columbia, that continued into future acts of generosity and exchange. According to Avaiki, using the money raised at the event, the girls' rugby team traveled to Fiji to learn more about Fijian rugby. The description of this event demonstrates how dance, as a process for becoming cultural in Canada, produces long-term, gendered, and intercultural webs of relations between Indigenous peoples of the South Pacific and non-Indigenous Canadian settler populations.

Conclusion

Dance among the Fijian, and broader Oceanian, diaspora in Canada is an embodied and interactive negotiation of identity that, while haunted by legacies of colonialism, challenges simplistic notions of culture, ethnicity, and identity as fixed and cohesive by widening danced participation. Conversations, physical encounters, and observations of meke and Oceanic dance revealed the migratory dimensions of identity through expressions of religion, ethnicity, power, indigeneity, and gender. Examples of Fijian and Oceanian dance in Canada show how the constructed and politically divisive ethnic groupings established during British colonial rule and explosive, postindependence, nationalist politics continue to inform the experiences and expressions of Fijian migrants living in Canada and how Canadian multicultural policies perpetuate ethnic classifications and gendered divisions. But multiculturalism is not simply imposed upon Fijians in diaspora. Rather, these examples reveal how Fijian Canadians strategically deploy depictions of Fijian culture as discontinuous and mutable and, at other times, as cohesive and stable. This seemingly contradictory process is important for Fijians living in Canada in terms of negotiating Fiji's past and present realities while, at the same time, adjusting to new connections and relations in Canada. In making new connections, danced experiences and expressions, which migrate and are exchanged and shared, are important aspects of developing long-term social relations with wider North and South Pacific Indigenous and non-Indigenous settler populations.

Alongside those who dance, there are Fijians in Fiji and Canada who do not participate in meke because of local manifestations of religious and political tensions that have also migrated from Fiji. Understanding the choice not to participate in meke was a new anti-meke terrain that required mapping. The new terrain, emerging from the flood of charismatic and evangelical churches that reject traditions, threatens older hierarchical political, religious, and social formations. As anthropologist Charles Piot, quoting sociologist Nikolas Rose, put it, what presented itself was the need for a cartography that "tracks the unmaking and remaking of an entire social world and takes seriously the wager of a people willing to trade a past for a future still unknown."[64] Those rejecting the past are gaining power and influence while those who were once preeminent are finding ways of holding on to that power. This was a source of tension between Fijian churches in Vancouver, and this is what my consultant at the iTaukei Institute of Language and Culture (chapter 2), wittingly or not, shared with me in his cautious questions, doubts, and whispers about religious tensions in Fiji. Amid what appears to be the development of a so-called witch hunt mentality in Fiji and among Fiji's Canadian diaspora, growing associations between meke and "devil worship" and the resulting rejections of meke indicate the "unmaking and remaking of an entire social world."[65]

To understand the decision not to participate in meke, I turn to new questions in the next chapter: When dance is so ubiquitous among Fijian and other Oceanian groups as a form of widening exchange and social relations, albeit along certain parameters of inclusion and exclusion, what religious and political reasons inform a choice not to participate? And how do these choices also relate to colonial legacies amid new formations of politics and religion in Fiji?

CHAPTER 4

Spiriting Meke

Generating Stability, Tension, and Transformation

A FEW DAYS BEFORE TRAVELING with my family to a "home stay" to study meke in a village called Namatakula in the Western Province of Nadroga-Navosa, Viti Levu, I called our hostess, Judith Batibasaga, to confirm that she was okay with the length and timing of our stay and to work out an appropriate amount of money to give her.[1] We agreed on a rate and she gave me directions. She told me to come to the green house at the end of the first road into the village. I questioned how we were to know we had the right house. She was confident it would be obvious to us, and she was correct.

We arrived in the village situated on the coral coast, which protects the village from strong ocean currents and waves, most of the time.[2] The house was located on its own at the far edge of the village, separated from the other homes by a long and straight cement path. It was also constructed differently. There were Western-style doors that swung open into a lobby-like entrance, and the house was constructed from brightly painted, green cinder blocks that distinguished it from the unpainted, gray cinder block homes nearby. Unlike the interior open spaces of other houses in the village we visited, the interior of Judith's home was organized into separate rooms for sleeping, eating, cooking, and recreational TV watching.

From the moment we arrived, I felt immediately comfortable with Judith. She had been a school teacher who was forced into a quick retirement when the current prime minister, Bainimarama, announced in 2009 (three years after he had taken military control of Fiji), with little notice, that the compulsory retirement age for public sector employees would be reduced to the age of fifty-five. She told me that she, along with hundreds of public sector workers, was given two weeks' notice of her forced retirement. The situation left her needing money; her home provided a solution. A hub of activity for friends and family, it became a home stay. At the time of our visit, she ran her home stay for tourists with the help of her husband, who did guided tours, her daughter-in-law, who did most of the cooking, and others who took part in cleaning, cooking, and caring for visitors.

She sat and talked with us about the world. There were so many problems with the world. She was happy to stay in Fiji. Would she visit her son in Vancouver and his six children, I asked? No, she was happy to stay in Fiji. There was nothing frivolous about what she had to say. Her movements were the same: slow, direct, and as needed.

Later in the evening while sharing a meal with her and her husband, Saimon, I asked her about meke in the village. She was evasive and reluctant to discuss meke. She said vaguely, "They used to do it over at a resort down the beach." I asked why meke was no longer done in the village. She attended a Pentecostal church, the Assemblies of God, she explained, and when Saimon's father, who was the village chief, joined Assemblies of God, his conversion obligated the whole chiefly family to convert. Judith told me that Assemblies of God does not allow traditional meke to be performed. I asked her, "When was the last meke done in the village?" She answered, "The last meke was fifty years ago."[3]

Although those living in Namatakula were not performing meke in the village, I quickly discovered that some of the Methodist village inhabitants were performing meke in a nearby resort. Within one village, there seemed to be a double story: Assemblies of God churchgoers who did not do meke; and Methodists who did meke anyway, outside the village. Such contradictions indicated a haunting tension around religion, ancestral spirits, colonial conflict, and resistance in relation to meke. Even more, they indicated a double spectrality—ancestral spirits were subversively threatening to destabilize the colonial order that still impacted the embodied present.[4]

Spirits are contentious in the ways they enflesh Fiji's colonial history and intersect with Fiji's current realities. As explored in previous chapters, haunting, felt affectively as tension and friction, indicates the ambivalence of articulating, or replicating, colonial legacies and resistance to such legacies in and around performances of meke. The appearance of Pentecostals breathing new life into white colonial legacies of religious practices, economics, and political individualism in a postcolonial context, for example, is a form of haunting. But living memories also resist colonial legacies in the transmission of meke movements, protocols, and techniques. Ancestor spirits also haunt the embodied present by blurring the distinction between the corporeal and the noncorporeal. While such spirits are experienced in contradictory ways depending on religious orientation, they are efficacious in the sense that they enter bodies, affecting them in a range of destructive and enabling ways. Thus, spirits are at once haunting reminders of colonialism as well as reminders of resistance to it—they are the dead or dangerous moments of subversive memory that blur past, present, and future imaginings, desires, and strivings.

This chapter examines spirit and religion as resistive methods of embodying meke within the context of local Fijian traditional beliefs. I focus on the ways Christianity has retroactively charted its way through pre-Christian traditions in defining Fijianness. But as I was to learn in my interviews with iTaukei about meke, ancestor spirits ordered Fijian life in ways that colonials did not understand, even as colonialism dismantled and threatened such long-term ancestral systems of social relations.[5] With this in mind, I explore evangelical rejections of meke, Methodists who are haunted by ancestors when performing meke, and the processes of one Roman Catholic who actively generates and transforms spirit in meke. All three approaches demonstrate disparate methods for embodying spirit in meke that stabilize and resist the legacies of Christian colonialism within Fijian traditional space. Ultimately, spirits, including ancestors, offer a politically conscious possibility for linking the past, present, and future and allowing for the nonmaterial to exist within the corporeal.

Choosing Not to Practice Meke

The many questions that emerged for me while staying in Namatakula expose some of the complexities of meke as a traditional practice in relation to spirituality, religion, and the economics of hospitality and inclusion in Fiji. My Assemblies of God host and hostess, Saimon and Judith, saw traditions as backward, perpetuating Methodist hegemony, and connected with devil worship. They did not desire or uphold meke as important to Fijian culture and identity. Rather, they viewed meke, like drinking yaqona, as having a potential demonic aspect and distanced themselves from traditional practices they associated with ancestor worship. But their rejection of tradition, in part by turning their home into an income-earning tourist accommodation, was also a political choice to reject the status quo.

The long-standing and strong hegemonic relationship in Fiji between Methodism, governance, and Bauan dominance maintained through traditional practices provides context for this different perspective on tradition.[6] In its early days in Fiji, the Wesleyan Methodist Church, which sent some of the first missionaries to Fiji in the 1830s, interwove itself within the vanua (the iTaukei customs and practices of the land). For various reasons, Fijians began to identify themselves and their connection to customs and the land as Christian.[7]

There has also been a long history of challenging this hegemonic authority by joining non-Methodist Christian churches. In the years following cession to Britain, joining a rival Christian denomination, such as the Seventh-Day Adventists, Assemblies of God, or the Roman Catholic Church, was a way to undermine colonial, Bauan, and Methodist authority while maintaining one's legitimacy as Christian.[8] Fiji scholar Nicholas Thomas, who did ethnographic research in Fiji's western interior in the late 1980s, noted that religion in Fiji's Western Province, such as Adventism and Assemblies of God, continued to act as a cloaking device for political maneuvers.[9]

Judith and Saimon appear to destabilize Methodist authority in part through their rejection of tradition. While missionaries and colonials once imposed eradication of Indigenous dances across the Pacific (see chapter 1), today in Fiji, the rejection of meke and other Indigenous traditions is typical of iTaukei evangelical and charismatic Christians.[10] In this sense, rejections of tradition can be viewed as acts of agency and decolonization, freeing up individual (as opposed to communal) economic and leadership opportunities. As anthropologist Charles Piot explained, "It was colonialism that 'invented' chiefs and village tradition as technologies of power, projects and technologies that were reissued by postcolonial dictatorships. Charismatics see themselves as attempting to free themselves from the weight of this (to them) oppressive tradition."[11] Although early Western missionaries and colonials did not completely eradicate meke, evangelicals and charismatics, who carve out their own resistive yet Christian legitimacy and authority, impose an element of erasure on meke.

Though such resistance to tradition is haunted by colonialism, in that it ambiguously mimics and resists colonial legacies, the current Pentecostal Christian discourse on spirit also influences church members' perspectives on tradition. Anthropologist Jacqueline Ryle noted that for one influential Pentecostal Fijian minister, Reverend Kurulo, the haunting of ancestor spirits could be detected by "misery" and "dirtiness."[12] In Kurulo's view there was a danger in feeling the wrong things: feeling bad could indicate the presence of the devil and an "unclean spirit"; good feelings, on the other hand, indicated the presence of God and a "clean spirit."[13] Pentecostal Christianity in Fiji has led to a present-day proliferation of ideas about devilish spirits, sorcery, witchcraft, and devil worship, which are used to explain occurrences of unusual behavior and misfortune as "evil" behavior, the result of not being devoted to God.[14] Spirits, and not inequitable colonial and postcolonial systems, are sources of suffering to the extent that "sickness, poverty, lack of education, difficulty getting married or having children, and general failure to prosper" can all be indicators of the effective and malicious presence of ancestor spirits.[15] Since anxieties about ancestor spirits persist, some Fijians are concerned with generating "good" Christian feelings and values by rejecting all traditional practices associated with ancestor worship. As a result, even though Methodists who practice meke say they are Christian, our Assemblies of God host and hostess, along with other evangelicals in the village I spoke with, do not consider them to be truly following the Christian faith because, in line with the larger religious politics of Pentecostalism, they associate such traditions with devil worship.

Judith reluctantly described the history of meke in the Western Province village but used the opportunity to proudly weave into the story information about how Saimon and his father had carved out a very different way of life than the rest of the villagers by not participating in the traditions, religious practices, and economics of the village. This separation between Saimon's family and the rest of the village extended back to a time when people in the village still did meke for tourists. Judith explained that during British colonial rule, there was a nearby hotel called the Korolevu Hotel (opened by a man named Hugh Ragg in 1948) where members of the Vusu lineage from Namatakula, Komave, and Biausevu would perform every Saturday.[16] The hotel would pay performers, who would use the money to build their houses out of bamboo (which grows nearby in Biausevu). As a result, everyone in Saimon's village had bamboo homes except for Saimon's father, whose house was made out of wood. According to Judith, he was the only member of the Assemblies of God at that time. He did not participate in meke, even though the rest of the village did. When Saimon's father became chief of the village, his family and others in the village also stopped meke out of respect for his beliefs.[17]

Thus, some evangelical Fijians, like Saimon and Judith, appear to emulate Western values and practices when they reject traditions, such as meke. But in so doing, they also resist colonial legacies by destabilizing the hegemonic authority of the Methodist Church, to which many other villagers belong. This choice to separate themselves from the rest of the village is in line with Thomas's observation that in rural areas, such as those in the Western Province, those who adhere to Assemblies of God often live outside villages.[18] Not only was their home separated from the village by a cement path created by Saimon's grandfather; they also adopted individualistic economic strategies. Tourism allowed them to build a home business that enabled them to acquire technologies that others may not have been able to afford (such as a large flat-screen TV, electricity, and a small degree of plumbing). Their economic status reinforced their social, religious, and spatial distinction from Methodist villagers, as did their separation from the social dimensions of customary practices.

Contradictory Relations with Ancestors

Unable to see meke in the village, my family and I visited a nearby resort in Navola, called the Warwick Hotel, to watch a performance by the Nasikawa Meke Group, some of whose Methodist members also lived in Namatakula. We entered a large banquet room where resort guests were just ending their Fiji-themed feast. Many of the guests seemed drunk, happy, and boisterous. An emcee appeared and introduced the meke group. Four men took their place on the stage to do a meke wesi-wau (spear and club dance).[19] The stage was postage-stamp small, and the dancers improvised a comedic response to their plight of having to perform a "war" dance on it. They bumped into one another intentionally and shoved each other out of the way to demonstrate, through humor, that they lacked space to dance. But then, the rhythm of the chant doubled in speed and lifted in pitch while dancers turned to face their rowdy crowd to perform intense, focused, and precise movements relating to combat.[20] Two men drove their spears forward and the other two spun to miss them. They took turns doing fast steps from side to side to miss spear thrusts and to create rhythms. "The lali has to be fast or you get hurt," explained Jiuta Tokula, an elder in the group, in a postperformance interview.[21] The performers held long spears in front of their bodies and manipulated them so the spears would vibrate. The men quickly jolted their arms and shifted their weight. Then they slowed down as they drew their spears back over the top of their right shoulders. Slowing down more, and building anticipation, they pulled back their torsos and used their fans to take aim. On the final beat of the lali, the dancers thrust their spears at members of the audience. The vivid and intense focus of the meke slid quickly into the next entertaining trick or joke.[22] It seemed they were subtly taking aim at Western tourists. But I learned there was much more to this meke and much more knowledge about meke in Namatakula.

∼

Although evangelicals in Namatakula expressed disdain for traditions, Methodists in the village saw traditions as part of their culture and heritage and their Christian identity. For example, Asesela Vasutoga, a young Methodist dancer from the Nasikawa Meke Group, explained he had no conflict being Christian and practicing traditions such as dancing meke and drinking kava.[23] Although both practices were once a part of worshipping the land spirits, he believed they were now cultural heritage given by God. He explained, "God gives kava and meke. Seventh-Day Adventists and those with Assemblies of God act from human motivations, not godly ones, when they stop meke and kava. Now meke is about tradition and culture anyway; it is no longer spiritual. The land god is the devil."[24] Thus, my interviews and encounters with meke in the village demonstrated a real conflict between Christians who wanted to include tradition in their lives and Christians who did not.

I had the opportunity to interview some of the group's elder members about their meke, and I began to understand the long and complex colonial and precolonial history between the inhabitants of the village. Tokula explained that the Nasikawa Meke Group was comprised of members who were descended from the Nasikawa people who came from the Sigatoka River area to settle in four coastal villages: Komave, Namatakula, Navola, and Navao: "They came to the coral coast to stay away from the fighting, but their foundation is in the mountains." He then traced the history of the Vusu people (to which Saimon belongs) and the Nasikawa people. He explained, "Both groups traveled across Nakovandra mountains in the north and came down to Navosa. The Vusu chief's uncle is the Nasikawa chief, but the uncle is the big man—he leads."[25] Tokula did not clarify when the Nasikawa people left the Sigatoka River area. But at some point, they were displaced because of war and scattered between villages.

Tokula's reference to war and the consequent displacement of the Nasikawa people from their Western interior village in Navosa aligns with a heavily documented history of resistance to subjugation by other Fijians and British colonizers. According to anthropologist Adrian Tanner, one of the defining features of the region is the way western interior peoples identify with war against coastal people beginning around 1867 and subsequent war with the British after colonization in 1876. The people of this region did not sign the deed of cession and fought to resist subjugation in what they termed "The Church War."[26] Eventually, the British (who referred to western interior peoples as the "devils") and other Fijian coastal groups who had sided with the British took control of the region.[27] The British then moved the peoples of the interior to the coastal villages to allow them more access and control.[28] Whether Tokula's ancestors fought with or against the British is not clear. But the displacement of the Nasikawa people to a number of village sites suggests subjugation. That the Nasikawa people continue to gather from their varying villages to perform their meke suggests, at the very least, a resistance to their dispersal and a desire to keep their history alive.

Meke, as a living mode of expression, contains historical, political, and spiritual knowledge of the past. In my interview with Tokula, I learned the Nasikawa Meke Group has a long history of performing in tourist resorts for foreigners. But despite the current commercial application, their meke were created several generations ago and tell histories specific to the Nasikawa people. He explained, "The spear and club meke was a gift from chief Davutukia to the Nasikawa people in the early 1900s because his daughter married one of the Nasikawa people."[29] This meke performed by the Nasikawa Group could be viewed as "living memory," which, as argued by Joseph Roach, is resistant to forgetting "through the transmissions of gestures, habits, and skills."[30] The spear and club meke they performed was a documentation of political relations between groups—it recounted a local history over one hundred years old.

As an embodied repertoire, or reproduction and transmission of historical knowledge, the Nasikawa Group performs meke that are also mediated.[31] The transmission of historical knowledge works alongside other performance pressures. The hotel paid the dancers to entertain the tourists on top of a very small stage. And the dancers transmitted their history through a Christian lens. Their performances indicate a double haunting. On the one hand, their meke suggest a resistance to colonial subjugation and control. On the other hand, their performance of cultural entertainment on a postage-stamp-sized stage is the result of colonial constructions of native Others intruding on the present.

Adding to this contradictory layering of memory and history, despite their disavowal of ancestor worship, the Nasikawa members I spoke to still practice traditions tinged by perceived dangers of vengeful land gods.[32] Tokula made this evident when he emphasized the importance of seeking permission from a daunivucu to do meke: "If permission is not sought in the proper way (with an offering of kava) then the dancers will get the lyrics, movements, or accents wrong and could die. But if you get permission, then you learn the dance the right way. It will be taught to the village and it will take a lot of practice to get it right, but the verses, movements, and accents will all be right."[33] Although primarily composed of Methodists, the way the group follows protocols for their meke tells me that, for them, the land gods are still present and powerful. Tokula went on to explain that after they perform their meke, they drink yaqona together to say thank you and they cobo (cup-clapping the hands) once for each dancer. He admitted that drinking kava is a small sacrifice to appease the land spirits so that the meke performers do not get sick. This protocol, he told me, has been done for generations.[34]

In addition to the comments of the Nasikawa Meke Group members, ancestor spirits, as sources of power and efficacy, continued to emerge in my conversations about the practice of meke with other iTaukei who lived in Namatakula. Kelera Bale, whose husband's father (Saimon's brother) was the recently deceased village chief at the time of my visit, spoke to me about her passion for and knowledge of meke, despite the fact that she did not practice meke in the village out of respect for the chiefly family into which she had married. She comes from the district of Rakiraki in the northern part of Viti Levu, and she referred to herself as a manu manu ni meke, whose grandfather was a daunivucu. According to Bale, dancers get their vitality and energy from the daunivucu, who in turn gets spirit, energy, the chant, and the movements from the land spirits:

> For some, their bodies just respond to the chant. Their heads will just go with the chant. They don't have to think about it. In Fiji, the daunivucu provides that energy and vitality by consulting with the spirit gods. Consulting the spirit gods is difficult because the daunivucu will have to perform the kava ceremony to ask for the meke. The daunivucu will consult with the

spirit gods and the spirit gods will then give the understanding of what words to create and the daunivucu will just write because it is going to come. After that, he will learn it. When he comes to teach the meke and give the meke to the people of the village to perform, then automatically, it just comes, the villagers don't need anything else. When we practice every day, it is not that strong, but when we perform it to an audience, it [the energy and spirit] automatically just comes, and then you show everything.[35]

For Bale, movements and bodies are directly linked to the ancestral spirits in meke through the daunivucu. Energy also comes from the spirit gods outside the body via the land. Moving bodies resist containment when they are perceived to be porous vessels or conduits for the transmission of that vitality and energy from the spirit world.

For iTaukei, Christianity is centered on the land, but ancestral spirits also haunt the land, making it a source of danger, anxiety, and suspicion. Using his own ethnographic research experiences, Tomlinson has stated that the lands of old village sites are imbued with the mana of the ancestors, who are particularly dangerous and daunting to those who enter it. "People," he wrote, "spoke of the ancestors' strength and violence and worried about curses from those ancestors that afflict people in the present. The signs of ancestral strength were embedded in the soil: people could become ill by digging a taboo patch of earth."[36] In the following instance, the presence of ancestor spirits generated uneasy, yet enabling, physical feelings in the body.

Epeli Tuibeqa, a Suva-based meke performer, described the feeling of powerful ancestral spirits entering his body from the land during a meke performance. The performance was at Thurston Gardens (near the Fiji Museum in Suva) for a domestic tourist event. Thurston Gardens (named after John Bates Thurston, governor from 1888 to 1897 and forcibly against ancestral worship) was once the location of the old village of Suva.[37] According to anthropologist Marshall Sahlins, the Rewa chief Ratu Qaraniqio attacked the village in 1843 and many of the inhabitants were killed.[38] Tuibeqa explained how the dancers dealt with the felt presence of the ancestor spirits: "There are spirits roaming around the museum and we didn't believe it until we performed there. So, we had to keep the chanting low in respect of the burial grounds near there." Tuibeqa added that the dancers who performed felt confusion and an unnerving feeling. But as the dancers followed the proper protocols of respect for the ancestor and land spirits, the spirits gave them greater physical strength and ability to do their meke:

Performing there, it was totally different. Even those who were chanting said that our jumping was like nothing we have ever done before. Our jumps were higher and the moves were more accurate and strong. They said they had never seen us perform like that. [Our heightened abilities came to us] because we respected the place and we maintained the silence [a common practice at burial sites in Fiji] until the meke. This made the spirits happy and they came to join us in the dance. It felt normal but we were just doing extra moves, we had more energy. After we came out of it, we saw the bruises on our knees, but throughout the meke we didn't feel it at all.[39]

Tuibeqa described an experience of ancestor spirits entering bodies in an enabling and powerful way to increase the spirit, physical vigor, and energy of the meke. This example shows the daily negotiations in space/place infused with Christian colonial civilizing legacies that strove to contain bodies and diminish the powerful and life-affirming Indigenous spiritual possibilities of the ancestor spirits. Such ghosts connect the past with the present.[40] In their felt/sensed dimensions, ancestor spirits make traceable histories of resistance and enable a vitality that blurs the distinction between life and death.

For some iTaukei, closeness to spirit creates discomfort and they wish to avoid encounters with ancestors while performing meke. Members of Kabu ni Vanua of the Conservatorium of Music explained that meke is a form of entertainment or a representation of culture and heritage and that meke is no longer a spiritual act (in terms of kalou worship). Instead, they infuse their dancing and the stories the movement evokes with "good" feelings that support cultural preservation, national pride, and Christianity. For example, one dancer with the Conservatorium told me about a seasea (women's standing dance) performed by the women of the group called *Sa Lutu a Caucau Vanua*, or *Morning Mist of the Land*. The dance is from Vanua Levu (the second largest island of Fiji, north and east of Viti Levu) and is about celebrating the land with Christianity.[41] The first verse of the chant is as follows:

Caucau e lutu mai uluda
Caucau e lutu mai uluda
(Early morning dew has descended upon our heads)
E tadola a lomai vuravura
E tadola a lomai vuravura
(The Earth has opened up the beginning of a new day)

Soqo levu ka sa maqusa
Soqo levu ka sa maqusa
(Speedy preparations for a special occasion has come upon us)

E totoka dina na siga ni kua
E totoka dina na siga ni kua
(Today is just a beautiful perfect day)[42]

The women illustrate this chant with their hands and smiling faces. The dance ends with the dancers on a diagonal performing joyful leg kicks while hopping from one foot to another. As they move their legs, their hands and arms circle fluidly down, out, then up, closing in quickly to bring their hands together in front of their chests, rhythmically accenting each quick kick. Master Lai, the director, had the women repeat these movements several times in a rehearsal I visited, coaching them to express more joy. The men of the group, the chanters or vakatara, shouted out to give the women more energy. After rehearsal, Selai Eramasi, a dancer and a teacher at the school, explained that this vocal support helps dancers generate more spirit and energy. She explained, "The big challenge with meke is getting energy without the use of being in a trance or possessed by spirits—the evil side." She continued, "A long time ago, people would go to the graveyard to connect with evil spirits and become possessed and then the meke would come naturally. Now, old meke are performed with new energy."[43] The director sought to increase the spirit and energy of meke in ways that celebrate and reify Christian/Fijian sentiments of welcome, generosity, happiness, and peace. The performers thus must negotiate an approach to meke under multiple pressures. They are expected by the government to preserve an authentic iTaukei past for tourists and foreign officials by performing meke in a traditional manner, a pressure that also positions Fijians as culturally Other as part of the colonial legacy. Yet they still find ways to express their contemporary Christian beliefs in their dancing. They negotiate being culturally "authentic" while resisting being bound to the past.

During my time in Fiji, I observed both reluctance to meke and confusion about how one should meke. Those who did meke, however, were carefully engaging tradition and spirit in varying and resistive ways. Such an ambivalent process of negotiating agency and cooptation in and around meke does not result in a loss of meaning; instead, meanings for meke shift.

Generating Transformation with Meke

Vilsoni Hereniko, who was the director of the Oceania Center for Art, Culture, and Pacific Studies at University of the South Pacific, had invited me to attend his production *Drua: The Wave of Fire*, full of newly created meke. A few days after we arrived in Fiji, Hereniko asked my partner, Aaron Kelly, a theatrical lighting designer, to assist with the production in the then new Japan-Pacific ICT (Information, Communication and Technology) Center.

We were in the black box theatre when I watched the meke dancers arrive and prepare for the dress rehearsal of the upcoming production. The dress rehearsal was, in a sense, their sevu ni meke, an important protocol that would traditionally involve presenting the new meke to the chief of the village who requested it.[44] Instead, in this urban, theatrical context, they presented their new meke to the directors of the production.[45] The Fijian dancers, who were Christians of iTaukei and Indian descent, had been observing tabu, restricting their diets and behaviors to collectively build strength so the meke would be the best it could be.

The scene opened with fierce warriors under threat of attack. The male warriors, black paint marking their faces, pounded their feet on the stage while shouting a challenge to their enemy intruders and waving war clubs. Their stances were low; with wide bent legs and upright bodies, they showed strength and readiness. A prerecorded steady and simple lali rhythm, accompanied with a low, booming voice, chanted out, calling their bodies into motion with intensity and urgency. The vocal coloring demanded attention, a powerful wailing that evoked mourning. Heads tipped sideways to sharply accentuate the rhythms of the chant and the movements. In contrast to the sharpness of these accents, their heavy clubs swung with the momentum of their weighted bodies. The rhythm changed as the lali and the chant quickened and bodies picked up speed and percussiveness. Throughout, the dancers moved with a tremendous range of motion, strength, speed, and focus. They made deep resonant cries over the top of the recorded chant, bringing the energy of the dance to even higher levels, producing a strong visceral pull inside my own body.

Though the dance began with the dancers moving in sync, they soon broke away into new formations that were less linear and more three dimensional and multidirectional. These shifts in formation not only transmitted the power, strength, and energy of the group but also the strength of individuals motivated to act toward a common purpose. One man stood apart: he was a manu manu ni meke and the daunivucu of this meke. Charged with spirit and energy, he transmitted this energy to the dancing and viewing bodies. Then, with a shift in the tone of the chant, the scene changed and the staged warriors, who began as fierce defenders of their land, discovered they had encountered friend, not foe. The manu manu ni meke knelt with the leader of the newcomers, they briefly held hands, and they cup-clapped their hands as a sign of mutual respect. The two groups danced together, each group with their own unique steps, and a reconciliation took place.

After the meke rehearsal ended, the daunivucu and I sat down to talk. "I come from Nanenivuda in Seaqaqa," he told me, "a town that is twenty kilometers away from Labasa, Macuata province in Vanua Levu. Nanenivuda literally means the 'footsteps of our ancestors'; nane is 'footprint' and nivuda means 'of our ancestors.' My great-grandfather Elia Sawesawe had accepted Christianity when the last cannibalism in Seaqaqa took place.[46] My meke has been inspired by the new spirit he worshipped and that is the Holy Spirit."[47]

∼

While many iTaukei sense toward secure Christian feelings in meke performed for Fijian culture and heritage, the third approach to meke I discuss comes from my encounter with daunivucu Damiano Logaivau. In his creative process, Logaivau generates intensities that sense toward the complex and unknown. Sensing toward security and sensing toward uncertainty are not bifurcated emotions but indeterminate processes with different directions and clusters of relation. Some Fijians produce meke that fit identities and bodies into essential or homogenous categories to make meke representative of Fiji. Logaivau's meke process supports his own political desires to celebrate difference and an ontology rooted in an integrative body, whereby bodies emerge through movement in relation to other human and nonhuman copresences. In addition to my extensive conversations with Logaivau about meke, I interviewed several of his dancers and observed three of his meke (as well as participated in one) over the course of my five months in Fiji. After analyzing these sources, I found that his process incorporated traditional and nontraditional techniques for creating and performing meke that resulted in a wide range of feelings from those responding to his intensity in rehearsal and performance. The responses expose tensions within his meke process, which involves transforming spiritual protocols centered on ancestral spirits to ones centered on Christianity.

Logaivau defies the norm in many ways, but one key act of defiance has to do with his spiritually intense relationship to tradition, which involves enriching his meke through the lens of his Christian faith. For example, he asks his dancers to observe tabu (such as not drinking alcohol or kava and not smoking). Although the spiritual significance of restricting diet and behavior once related to pleasing the ancestor spirits and ensuring that the meke would be the best possible, Logaivau, an ecumenical Roman Catholic, uses tabu to increase the spirit from God as well as the strength and energy of the meke mata (meke team) and brings them together as a group.

Logaivau's investment in and inspiration from his Christian faith is also untraditional (in that he does not acquire meke from the ancestral or land spirit gods) but essential to his method and central to the tensions within it. For example, he often begins with a Christian prayer, asking God to enrich his meke:

> You have read about the process of meke creation with regard to witchcraft. I don't know exactly what occurs; I was not part of my extended family's processes. I ask God for his blessing and the use of the intelligence and wisdom I have to give life to the people who will see the meke and to bless the people with whatever they can learn and especially with the ability to live life to the full [bula] as much as they can. I thank God for providing health and happiness for all involved in the meke and to spiritually bind the meke group together for the present purpose of creating a new meke. That is the prayer that I normally say. And to thank God also for the gift that I am just able to create and choreograph with the power, the mana, that has been given to me. I think the bottom line is to pray to God to continue to give me the strength to do that always. And two things I always ask for: one is to emphasize the courage to forgive and the other is the courage to ask for forgiveness. Those two things are in the prayer I normally do because I am conscious that when people see the meke that I do, they are automatically going to think this is witchcraft. I pray for the mana, enriching the mana for the meke I do.

In his prayer, Logaivau is asking God to bless him with the ability to bring his Christian faith together with notions of bula (expressed in wanting to give life to all involved and for them to be able to live life to the fullest) and forgiveness (to reconcile meke's past connection to ancestor spirit worship) in his meke. But this quote also indicates an anxiety about responses to his meke linked to the colonial legacies that inform his process.

Instead of entering a yaqona-induced trance state to invoke the land spirits (something he explains he will never do because it would mean crossing the line into practicing "witchcraft"), he allows the spirit of God to enter his body through prayer, putting him into a creative trance state. Once the spirit of God enters him, he is inspired to create: "I feel really empowered with energy in my head and my whole body, alive with creative energy. That energy just comes after I pray, and I need to sit in front of the computer or with a pen because right away it just comes and within two minutes the lyrics are there. The prayer is very important, if I don't do that, I feel I can't move. I need to center the focus of my thinking to God."[48] Even though he uses nontraditional elements to invoke spirit, he nonetheless views meke as a living traditional practice that is creatively and unpredictably spiritual and religious.

Logaivau also uses traditional and nontraditional elements to create his meke chants. He follows the harmonic, stanza, and strophic style of his province while also using his own creativity and affective memories of village life to give his meke intensity. He explained: "The sound of people mourning in the village inspired my creativity in one of my chants. There is lots of emotion in the sounds of villagers engaging in village life. I weave those sounds into the beginning of my spear dance, I set the tone with the sound of grieving. Villagers have different tones and pitches and I picked one just to set the scene."[49] He draws from these intensely emotive qualities to pull at the felt responses of his audience.

Logaivau gained inspiration for his approach to creation from watching his family create meke. His mother, for example, created without rituals and protocols, while his paternal grandfather sought traditional connections to the land spirits for his meke:

> I have witnessed my paternal extended grandfather at work during rehearsals, but I have never seen the actual spiritual calling in the primary stages where the core of the daunivucu's followers will be present with him. The extended ritual requirements are the drinking of yaqona and the renewal of a garland every day until the sevu ni meke [presentation of the new meke] and actual performance is done. I observed that every morning or day of

practice, one of the rituals is to have the daunivucu wear a new salusalu vono [a Fijian garland made of a plant called vono] or any salusalu. As long as it is fresh every day, it is a sign of spiritual strengthening for the daunivucu. The garland is of great significance as I observed. I asked my uncles, "Why does the daunivucu wear a fresh garland every day?" They say it's a sign that the spirit is in the daunivucu. As well, the wearing signifies the honoring of the spirit as it works through the daunivucu.

I was informed that his walking stick holds a lot of mana and spiritual strength as well, and it allows him to channel power to teach. Whenever the meke team forgets a meke move, they will refer to the daunivucu. He then calls for his walking stick and uses it to refresh the meke mata [meke team]. It is more or less the first-hand spiritual connection and a sign the spirit is around. It is almost subtle in the eyes of those who are not sensitive about the spirits but commonly known that the daunivucu always follow their spirits that dictate the lyrics and moves for them or refresh them when anything is forgotten. In a simple form, they do not hold the freedom to create but they hold the freedom to choose to call on the spirits that manifest their power in them and give the lyrics and the choreography.[50]

Though respectful of his grandfather's spirituality, he clearly roots his own practice in Christianity and the "one true God." As he told me:

> My cousin had just visited me last month when I was choreographing for the "Drua Meke." At one point he shared that our extended grandfather did find it difficult to get the meke moves given that my cousin quietly drew a sign of the cross on his walking stick. My cousin was curious if the spirit in the walking stick would remain when the sign of the cross was drawn on it. According to him, he said that our extended grandfather had to unfortunately call for another stick to bring the spirits back on again.[51]

This story was important to Logaivau because it legitimized his spiritually intense meke process as Christian and demonstrated his belief that the "one true God" is more powerful than other spirit gods of the land.

Thus his connection to God informs his meke creation process, yet he is anxious about the external pressures and judgments of those who question his spiritual orientation and motivations. The tension is indicative of the past and present coexisting. While some Fijians seem to be giving new life to Christian colonial legacies that condemn Indigenous spiritual practices of political and ritual authority, including meke, Logaivau continues to practice traditional meke protocols and practices with Christian spirit and to transform that tension with the past into dynamic action.

Christianity plays a big role in transforming bad feelings from ancestor spirits to good feelings, and Logaivau wove this belief into his three-dimensional choreography. He explained that the reconciliation process of transforming bad into good involves mana, whereby what is said is made true:

> We believe that when you say something bad, it goes with its mana [bad spirit] and when you say something good, it goes with its mana [good spirit] too. When you say something, that mana stays there unless a ritual of reconciliation is performed to transform the mana. If the ritual of reconciliation is not performed, the bad or evil spirit remains and is felt as a barrier—a kind of discomfort between people. Good spirit allows people to open up and share things openly. If one is hurt by another, good spirit opens an atmosphere of reconciliation.[52]

His faith in reconciliation is evident in his meke wesi-wau for the production *Drua: The Wave of Fire*. Through movement choices and changes in the rhythm and tone of his chant, he evoked a transformation from bad warring spirit to good Christian spirit. The rhythm slowed, the chant changed from a minor to a major key, and the dancers shifted from antagonistic movements of fierce attack to movements that signaled generous care and respect, such as kneeling in front of one another on stage and grasping each other in an embrace. Logaivau's pattern of speech and his choice of sounds and movements for his meke exemplify his work of infusing his meke with "good" spirit, ensuring they are aligned with his Christian faith.

This process for transmitting "good" spirit was also about being vulnerable and open to sensing spirit. In his sensing, he was not reaching toward a destination but a direction formed by his readiness, generosity, respect for difference, and inclusivity. As he put it, "Curumi konaio ni meke," or let the true spirit of meke come in you. He continued: "Curumi konaio ni meke means for the dancer to really be in the moment and get into the meaning of the words and the emotions attached to it and the emotions attached to the harmonic and melodic dynamics. And, that the full expression that is there must arrive at the audience. The audience must be able to capture that deep emotion and meaning of the moment."[53] Curumi konaio ni meke is his emergent process: a process shaped not by singular definitions of what it means to be Christian and Fijian but by his sensory and relational experiences and memories. As a result, the sentiments he expressed were not secure but fluid, felt differently with every encounter.

Logaivau used techniques for increasing a fluid, transmissive spirit in performance. In addition to being a daunivucu, he is a manu manu ni meke. While his meke mata moved together, he used his voice and movements to heighten the energy of the dancers and audience. "I play with the rhythms to get the energy up higher," he stated. "That is my role as motivator, to keep them going—always strong, really driving the energy." He controls the shape of the meke by shouting "laga viro," meaning to go again or repeat a section, or "biu khari" or "tana khari" to move on. In his vocals, rhythms, and movements, he attempts to actively generate and shape the relational spirit of his meke.

He also generated supportive, multidimensional feelings and spirit in rehearsals with constant assurances made through utterances of "io," "isa," and "with all due respect." With io he was expressing yes, in agreement with, you are on the right track, and evoking a feeling of generosity and encouragement. With "isa" he was expressing empathy and solidarity in misfortune, a desire for connectedness, and common vulnerability.[54] And, "with all due respect . . ." he expressed dissent without negating other ways of thinking or other approaches; he showed his respect for difference by affirming diverse and varying opinions and feelings. He appeared to be living life to the fullest (an expression of bula) and wanting to share his life and knowledge about meke. He encouraged the same fearlessness in those around him. In these utterances, he was actualizing a kind of energy and spirit into his group's interactions while setting up the potential and possibilities for future connections and relations.

Responses generated by these meke performances were complex, incorporating seemingly conflicting values and beliefs shaped by the historical containment and control of meke. I interviewed a number of dancers, dance directors, and community members who said that the spirit and energy expressed in Logaivau's meke performances transmit a powerful and unpredictable intensity.[55] The uncertainty of spirit and energetic intensity was, however, confusing for a couple of my interview subjects. One dancer, a born-again Christian, described his experience of watching Logaivau: "He is a very traditional man but at the same time very spiritual. I don't know how that works for him. He has a mix of both worlds. He scares me actually because he is very intense."[56] This iTaukei dancer perceived Logaivau's intensity as generating an unnerving quality and possibly the result of a connection to the world of ancestral spirits. This response rejuvenates negative Christian colonial constructions of ancestors. In contrast, a Methodist meke performer described getting goose bumps from Logaivau's meke. In this account, Logaivau's expressive energy generated a profound physical response that was positive: "He does everything with a clean spirit and an open heart and everything comes out sounding good. He has this old Fijian soul. When I bring his chants home everyone gets the same reaction of goose bumps. Listening to his chants got me back into meke again. Logaivau is a very inspirational person to be around. I have learned two meke from him. . . . He's one of those gang who just brings so much energy."[57] In this sentiment, Logaivau's spirit and soul are connected to Fiji's past because of his expressions of intense spiriting feeling and energy. The meke performer also described Logaivau as having a "clean spirit." Recalling the words of the Fijian Pentecostal minister, Kurulo, that a clean spirit is a Christian spirit, this dancer's choice of words makes it clear that Logaivau is Christian despite his "old Fijian soul." While most described Logaivau's intense energy in positive terms as generated by his generosity, one's religious orientation might make his intensity seem more or less threatening. Regardless of orientation, Fijians I consulted with indicated they rooted his intensity in the past and Fijian tradition.

The many different responses to Logaivau's performances and his meke tell me that he was effectively generating a space to reconcile, without reducing, past systems of inequity within current expressions of spirit. Logaivau's approach to merging his Christian faith with traditional practices and protocols generated expressive intensity, and that force moved people to respond in differing ways, which was his intended purpose—to respect and support difference. In conscious resistance to those who have tried to unify and dominate Fiji by imposing their own cultures, traditions, and beliefs, in my interviews with Logaivau, he insisted on maintaining multiple definitions of "meke," "tradition," "Fijian," and "iTaukei" simultaneously. Instead of narrowing and fixing an understanding of these concepts and their influences on identity, he encouraged a proliferation of unfixed meanings. This was his ethics of difference, grounded in intensities and repetitions of uncertain spiriting affects, upon which a politics of expression in a generative theory of culture and identity comes alive.

Conclusion

In this chapter, I demonstrated how three different approaches to meke have emerged as ways of dealing with anxieties about how to negotiate ancestral and land spirits and Christianity in traditional space. As Nicholas Thomas put it, "Tradition can be an objectification of the heritage one has but wants to be rid of; as a resource, it is as necessary to progressivist projects of nonconformity as it is to those of cultural affirmation and preservation."[58] Within such contradictory negotiations of tradition, zones of indeterminacy are created that allow identifications with Fiji and Fijianness to shift.

This chapter explored how distinct nonconformist ways of engaging with meke actualize expressions. Judith and Saimon, who choose not to meke at all, rejected traditional protocols and rituals as a way of pushing against Methodist/traditional hegemony. At the same time, some Fijian Methodists who demonize the spirits of ancestors also feel them in powerful, physically enabling ways that demonstrate bodies resistant to colonial legacies of subjugation. Logaivau resists colonial legacies of codifying Fijians with his own approach to meke that respects difference rooted in expressive complexity—incorporating seemingly conflicting values and beliefs. The dance, however, transforms that seeming conflict into dynamic multidirectional action. All three approaches to meke show that meke takes on resistive dimensions in the way it is performed as a tradition.

The politics of spirit I argue for here connects the material body with the nonmaterial and gives form to a sense of culture and identity. Haunting, of colonialism and spirits of ancestors, shows how the material and ephemeral are linked, and not bifurcated, within an ontology of the body as integrative with nonmaterial copresences. Expressions of spirit in meke blur past, present, and future since they are at once impacted by colonial legacies and impacting current social relations and future directions. Expressions that generate certainty or security are just as emergent as those that generate a sense of uncertainty or insecurity; one is not more "natural" than the other. Along the continuum of certainty and uncertainty are spaces of indeterminacy. These are the complex dimensions of contemporary meke practice and a part of how iTaukei reconcile non-Christian spiritual beliefs and practices with Christian ones.

CHAPTER 5

Generating Efficacy

Countervailing Rhythms of a Contemporary Meke

AFTER MY MOM PASSED, I dreamed, planned, and imagined myself going to Fiji. I wanted to do something to respond to her powerful memories of Anna Qumia, memories that helped my mother through difficult times. I wanted to give a gift of gratitude. But was it possible to return a gift to someone I did not know, who was likely no longer alive? And what did the loving memories really recall? They were, after all, the result of a colonially imposed system of Euro-domestic service. Was it possible I would repeat the uneven power dynamics of those colonial relations in returning a gift that could not actually be returned? How might I instead work productively with the legacy of those colonial relations to expose mechanisms of political and economic power? My research compelled me to respond to the unsettled feelings pulling and pushing inside me. I could not ignore them, for if I did, they welled up inside and manifested in even greater levels of urgency. I reached out to my mother's Fijian friends in Canada and Fiji and spoke with them about my desire to keep pressing on these unsettled feelings and memories through researching meke. I asked a lot of questions. They encouraged me to proceed, so I did, planning how I might do so in a way that did not diminish or ignore the complexities and problematics of this endeavor. But I still had a long way to go in terms of figuring this out.

Four years later, after extensive planning and grant writing, I arrived in Fiji to research meke. Within days, I was introduced to Damiano Logaivau. I told him about my mother's memories of Fiji and my intent to research meke. The remnants of colonialism, however, inevitably shaped our relations. In contrast to the economic and political restrictions Fijians faced during military rule, as a white Canadian, I was in a privileged position to get grants to travel across the globe to conduct research. Nevertheless, he seemed genuinely moved by my mother's memories and my own interest in writing about meke. In response, he unexpectedly offered to create a meke that would activate and extend Qumia's legacy of care through the Fijian notion of loloma, or kindly love and affection, for me to take back to Canada. Although the specter of colonialism haunted our arrangement, his offer did not seem like an empty promise. His words indicated that he was prepared to make a major commitment to follow through, and his motivation appeared to reflect an interest in exploring Qumia's impact with his own expressive and creative acts. We talked about possible titles and settled on *Mekhe ni Loloma*, meaning to sing and dance about the gift of love. And yet my body and identity, my whiteness, was also a reminder of a colonialized, multigenerational economy of exchange. Despite my desire to give back to Fiji, Logaivau's embodied labor and care replicated Qumia's (and my own romanticism of it). Was I returning a gift? Or was I the beneficiary?

Our rehearsals and conversations were driven by a commitment to knowledge sharing and felt like mutual exchanges. But how could our exchange be neutral when my presence was not? Was I placing him in the role of the Indigenous master, with me as the white foreigner novice? Despite the history that shaped our relationship and his labor, he nevertheless created the meke chant and invited me to join in the creation and to record the process. Logaivau started with a prayer in his own Fijian dialect from Macuata, Vanua Levu, that connected all who had come together for the intended purpose of creating this meke, including Logaivau, his nephew and assistant, Livai Baravilala, and my family. Within minutes of the prayer, he had created the chant, with words full of wisdom, spirit, and life energy that bound us by the principles of living life to the fullest and activating and extending Qumia's loloma. Logaivau, Baravilala, and I then spent time together locating the rhythm and speed of the chant, which became fast and vigorous. We added in the cobo, and Baravilala's voice found a harmonic complement. Baravilala was quick to remember and repeat small adjustments and additions to the rhythm and the chant. Logaivau added the lali rhythm to the cobo and the chant. The three of us recorded ourselves while we practiced repeatedly to remember the rhythms that eventually took hold.

Language shifted between English and Logaivau's own Fijian dialect. He was politically invested in using his own dialect to express himself and effect change on Indigenous terms. He used English because he wanted me to understand the enabling process of iTaukei ritual efficacy. Given my identity, however, did teaching meke to me in English also risk diminishing Indigenous change on Indigenous terms? Logaivau led us into the chant using English each time: "Set, let's take it . . . One, two, three, four . . ." Then we switched to his dialect and chanted, "Curumi au bula ni lomalomarua . . . ," to say that once the life was double minded. Flipping between English and Fijian, we went over the chant, lyrics, and rhythms to craft and establish them. Every repeat added to the tempo and energy of the expression. We invested ourselves (in English and Fijian), and as a result, also infused the meke, with that spirit and energy—caught in/between/beside colonial, postcolonial, and post–2006 coup tensions and residues—like the meke was a repository for all that we put into it, to then be the expressive force that emanated from the meke when performed. This expressive force was full of countervailing pressures built from the flipping between rhythms and language—our bodies became contact zones for negotiating colonial legacies and postcolonial realities of language, rhythm, and identity. There was colonial residue all over this, and my own body was deeply implicated. Our meke encounter was bringing out these remains, full of past and present power imbalances, and a desire to move with and through them.

∼

Reflecting on my fraught ethnographic experiences and interactions with Logaivau during the 2012 *Mekhe ni Loloma* process, this chapter explores expressions of the Fijian spiritual life-energy concept mana (power to effect or bring-into-existence) as a political form of reciprocity that plays an active role in negotiating inequitable power dynamics embedded within social relations locally as well as translocally. Western and Indigenous Fiji scholars have written extensively about mana, as situated within an iTaukei Methodist discourse of loss, powerlessness, and decline of effective ritual political authority and as a supernatural gift from God, but rarely as it relates to the movements of the body.[1] This chapter intervenes by showing how Logaivau, an ecumenical Roman Catholic, seeks to reclaim mana as an embodied relational process of achieving an intended purpose to contribute to a deeper understanding of the politics of agency in post–2006 coup Fiji.[2] Drawing from five months of intensive interviews, observations, and rehearsal interactions, and building on previous mana scholarship, I show

how Logaivau activated mana communicatively and expressively through the chant, choreography, sounds, rhythms, and pedagogical transmission of *Mekhe ni Loloma* as a strategy for moving with and through systemic colonial and postcolonial power imbalances to generate inclusion, reciprocity, and resiliency on Indigenous terms.

As part of this intervention, this chapter critically examines how Logaivau conveyed loloma and mana in the chant and choreography of his meke as circulating gifts, which were, owing to my own presence, deeply implicated in uneven relations of power.[3] He narrated loloma in *Mekhe ni Loloma* as a freely given gift, Christian communal caring, and interwoven with Fijian mana as a source of human agency and efficacy as well as a gift from God. He sought to transmit loloma and mana—both notions that have evolved with shifting relations of power, economics, politics, and religion—through meke using a close pedagogical process of transferal from one body to another as well as exchange between Fiji and its diaspora, activating a long-term, long-distance responsiveness between bodies. His belief that expressive bodies extend across time and space reflects Tongan scholar 'Okusitino Māhina's and Fijian scholar Unaisi Nobobo-Baba's assertion that bodies are part of a continuum between past and future in relation to spiritual and environmental realities.[4] In *Mekhe ni Loloma*, bodies have an uneven capacity to extend. My privileged body traveled freely to Fiji to pick up a meke and then take it back to Canada, animating a colonialist legacy of privileged global mobility as well as replicating the dynamic of Westerners taking and receiving from non-Western cultural sources of rejuvenation. Thus, the translocal or transcorporeal capacity of the meke is also co-constituted by these uneven transmissions, communications, and relations between bodies across time-space.

Despite the large presence of mana in my discussions with Fijians about meke, initially I felt it was inappropriate to write about mana because of my being a non-iTaukei, Western scholar with familial links to colonial Fiji. My family's past colonial exchanges, as well as my own in Fiji and in the Canadian diaspora, are implicated in producing a potential loss of mana through inequitable exchange. Ultimately, I decided Logaivau's approach to activating mana in meke needed to be explored because it demonstrates an embodied form of power and agency that Christian colonialism did not manage to suppress. Yet this came with the danger of speaking for his experience and getting it wrong. To mitigate this, I shared this chapter with Logaivau throughout the writing process. Recognizing the limits of my knowledge, this chapter highlights his use of mana as an active and effective, relational and responsive embodied process of achieving an intended purpose.[5] In addition, by including the details of my own relationship to this research, writing, and dancing, I aim to show how danced expressions can reveal the embodied seams of contradictory and diverging decolonizing efforts and colonizing residues.

My body extends across two very different decolonizing strategies. On the one hand, honoring the Fijian notions of spirit and mana that have influenced (and some could say even compelled) this research pushes against Christian colonial erasure of mana as active and effective as well as challenges Western bifurcated notions of materiality and spirituality. Furthermore, honoring the larger translocal spiritual, philosophical, and agentive potential offered by the notion of mana as a research paradigm also honors plural Fijian knowledge, practices, and values such as Fijian notions of respect, resilience, and reciprocity. With each of these notions, I am responsive to, and critically aware of, Fiji's changing political context. On the other hand, in light of my colonial/settler heritage, assuming a personal connection to Fijian concepts of spirit and mana comes dangerously close to recolonizing through appropriation and romanticism. It is my intention to honor Logaivau's powerful thoughts and feelings about mana while also remembering that Fijians are not (and have not been in the past) homogeneous, local, kin-based, noncapitalist gift exchangers.[6] In Fiji, neoliberal and gift economies interpenetrate and connect to larger global economic, political, and religious processes (a reality emphasized throughout this book). Thus, throughout the chapter I negotiate these decolonizing strategies that are seemingly at odds with one another to discuss some of the specific ways in which Logaivau strove to activate the complex Fijian concept of mana in *Mekhe ni Loloma*.

From Loss and Decline to Active Responsiveness

Although Fijian mana is canonically a verb denoting effective action, bringing-into-existence, and action that creates truth,[7] according to Tomlinson, the perspectives of early British Wesleyan Methodist missionaries and later British colonizers turned mana into a kind of supernatural substance for the last two centuries.[8] The outcome of loss flows from the following principle: by turning an action into a substance or thing, actions lose power and can be lost, or taken.[9] The shift from action to substance interwove its way into Indigenous customs and traditions and impacted early nineteenth-century Western accounts of Fijian mana as well as the twentieth-century perspectives of several European and iTaukei Fijian scholars.[10] In describing mana as a vague and impersonal supernatural or invisible medium of power, these scholarly accounts also nominalized mana (turning mana from a verb into a noun) and sometimes substantivized it (giving mana the grammatical role of a noun). Treating mana as a supernatural power supports a bifurcated approach to vitality and materiality whereby the body and its movements remain somewhat passive: spirit enters the body rather than the body generating spirit. Tomlinson suggested that the Methodist colonial role in distancing mana from human action has played a significant role in the sense of loss associated with mana. Methodists took power out of the realm of human agency and placed it with God and those in the service of God (such as Methodist missionaries), "developing a 'perpetual lament' about decline and loss in Fiji," especially with regard to chiefly authority.[11]

Three recent changes to traditional practices and protocols in post–2006 coup Fiji would seem to support Tomlinson's assertion. First, increasing numbers of iTaukei have been converting to evangelical and charismatic churches and rejecting Fijian traditions, including meke.[12] Second, to counter this pressure on chiefly traditions and protocols, Methodists have positioned Fijian culture and heritage as a way to situate iTaukei as preeminent arbiters of a Christian, Fijian nationhood in Fiji and Fiji's Canadian diaspora. Yet this approach reifies meke, turning meke into an object representative of Fijian culture, reducing meke's active and diverse socially responsive aspects. Third, with the post–2006 coup shift in governance under the banner of multiracialism and the dissolving of the Great Council of Chiefs in 2012 by government decree, iTaukei are increasingly concerned about the protection of land and the mana within it. These major changes to governance and concerns over land ownership are deeply distressing for iTaukei, especially those who have lost power and privilege, with major impacts to social structure, subsistence, identity, and culture.[13]

Nevertheless, post–2006 coup shifts in Fijian governance and politics appear to be fostering a space for reclaiming mana through meke in order to actively and effectively move with and beyond Methodist colonial legacies of divisiveness. Logaivau has a complex approach to mana—at once a source of human agency and effective, a supernatural substance from God, and an expressive, translocal gift that widens involvement by extending social relations and obligations of return beyond Fiji's race-based categories of identity. In other words, his notion of efficacy arises from the colonial and postcolonial arrangements of power it seeks to challenge.[14] His meke, as a source of ritual efficacy and political authority, develops an expressive force that moves with and resists inequitable power formations. In *Mekhe ni Loloma*, he sought to generate mana expressively between bodies to form an active and effective resilient space capable of addressing inequitable relations of power. *Mekhe ni Loloma* responded to the colonial dynamics between my mother and her nanny and between me and him. Thus the meke actively negotiated countervailing postcoup and postcolonial pressures, seeking to enable multilayered and diverse iTaukei notions of mana to thrive culturally.

Chant, Choreography, Floating Notes, and Rhythmic Irregularities

The *Mekhe ni Loloma* chant lyrics evidence the myriad ways in which Logaivau generated efficacy. The chant is in his dialect from the Macuata province of Vanua Levu (near Seaqaqa), though he provided me an English translation of the chant, which follows the Fijian text. His explanations of the lyrics are in parentheses:

Vahasoho:
A oku I alnoa vou meu alanoa vahina mata
Ai alanoa ni loloma alivahi vahare ahi hina
A oku ovo ni vanua lua hei na vei ha sa sivi ake
A hena yalo curumi au, au u vaharau me u wasea a oku loloma
Mena tau solia a vahacegu hei na sau u' na vei gauna
Au na laga'a iho au na meke ahina
A vuhu yaloma'ua hei na hena yalo re
Mena tau solia a bula
Mena tau solia a bula
Mena tau solia a bula ni vei gauna mamuri.

Usa lesu mai meu mai solia
Usa lesu mai meu mai solia
Usa lesu mai meu mai solia
Meu mai solia solia solia
Meu mai solia solia solia
Solia lesu wake ni miau bula

Solia lesu wake ni miau bula
A bula miau ma solia mai
A bula miau ma solia mai
A solia lesu wake mei sau ni bula
A solia lesu wake mei sau ni bula
Mei sau ni bula
Mei sau ni bula
Ai sau ni loloma ma soli mai vei au
O Vi'i lomani a oku Vi'i lomani
Au sasolia, solia solia solia, solia lesu ake a bula

Curumi au bula ni lomalomarua
Voto voli mai na meli silima ua ni koloni au vaha curuma
Curumi au bula ni lomalomarua
Voto voli mai na meli silima ua ni koloni au vaha curuma

Au vakakare voli siga a bogi a vanua
Au vakakare voli siga a bogi a vanua
Amu utei sara u a oku bula
Amu utei sara u a oku bula
Liwa mai a cagi vou veisau a mua sa sira mai a marama ni vanua
Liwa mai a cagi vou veisau a mua sa sira mai a marama ni vanua
Na buhebuhe me lave'I ha'aha'a oku bula main a liwaliwa

Au sana maka ni kai suha sa mua a oku waka vou
Cirri I lagi a hena hubou voto mai Lua na yaloku vou
A yalo ni tau valu se dredre cava ga au na curu basiha'a
A bula solia mai o Ana Qumia hena hawa hei vi'l viroga ni ma'aha
Sobu a hena mana, sobu a hena mana, sobu a hena mana.

Usa lesu mai meu mai solia
Usa lesu mai meu mai solia
Usa lesu mai meu mai solia
Meu mai solia solia solia
Meu mai solia solia solia
Solia lesu wake ni miau bula
Solia lesu wake ni miau bula
A bula miau ma solia mai

A bula miau ma solia mai
A solia lesu wake mei sau ni bula
A solia lesu wake mei sau ni bula
Mei sau ni bula
Mei sau ni bula
Ai sau ni loloma ma soli mai vei au
O Vi'i lomani a oku Vi'i lomani
Au sasolia, solia solia solia, solia lesu ake a bula

Ula lei o Ula lei o Ula lei o Ula lei hi

[Prologue:
Allow me to tell my new story
It is about love properly weaved
It is about my culture, tradition, and history that has been created
Its spirit comes in me
I am ready to share my love that will always give peace and mana all the time
I will sing about it and meke about it
It is about wisdom and all the good spirit
Let it always give life
Let it always give life
Let it always give life all the time in the future

Chorus:
I'm coming back to give
I'm coming to give. I'm coming to give
I'm coming to give life in return for the life you have given
To return the love that was given to me
I'm giving back in return of the life you have given to me
To return the love that was given to me
For beloved Fiji, for beloved Fiji
I'm giving it, I'm giving it, I'm giving it, I'm giving life back to you (Fiji)

Verse One:
Once the life was double minded (she was caught in colonial/settler struggle to belong).[15]
I am riding on the vessel with the wave of colonialism (she was born into colonialism and it impacted her life)

Verse Two:
My life is not really firm (she is disconnected and searching for something)
But the new wind direction comes and it changes my whole life (mana—the wind—changes her life)
A new wind direction comes to my heart. The lady has come down (mana—the wind—comes into her heart from Anna Qumia—the lady)
From Namosi she came to lift and warm my life up from the cold (Qumia lifts her out of a life of colonial cold heartedness)

Verse Three:
I am on a new boat now and I am not returning to the past (she is firmer now; like a warrior, she is going to go forward in life on a firm footing)
The smoke of this boat floats away in the air (the smoke refers to heaven because the smoke goes up)
My new life has come (through courage, colonial mentalities float away and she can live in a new way)
I have adopted a new life of battling the difficulties (the spirit of a true warrior is in her; she is ready to battle the challenges that come)
All the spirit of Fiji comes to life with the life that Anna Qumia gave and with what all of the descendants of Fiji have given (all people born in Fiji generate mana through their generosity and giving regardless of race)
All the mana is coming down into it, all the mana is with it (a Fiji blessing for the meke)

Chorus:
I'm coming back to give
I'm coming to give. I'm coming to give
I'm coming to give life in return for the life you have given
To return the love that was given to me
I'm giving back in return of the life you have given to me
To return the love that was given to me
For beloved Fiji, for beloved Fiji
I'm giving it, I'm giving it, I'm giving it, I'm giving life back to you (Fiji)

Epilogue:
Jump, jump, jump (the chant finishes with a big jump to increase the energy of the meke)]

The story of the gift of love told by the chant unfolds from the opening prologue, a chorus, three verses, a return to the chorus, and a short concluding epilogue. The prologue expresses the notion that Qumia's loloma, full of the spirit of mana, has been transmitted to me via my mother and is compelling me to respond by coming to Fiji to return Qumia's loloma. Logaivau's chorus suggests that by coming to Fiji to share the story of Qumia's loloma, I am returning that mana to Fiji in the spirit of life (bula) and love. The three verses that follow the chorus shift to the perspective of my mother growing up in Fiji. The first verse addresses the colonial realities she faced and her feeling of being split, or double minded, between worlds. In the second verse, my mother's life changes for the better in response to the love given by Qumia. The third verse breaks down colonial divides on Indigenous terms by connecting my mother to Fijian mana through Qumia's loloma.

Logaivau's *Mekhe ni Loloma* chant effectively brings into existence spiritual agency from an uneasy space of contact between Indigenous Fijian notions of generalized reciprocity and Eurocolonial economic notions of material private property. He also communicated his own worldview based on iTaukei-Christian notions of loloma and reciprocity, demonstrating how conflicting notions of loloma/love are central to this uneasy space of indeterminacy. The chant defines loloma as kindly love and affection, freely given, socially relational, and spiritually active. He sustained these notions throughout the meke chant. For example, the text in the chorus that begins "ai sau ni loloma," which refers to returning the love that was given to me, conjoins loloma with the word "sau." According to linguist Paul Geraghty, Fijians often prefer the term "sau" over "mana" when referring to exercising spiritual power.[16] By adding the word "sau," Logaivau incorporates spiritual agency that, in this case, suggested that Qumia used her own spiritual agency to give loloma. Further, the lyrics suggest her giving was spiritually effective in that it initiated responsiveness and reciprocity between bodies that was so strong it compelled me to travel to Fiji to return the gift decades later. Yet narrating loloma as a freely given gift of kindness and love erases the power dynamics involved in the economic obligations tied to Qumia's loloma, whereby my family contracted Qumia to care for my mother. Although my mother developed a core sense of inner strength and identity built on memories of Qumia's kindness and affection, there is no way to confirm how Qumia felt toward my mother or my grandparents. As discussed in the first chapter, in their British colonial home, Qumia's domestic care was also her labor. Looking at loloma within this colonial context reveals that Qumia's loloma is complexly interconnected with formations of power and diverging notions of reciprocity.

If, however, Logaivau framed Qumia's loloma as entirely governed by colonial power and an economic obligation for her paid domestic duty, her loloma would lose spiritual agency and, as a result, its efficacy—it would turn from active verb to a passive thing that can be lost or taken, elevating colonialism's destructive power to undermine or successfully suppress the social and spiritual potential of iTaukei reciprocity. Instead, Logaivau's choice of lyrics in the chant demonstrated his interest in telling a story of spiritual agency. Choosing not to include the colonial economic obligations of Qumia's love in the chant could have been a tactic for increasing the potency and success of Qumia's loloma. The chant complicates the notion that loloma, as a freely given gift, can be purchased and even taken by rerouting it back into a system of reciprocity and a spiritually active responsiveness between bodies. It suggests that Qumia gave loloma to my mother knowing that the gift would in the future necessitate a response informed by her self-donated transmission of affect. Logaivau brought into existence a meke that is capable of exposing and negotiating conflicting iTaukei, colonial, and postcolonial acts of transfer while generating an active responsiveness between bodies based on iTaukei terms.

The meke combines multiple meanings of mana—at once a source of human agency, a supernatural substance from God (connected with Fijian land), and an expressive gift. This complex approach to mana is evident in the chant lyrics when the spirit and life energy, or mana (referred to as "the smoke" and "wind"), gives my mother strength to battle life's difficulties and challenges and to move forward in life on new iTaukei terms. Mana, here, is a supernatural gift from God. But it is also manifested materially as part of Fiji's environs (in the smoke and the wind). Yet Qumia's transmission of loloma as "a new wind" that comes into my mother's heart, frames Qumia's transmission of mana with human agency while also transferring a sense of agency and power to my mother. The final line of the third verse continues to suggest Logaivau's intention of using mana as a verb and a gift from God. The lyrics "Sobu a hena mana" are translated as "all the mana is coming down into it." Here mana comes down from God and the heavens above. But Logaivau added to his own English translation "all the mana is with it," meaning mana is also generated by the meke.

Beyond the use of the word "mana" in the chant, the other lyrics of the chant also open a space for widening participation through action-oriented spiritual efficacy. Meke is itself presented as a verb in the vahasoho lyrics "au na laga'a iho au na meke ahina," meaning I will sing about it and meke about it. Here meke means to perform, transmit, communicate, and engender by activating a story through chanting, singing, and dancing. Using these terms together, Logaivau asserted an important, vital spiritual dimension to the storytelling. This is supported in the following line of the prologue (line seven) by the use of the term "yaloma'ua" (yalomatua in the Bauan spelling), which refers to a spiritual wisdom, or knowledge and skills learned from elders. According to Fijian scholar Dr. Tupeni Baba, yalomatua increases efficacy in life and involves a sense of purpose and fulfillment in contributing to community.[17] Logaivau's lyrics suggest that such spiritual wisdom adds to the intended purpose of the meke by generating a life-affirming spirit that can build community across borders.

While these Fijian terms, in his Macuata dialect, are critical to sustaining long-term, long-distance energy and efficacy, Logaivau integrated English into the *Mekhe ni Loloma* process and translation to increase communication and understanding. As an official language in Fiji, English is the result of almost a hundred years of colonial governance. While some in Fiji prefer not to work in English as a decolonizing, postcolonial reclaiming of Fijian culture, his rationale for teaching *Mekhe ni Loloma* in English reflects a strategy to undermine the remnants of colonial policies that divide people. This became evident during rehearsal one day when he stopped creating to note how strange it was to teach meke in English: "This is probably the first time we are teaching meke in English. But that is okay. The ancestors have done so much for us—for this generation, we need to move beyond that. It is our job to do great things too, to lift the meke and teach it at different levels. We are sharing meke with the whole world family, and we are sharing cultures and movements with each other. [We are using English to] teach the Canadian Fijian team the meke."[18] Thus, he chose to speak in English as a way of bringing me, along with others living abroad, into a meke experience that fulfilled his multiracial ideal of peace, harmony, and inclusion; but his use of English was also a testament to the impact of British colonialism in Fiji. As he stated, "This is a collective choreography with Evadne's own story—it's a hybrid/fusion meke." The hybridity of this story is not about an equal merging of culture; it is about historically uneven rhythms of privilege and power being perpetuated by my presence.[19]

While the use of English caused barriers to his creative flow, he explained that he used English to generate inclusion. Moreover, he chose to decentralize the Bauan Fijian dialect—a dialect instituted by the Christian colonial administration—through combining English, Bauan, and his Macuata dialect to communicate within and beyond Fijian-speaking communities about the life principles that inform his meke creations. The hope seemed to be that these decentralized, inclusive, life-affirming principles would migrate around Fiji and to other parts of the globe. Thus, he hoped this meke would be a gift to those who identify with Fiji regardless of descent.

After creating and developing the chant and its rhythms, there was a vibrant energy in the room as Logaivau launched into the massive creative endeavor of developing the choreographed movements. His nervous system was highly tuned and energized by a full commitment to meke. He was specific, intentional, while also being light on his feet. Intention existed in the physical force and the muscularity of his body movements. His knees bent deep—suggesting his preparation and engagement. His strong, confident actions with his spear solidified connections between body, spear, and space-time. He moved quickly, sharply—with clarity and directness. Then he put on the brakes, slowed down, and settled into a stance in which his torso geometrically angled back from his pelvis—a posture that evoked power, pride, and vibrant energy, with strength traveling up, down, out, across, and between our bodies. The thick, humid air rushed around his body-fan-spear so quickly it created a breeze. Wind emanated from his movement and moved the hair on my skin as well as the skin of others—expressing responsiveness between bodies and "amu utei sara u a oku bula," referring to the wind blowing in a new direction that can change a life. He showed no signs of fatigue. With his intended purpose fully charging his moving body as well as our own bodies, he was generating a life energy that was effecting change, felt in, on, and between our bodies.

I attempted to physicalize what Logaivau imparted, but he encouraged me to find my own personal connection to the movements. We worked on the meke iri (fan) section first, followed by the wesi (spear) and wau (club) sections. He taught me to hold the fan high and snug around the handle with my right index finger pointing up the fan, and how to move with it. I learned to feel the movement and position of the fan as though the fan was an extension of my arm and torso. Sometimes the fan took precedence—

my wrist extended back as far as it could go so I could pull the heel of the fan down with the full face of the fan pressing forward toward the audience. The fan took on multiple meanings. There was power and grace in the fan. There was spirit in the fan. And the fan was a part of Fijian culture and heritage. Logaivau's fan came from the Macuata Province, Vanua Levu. It had a teardrop shape and was not woven like many of the fan designs from Viti Levu. It was made from a single Fiji fan palm leaf with the stem of the leaf split at the base of the fan, folded back, and tied at the top to create the outer rim of the fan. He told me that Macuata fans held deep personal significance for him, forming part of his identity.

In each section of *Mekhe ni Loloma*, I learned to dig, hit, strike, swing, slash, flicker, and dab the fan/spear/club with full commitment. When we switched to the meke wesi (spear) section, we grasped the spears in our right hands and the fans in our left. Logaivau demonstrated clapping the spear and fan together and then swinging his arms down, apart, and back with fan and spear tips pointing up and his torso folding forward. I started to feel the edges of the fan and spear like they were the edges of my fingertips—knowing just how far to reach without accidentally hitting Baravilala, Logaivau, or myself. In the meke wau section, the club felt heavy and it pulled my body with it. Now I understood why some of the most powerful meke memories of my interlocutors had come from watching meke wau so physically demanding that the dancers at times passed out on stage from exhaustion. I was told Fijians run along the road and do extra physical training to prepare for meke wau. It requires a lot of strength and stamina to move a club fully and quickly. Still, holding a heavy club added more swing to our movements. Logaivau played with the club's momentum, controlling it, using it to add speed and force to his bodily slicing through space. The energy of the fan, spear, and club extended beyond their edges as they moved through space, moving the air around us as we breathed.

∽

Logaivau designed the choreographic process to increase the mana of the meke by shaping movements in relation to identity and personal truth. For him, mana increases the more deeply one identifies with the meke and communicates these deeper meanings and identifications:

> I am able to relate my struggles and challenges in life to moving through jungle. I remember moves like simple working through bush tracks, where

you have to squeeze in the thick of the forest to keep moving forward, and simple moves as cutting banana trees, lifting hands to put loads on our shoulders, protecting ourselves from wild animals, jumping over the logs where necessary, sliding, and surrounding wild pigs, or standing in line to work as a team to complete tasks like clearing each other's plantation. I want to share these moves that are based on survival strength.[20]

Such movement-based memories informed how he choreographed the meke. His legs are bent deeply to create a ninety-degree angle at the knee, the pelvis is upright, and his torso moves dynamically, quickly, with great range of motion. There is mana in the angles, dynamic movements, and rhythms of his body because these are the expressions of his felt personal memories.

In addition, the intention, effort, and care that we put into our movement choices directly impacts the mana that is produced. As evidence of this, when working on the third verse of the meke, Logaivau asked me to create some movements to add to the choreography, so I generated some based on the feelings I associate with my mother's memories of Qumia (figure 5.1). I also moved to share the colonial and postcolonial discord of those memories that, in this dance, forge a link between Fiji and Canada. Once I finished creating movement, Logaivau shaped them into a new form that aligned with the ways he imagines people moving through a battle (figure 5.2). In this case, it was a battle for finding inner strength and a readiness for life's challenges. My memories, rhythms, and angles became part of the energy and movement of *Mekhe ni Loloma*. But so did my feelings of clumsiness as well as my guilt about my family's colonial history and whether or not it was appropriate for me to even participate in this meke. My discomforts about appropriation remained and also became part of the expressive force of the meke.

Yet the meke was capable of negotiating uncomfortable, conflicting feelings. Logaivau generated an active, life-affirming rhythm-space in his meke through stories of resiliency and reconciliation—generating a common purpose open to mistakes and mishaps. During rehearsals, he taught us about his understanding of the resiliency that resides in the meke process. After periods of intense and rigorous physical rehearsal, he would give us small breaks to catch our breath. During the breaks, he would say something about meke and Fijian culture—always qualified within his own experiences. In one such break, he explained that when you make a mistake or break a rule, you say "orei" (penalty for infringing on traditional customs).

Figure 5.1. *Mekhe ni Loloma* rehearsal, Pacific Harbour, Fiji, August 2012. *Left to right*: Damiano Logaivau, Livai Baravilala, and Evadne Kelly. Video still by Aaron Kelly.

Figure 5.2. Damiano Logaivau in rehearsal of *Mekhe ni Loloma*, Suva, Fiji, October 2012. Video still by Aaron Kelly.

"It's a traditional and gentle way (for a daunivucu or chief) of saying you're punished—the spirit is away. We always respect that. But we can also have some fun if we make a mistake. When I was in the police band, if you made a mistake, you would hold your instrument above your head and yell, 'Come back my spirit' or say, 'I'm not feeling alright,' and then come back. That's why we, Fijians, are always happy. We can spring back any time. That's life for us."[21] Thus, the spirit of a meke is at its highest when the whole meke team is working toward a common purpose. Mistakes detract from achieving the common purpose and, as a result, are taken seriously, but there is also room to bounce back after making mistakes. He intended for this meke to be a space of respecting our common purpose as well as resiliency, making mistakes, and bouncing back. Thinking about this resiliency within the larger postcolonial, postcoup political context, Logaivau approaches his meke as a space to embody complex intersections of discord and find a way through them.

The club section movements for verse 1 provide evidence of how Logaivau choreographs a resilient space for dealing with conflict. In this verse, the words "curumi au bula ni lomalomarua voto voli mai na silima ua ni koloni au vaha curuma" express a feeling of being split between Eurocolonial culture and Fijian culture. Our bodies express this split by marching forward while swinging the clubs into the palms of our hands, then swinging the clubs in reverse while lunging backward in space. As we lunge backward, the clubs turn into firearms (conjuring images of battles for autonomy and control between Indigenous Fijians and British colonizers). The guns then turn back into clubs and we swing them above our heads, forward and back, adding accents with our heads that tip quickly to the side. We stomp our feet left then right and pull the clubs back across our shoulders prepared to strike—seizing the moment and living life to its fullest. From club to gun to club, and between forward and backward, side to side, the colonial/Indigenous battles and confusion play out in our movements. But iTaukei notions of living life to the fullest prevail in the final movements of the phrase—expressed in a deep lunge with club ready to swing into a new life despite of, and because of, all that has come before. This expresses a resilient springing back and moving forward from conflict.

Logaivau also situated meke as a choreographic resilient space that aligned with Fiji's post-2006 policies on multiracial harmony, diversity, and inclusion. In *Mekhe ni Loloma*, he designed a three-dimensional use of space and idiosyncratic use of rhythm to emphasize the uniqueness of identities.

He explained the reasons for his choreographic use of space: "This is to say that meke choreographies and lyrics are unique across Fiji, celebrating unique traditions and protocols, but we all have unity in the destination. Our one aim is to live life to the fullest, to apply life to the best. My whole approach to meke is based on these principles of life."[22] He strategically positioned dancers so they could fan outward and inward while cohering around muscular, crafted, and synchronized body angles, geometric lines, and movements. Diverse directions of movement accompanied with physical unity embodied a larger goal to create space for multifarious perspectives. In the end, the exact forms mattered less than the energy exuded through an ultimate commitment to expressing range of motion, speed, and sharpness. For example, on the final beats of the chant, we pulse our knees and press the palms of our hands down toward the ground and then leap, pulling our knees up high in a big jump of our choosing. Logaivau wanted all sections of the meke (fan, spear, club) to join together for this last line of the chant so that jumping together evoked respect for difference.

His choreography also constructed efficacy by dedicating a pathway between the body's movements and the land. In verse 2 of the club section, the words express disconnection due to colonialism contrasted by Qumia's connection to Fijian land. To embody these lyrics, we start facing stage right in a deep squat. We jump to the side, front, other side, and back to the first side, squatting low with our clubs pulled back behind our shoulders, expressing no firm direction. Then, divided into groups that travel separately to stage right and left, we migrate in opposite directions, suggesting double-mindedness. We jog away from each other with our knees pulled high for four runs over four beats. Then, we dig our clubs toward the ground and carve our clubs in a big arcing movement, ending with the clubs pulled back behind our shoulders as the lyrics express the arrival of Anna Qumia into my mother's life and a new sense of direction. Next, Logaivau choreographically suggests that Qumia's personal connection to land through Fijian mana is what gave my mother direction and identity. We point the tip of the clubs back down toward the ground and dab down for several beats across, in front, and between our legs, emphasizing with every dab the importance of the land. We gather that entire land acknowledgment and pull the clubs back over our shoulders for four slow beats to say a connection to the land informs a readiness for the future.

The efficacy of the choreography was also gendered. Once the men's sections were crafted, Logaivau worked with me alone on the women's section.

In this seated sequence, I began to understand how to embody femininity from his perspective on gender. Through demonstrating, he taught me to soften my chest, lean back, and relax my fingers while still moving quickly and clearly in the geometric choreography. This was in stark contrast to the physical readiness, and the forward leaning and upright torso featured in the men's sections. His muscularity softened in his demonstrations of femininity, as did his angles in space. And as his movements became more pliable, the space around his body did so as well, and he did not punctuate the rhythms. Even his manner of teaching changed. He showed less force in drilling the movement; the drills were gentler and less vigorous. Unlike the men's movements, which I could muscle through, my body could not quite figure out how to combine these qualities of softness with speed and precision. He instructed me to never settle in points of contact, to move through, to move with speed. Despite his clear demonstrations of the phrases, I could not figure out how to move as a woman. Interestingly, I was more comfortable expressing the complex politics at play in the meke through the men's movement phrases. Though the distinct men's and women's sections reinforced gender binaries, Logaivau blurred gender by choreographing movements for the men's sections based on my mother's experiences, thus transposing a woman's battles in life onto the concept of the Fijian male warrior. Our bodies, moving as men, imprinted the space with rhythms that surged outward with ferocious speed and intensity.

Given the prevalent gender binaries in Fiji, I kept wondering why Logaivau included me in the creation and learning of the men's sections. It is possible my educated status allowed me to temporarily transgress gender divides when learning the men's sections. Perhaps I experienced what iTaukei Fijian scholar Tamarisi Yabaki experienced in her research with rural iTaukei women. As an educated expert, Yabaki was treated as a leader and recognized as a "man" by the village men and elders.[23] Regardless of whether or not I was allowed more gender mobility as a dance researcher, or as a White westerner, I did not think through these gender dynamics during the rehearsal process. Over time, however, he made it clear that I should only perform the women's section, but the temporary transgression of gender boundaries in rehearsals draws awareness to the performative aspects of gender in meke. While surface representations of meke in Fiji seem to perpetuate gender binaries, inside the embodied performance, or repertoire, gender identities were not so clearly divided.[24] The fact that I did not know how to feel like a woman, or a man, dancing meke also calls into question my own performance of gender.

Once the rhythms and movements were established, we made a recording of the chant. We recruited Dave Lavaki, one of Fiji's celebrated hip-hop artists (Mr. Grin, Suva City) and recording artist at University of the South Pacific's Oceania Center, to record the chant, the cobo, and the lali. Logaivau sang the chant to Lavaki. Next Lavaki worked with Logaivau to set a synthesized version of the sounds and rhythms. The opening two lines of the chant required eleven beats, a three-beat break, and another eleven beats. Using a synthesized kick-drum beat (112 beats per minute), Lavaki added four recorded layers of us doing the cobo, which was double the speed of the kick-drum tempo. Logaivau played a lali rhythm that was six beats per kick-drum beat, over which Lavaki added four layers of lali recordings. Throughout, Logaivau coached me on Fijian diction, paying close attention to qualities and rhythms of sound, so I could also be included in the chant recording. We practiced singing "vaha curuma" in one beat over and over until I learned to end the opening phrase of verse 1 with speed, force, and volume. Next, we recorded the vocals. Between Logaivau singing the chant in low base, medium, and high pitches that spanned three octaves and my own vocals, there were a total of twenty-four layers of vocals. During these first two lines of the chant, the vocals created harmonies four pitches apart. The final layer added to the meke chant was Logaivau calling out into the microphone, "Vakarau! Vakarau! Meke!" to say, get ready to meke! These deeply resonant vocal calls added a rhythmic complexity through their seemingly spontaneous and improvised placement.

Logaivau referred to these vocal cries and calls as "floating notes" with "irregular rhythms" and included them to increase the spirit and connection between the dancers and the chant. "There are floating notes," he said, "that float across the main chant of the meke,"[25] which he demonstrated by making waves through space with his hand. Floating notes are a part of the music that cross through time and space with what he referred to as their own irregular rhythms (in relation to common Western time signatures), traveling from one dancer to another as a vocal call. He emphasized that calling out in this way is part of creating and transmitting a sense of spirit as well as emotional and psychological strength. When the chanting is live, the cries intersect with the meke in random and improvised ways based on the ebbs and flows of spirit and energy felt among the group. When the dancers need the energy, you hear the chanters and the dancers cry and call out more to increase it. As Logaivau explained: "When calling out, performers use chest voice to mimic heavy chest sounds in the village that are used to help each other out. For example, when planting in the fields, Fijians call out to each other and project to each other across a large space. Using chest voice and yelling out, the person far away will capture what is being said and the encouragement to keep going with hard work. This is something we have learned from our ancestors. We follow the same tradition in meke."[26] Performers yell and call out to send mana across to the other performers, and performers continue to respond—passing and building energy by yelling and calling across to one another—connecting bodies across time and space. The more the performance transmits energy and mana, the more the meke connects people together and brings them into the spirit of the meke.

The energy and resiliency of the prerecorded floating, irregular notes demonstrate how he designed *Mekhe ni Loloma* to move beyond the legacies of Western colonial perspectives that diminish and erase these energizing components of the form. According to Logaivau, "For Fijians, if the meke performers shout, that is music. But for Westerners that is not music. When Western scholars transcribe the meke music, irregularity of rhythm and phrasing get removed and lost."[27] Floating vocal calls cut across the chant and add rhythmic and tonal excitement into the chant. Instead of having live chanting, however, he records his chants so that his meke can be staged for theatrical performances outside the purposes and setting of a village. A small group sings the chants and vocal calls, but he mixes and records them in a way to make it sound like there are many voices singing. He invests vast amounts of time and energy in the process of recording so that the end result will generate a heightened sense of spirit. The use of technology enables a creative space for him to investigate and access dimensions of expression otherwise unavailable.

Despite my body's own Westernizing rhythmic impetus, the meke's rhythms and phrasing aligned with the cadence of the chant to generate collectivity. "In the village meke," Logaivau stated, "when we sing collectively, we don't mind if structures are there or not. It is more about the atmosphere."[28] Through his composition of such irregular rhythms, *Mekhe ni Loloma* has an expressive capacity to negotiate feelings and sentiments of conflict and opposition that move with countervailing rhythms to bring people together for a common purpose. For example, the first verse is sung in what my ears recognize as a 4/4-time signature. And yet the chant has eleven beats with a three-beat pause. Nevertheless, during the meke rehearsals, my body continued to try to produce my own Western interpretation of the rhythms in the phrasing of the movements. Interestingly, by design, the rhythms coincide with lyrics that address my mother being born into double-mindedness and split between Fijian culture and British colonial culture, thus capturing the complex dialectics at play. Thus, there is an expression of ambivalence embedded in the discord created by my reproducing contemporary Western rhythms over Logaivau's rhythms that continues to frame the dance and our interactions and captures the legacy of colonialism. Still, the rhythms are resilient, resistant, and capable of moving with and beyond the rhythmic impacts of British colonialism.

Migratory Gifts: Uneven Rhythms of Reciprocity

We worked for several weeks on creating this meke over the course of the next five months. As time passed I felt a growing pressure to find a way to give back. He was definitely giving more than I could possibly contribute to this exchange. I also knew that the traditional gifts given to a daunivucu were, in this case, inappropriate. He did not drink yaqona because he believed it was linked with the worship of the pre-Christian land spirit gods that he associated with witchcraft. It was also not appropriate to give him jugs of kerosene, yards of fabric, and large amounts of food that could be shared with his village, since he did not live in his rural village (Nanenivuda in Seaqaqa) anymore but lived in a single-family dwelling in a small, urbanized town called Navua. I felt increasingly deficient in my ability to reciprocate.

As a result, I consulted with his colleagues at the Oceania Center and found that he had been paid for his meke in a recently staged theatrical production. Those I consulted with agreed that money was not a suitable way to compensate him for his meke and labor, though money was always needed and appreciated. Feeling desperate to give back, I gave him money after rehearsal one night as a gift of gratitude. He was stunned, confused, and disoriented by my offering. He tried to give it back. But I insisted he take the money and I naïvely explained that it was the one way I could think of returning his generosity. I explained that I was not trying to buy his time or his knowledge, I just wanted to return a feeling of generosity. He understood my intent, and on the basis of that understanding, he accepted the money. But can feelings of generosity really be quantified and replaced with money?

Rehearsals and conversations were never the same again. Our meetings became driven by what felt like a desire on his part to deliver a finished product for me to own and bring back to Canada. I tried to remove that pressure of obligation by reminding him that it did not matter if the meke was finished, that the process of learning about meke was more important to me. But there was no going back to the way things felt prior to the monetary exchange. Now it seemed as if he felt he owed me something and that gave me a power I did not want (or highlighted the inequitable power I always had but had been blind to). It was clear that I could not disconnect myself or our relationship from the disruptive power and privilege of colonialism. *Mekhe ni Loloma* had transformed from an active, effective, and generative song-dance process to a thing that could be owned and taken away.

We made efforts to synchronize our rhythms, have them dance together in/between our bodies, but it didnot always work. Sometimes rhythms resonated in energizing and thrilling ways that allowed us to embody Logaivau's view of inclusion. Other times, rhythms collided, slicing and destroying the time-space in/between bodies, and exposing the violence of colonial and neoliberal mentalities—to turn intangible actant into passive thing—reducing the power of movements through space-time.

The basis of our relations, as framed by Logaivau and myself, was the spirit of return generated by the memory of Qumia's loloma. In some ways, I killed the love. But this experience was also a reminder that the love was always infused with uneven money and power due to the colonial economic relations between Qumia and my mother. I unintentionally changed the purpose of the endeavor, putting a stop to the interactive motion of exchange, stopping the momentum and transmission of force that extended and emanated up, down, out, across, and between bodies. Without that motion of return—the movement of the gift—the spirit changed. My response carried a kind of colonial and neoliberal no-strings-attached, never be beholden to or in someone's debt attitude about social obligations and relations. Nevertheless, there was something in Logaivau's meke more resilient than my abrupt, almost violent assertion of a new rhythm of reciprocity. He had built room in this meke to make mistakes, to trip and fall, lose contact, and still spring back and reconnect. The meke gift still pulls at me and wants to move, an important reminder that *Mekhe ni Loloma*, as a site for generating spirit, energy, and inclusion, is a resilient space that could, by design, accommodate conflicting and irregular rhythms—even violent colonial, neoliberal, and battling ones.

⁓

As a pedagogical transmission of kinesthetically expressed visceral sensibilities and movements, *Mekhe ni Loloma* generates efficacy as a kind of transcorporeal gift exchange, or responsiveness, that extended between our bodies. With regard to Marcel Mauss's observation that mana in the South Pacific is generated by the movement of the gift, dance studies scholar Mark Franko looks at the pedagogical transmission of dance as generating a force of response or return. According to Franko, "Teaching a movement is giving something of oneself, and this gift of movement indexes the force inhabiting the gifts as described by Mauss." In other words, the intangible gift of transmitting dance gains force through movement. "This force," as Franko explained, "involves the circulation of self."[29] The notion of "I" and the "present" dissolve as the "self" and the past become part of what is transmitted and transferred in movement. Put another way, movements extend through time, carrying the traces of those who transmit them. While this notion of transmission is not necessarily universal, Logaivau's meke contains the same integrative principle, whereby relational bodies extend between past and future. The final line of the prologue in the chant supports this perspective when the lyrics express, "Let the mana always give life all the time and in the future." Similarly, the second to last sentence of the third verse, which translates as "all the spirit of Fiji comes to life with the life that Anna Qumia gave and with what all of the descendants of Fiji have given," suggests all people born in Fiji generate mana through their self-donation and giving. Past acts of giving are extended into the future by acknowledging that Qumia was part of a greater decentralized web of giving generated by all the descendants of Fiji, regardless of where in the world they migrate and regardless of descent. The chant suggests that the circulation of gifts results in multiple interconnected relationships and that Qumia generated an assemblage of multilocal relations that connect bodies in Fiji and diaspora. These lyrics ensure that the efficacy of the meke does not fade; it continues into the future, extending in time and space, between, within, and across bodies.

But as Mauss asked, "What force is there in the thing given which compels the recipient to make a return?"[30] Franko suggested it is the self-donation involved in the process of transmission that compels a return to be made. In other words, movements transmitted, or given, between bodies generate responsiveness, a force, or mana, that compels return. While Franko described bodies in this space of interactive and interpersonal transmission, whereby "movement is given from one body to another," as sharing "the same kinaesthetic experience," I draw attention to the ways in which our integrative, relational bodies do not share the same kinesthetic experience.[31] Rather, in *Mekhe ni Loloma*, our bodies experienced our shared kinesthetic actions in singular ways because of different relations of power. Therefore, the transmission of *Mekhe ni Loloma* as gift within a teacher/student pedagogical relationship produced a force that compels a return, yet is implicated in political relations of power in ways that create countervailing rhythms of reciprocity. While these reciprocities between bodies in motion produced feelings of generosity and inclusion, they also produced doubts, discomforts, and anxieties about the reproduction of colonial and postcolonial power imbalances. These intensities are all important effects of *Mekhe ni Loloma*—a postcolonial rhythm-relation song-dance.

When, overwhelmed by a sense of obligation and in desperation of finding a way to reciprocate Logaivau's gift, I offered money, my actions instantly sucked the mana, the spirit and energy, out of our exchange. Perhaps Mauss was correct in his discussion of mana, and mana was at stake of being lost if I did not reciprocate the obligation appropriately.[32] I tried to fix our power inequity with money. Here I recall Tomlinson's observation that once a verb is nominalized (turned into a passive noun or thing), it loses power to act and can be lost (and taken). This point is central as it relates to Tomlinson's claims about mana being situated within a discourse of loss and decline. By bringing money into the equation, I introduced an element that he was unable to reciprocate. This act of "giving" on my part put an end date on our relationship. I turned our relationship into one of ownership over services rendered, and even worse, I set in motion a loss and decline of energy and responsiveness—once the product was finished, his obligation was over and so was mine.

My response to Logaivau's gift tokenized *Mekhe ni Loloma* and reframed our exchange in terms that were the antithesis of what Logaivau was aiming to do. As my analysis of the chant, sounds, rhythms, and choreography demonstrate, Logaivau is verb-oriented in his approach to meke as well as in his use of notions such as mana (efficacy), sau (spiritual power), loloma (kindly love), and bula (living life to the fullest) in *Mekhe ni Loloma*.

He used these life-affirming words and stories of resilience to actively and effectively bind us together to achieve our intended purpose—to generate inclusion and reciprocity and, perhaps most importantly, to make mistakes and rebound from them.

Had I been paying closer attention, I would have realized that he offered a structure of response, quoting Franko, "whose potential [was] grounded in the operations of transmission."[33] In other words, the pedagogical moments of transmission (expressed and shared in creation, rehearsal, training, repetition, and conversations) generated their own performativity or efficacious form of giving built on an active responsiveness between bodies that supports and compels continued social interactions into the future. I reciprocated his force of transmission in ways that might have reduced the potential for such a translocal social responsiveness. Instead, I was to learn, responding to this gift of *Mekhe ni Loloma* required another movement to extend the time and space of social relations and obligations—to continue the movement.

The transmission of *Mekhe ni Loloma* demanded active responsiveness, and the magnitude of what was shared required a response that resisted immediacy. The generosity and expressive energy that Logaivau gave required a much more long-term response, which I could not reciprocate directly or quickly. As Jacques Derrida has theorized, social relations are bound by the interval in which the gift is not yet repaid.[34] This theorization of reciprocity resonates with the visceral feelings compelling me to make a gift of return. And since the money I offered was not an appropriate response to his gift, I continue to feel compelled to respond to Logaivau years after he taught me about meke and entrusted me with bringing the *Mekhe ni Loloma* to the Canadian Fijian diaspora so that I could document and disseminate this significance of his meke-creation process. The intentions and relations of force behind *Mekhe ni Loloma* now form my responsiveness to Logaivau. The obligation to return extends translocally through space and into the future with a greater knowledge of the political power dynamics at play.

The experience of *Mekhe ni Loloma* was at once profoundly enriching while at times tense due to my crassness. Still, my misstep does not fully undermine *Mekhe ni Loloma*'s potential for transnational exchange. Here I recall Mauss's understanding of how the gift extends relations, including unequal ones, over time and space, "in perpetual interchange of what we may call spiritual matter, comprising men and things, these elements pass and re-pass between clans and individuals, ranks, sexes and generations."[35] This appreciation aligns with Logaivau's view that culture is not a "thing" that can be lost and taken. In the end, *Mekhe ni Loloma* could not simply or straightforwardly generate inclusion on Indigenous terms. Rather, its efficacy incorporates all the politics and unsettled feelings that went into it.

Conclusion

Despite, and because of, its ambivalence, Logaivau's *Mekhe ni Loloma* is evidence of a postcolonial, post–2006 coup approach to meke that is active and effective at negotiating multifarious rhythms. Mana (as efficacy) is not lost for Logaivau, and his meke are not vanishing. Instead, he continues to be busy creating new meke for a range of fraught and complex occasions, including a recent meke for the 2017 centennial celebration of the abolition of indentured labor in Fiji.[36]

Mekhe ni Loloma is not a chant-song-dance of cohesive, singular social rhythms. This meke is transcorporeal in that it is co-constituting and co-constituted by countervailing rhythms, movements through space-time, and sensory experiences. *Mekhe ni Loloma* offers an understanding of movements, sounds, and rhythms that emerge from relational feelings of intensity that are transferred between bodies in motion and implicated in formations of power. Sometimes the movements, sounds, and rhythms enabled vibrant, relational, kinesthetic syncretizations and sometimes they produced uncomfortable and even violent rhythms that threatened to disable long-term relations. That *Mekhe ni Loloma* has the capacity to maneuver through such countervailing pressures (and rhythms sometimes violent) says something about the resilience of the meke. Exploring the countervailing dimensions of reciprocity in *Mekhe ni Loloma* shows how bodily relations and transmissions move with, through, and beyond legacies of colonialism. Eventually, by taking my cue from Logaivau, this meke process has revealed methods and techniques for creative emergence in the felt and sensed transcorporeal relations of transmission that extend social relations and obligations translocally. But how would Fijians in Fiji and Canada respond to this meke?

CHAPTER 6

Performing Indeterminacy
Performance of Mekhe ni Loloma

THE DAY BEFORE LEAVING FIJI, Master Damiano Logaivau wanted to record *Mekhe ni Loloma* so I could take it back to Canada to teach and share with the Fijian diaspora. He had set up a four-hour block of time to film the meke at University of the South Pacific's Music Center, courtesy of Tuilagi Igelese Ete, head of performing arts.[1] He wanted to film us in costumes because he felt they would give the meke more spirit and energy. To this end, he also invited two manu manu ni mekes (who are especially gifted with communicating the spirit and meaning of meke), Livai Baravilala and Ledua Peni, to join us in dancing *Mekhe ni Loloma*.

On the way to the university, Logaivau requested we pick up meke supplies that he said would heighten the spirit and mana of the meke. He explained that materials for the costumes come from soil that is rich with mana. As a result, the costumes, which consist of grass skirts, masi, coconut oil (for covering the body when performing), and face paint, are all full of mana that intensifies the spiritual energy and effectiveness of the meke to communicate meaning. We stopped at the flea market in Suva and the Fijian handicraft market to gather a bottle of nice-smelling coconut oil (created by cooking the oil with flowers) and Kajol (black eye makeup) to use as face paint.[2] We then made our way to the Music Center.

Fumaru Fatiaki, who was the costume designer for the Oceania Center for Arts Culture and Pacific Studies, kindly gathered together a costume for me. Fatiaki told me that she is from the Bauan province and that her family is a chiefly family. She says in the past her family, which has a high degree of power and authority, would never do meke—they would only ever watch others come and perform for them as entertainment. Despite her family's chiefly status, Fatiaki, who is transgender, performs women's meke. Her dancing affirms connections between ways of moving in meke and the performance of gender in Fiji.

Piece by piece, Fatiaki generously helped me get into my costume. The costume included a thin piece of masi with a cream-colored cowry shell in the center, tied firmly against my neck, and a black cotton and strapless tunic that ended below my knees, with masi covering the black fabric from the waist down. Around my waist and wrists, I had vesa, an ornamental grass fringe held together and tied with magimagi or coir sinnet (string made from braided coconut fiber). Vesa, like the other costume pieces, was a meaningful symbol for Logaivau of carrying iTaukei culture and heritage close to one's sense of self. As Fatiaki helped me dress, she told me my costume was from Fiji's Lau group of islands and that it was normally used for seasea (a women's standing dance). She said I was the perfect height for the seasea and that shorter women usually do sitting dances. As she applied the Kajol below my cheekbones, she added that her mother knows everything about the face markings: "The forehead marking should be a rectangle if you are the son of a chief," she told me. "For the ladies, they just have two circles below the cheekbones, to highlight the cheekbones and beautify the dancer."[3] She applied the Kajol below my cheekbones, but this did not make me feel beautiful.

As she helped me with the costume, I felt more and more like an imposter, a sentiment that I shared with her. Most iTaukei have told me that the moment they put their costumes on, the meke spirit just comes to them and automatically enters their bodies. But when I put the costume on, the meke spirit did not come to me; no feelings of fighting spirit or living life to the fullest emerged. I caught a glimpse of myself in a reflection. I looked burnt out and tired compared with the brightness and openness of the iTaukei dancers in the room. I felt eyes watching me that seemed to assess my actions and intentions. I myself had no idea what my intentions were anymore. Logaivau told me he wanted me to be a part of recording this meke because the meke was a part of me. In his eyes, at least, I felt a sense of security. But outside of his assurances, I felt inadequate and incongruous in every way.

We started relearning our parts while wearing the costumes so that the full spirit of the meke would be communicated transnationally to the Fijians in their Canadian diaspora, who would one day be watching the video.

But artists from the Oceania Center were watching the whole process live, making our rehearsal and informal performance also part of a local relational exchange. I assisted Baravilala and Logaivau in relearning the choreography of the men's sections. Peni, the third manu manu ni meke, arrived and began learning the large volume of choreographed movement for the first time. Baravilala carried a fan, Logaivau held a club, Peni wielded a spear and fan, and although I am more familiar with their choreography and it was in my muscle memory from months of rehearsal, I did the sitting women's part that was relatively new and unknown.

Logaivau told me the gestural movements were less important than getting the energy right, but I felt incapable of demonstrating the right spirit of joy, strength, and love. I was totally preoccupied with relearning the choreography off my laptop while managing my ambivalence about performing an Indigenous dance tradition, albeit in an untraditional way. The result felt like a loose patchwork of failed attempts and possibilities. Once we were ready, we took our positions. I sat with the three manu manu ni mekes behind me and a growing audience of iTaukei artists in front of me. Normally, as a performer, I would be actively trying to extend my energy to all those around me, while also paying close attention to my own experience of dancing, to generate an intensity of expression and experience for all who are present. Occasionally, I could feel the intensity and the heat coming from the three bodies behind me. At these moments, I felt connected with their energy, and I enjoyed dancing to the chant. Other times, I struggled to connect.

After we finished, one of the artists generously invited us to have some yaqona. Out of respect for the offering, we joined for one bilo, or cup. We stopped at one because we were also aware that Logaivau was not comfortable with drinking yaqona because of its use by daunivucus in connecting with land spirit gods. As a gift of gratitude and a farewell, the artists in the room joined together and sang "Isa Isa." Their singing was very moving. "Isa Isa" has become a popular farewell song to sing to visitors as they depart Fiji, and we were leaving Fiji the next day. But the song was also deeply familiar. During my childhood, my mother sang "Isa Isa" to me before bed at night.

I am not sure how my mother learned the song, but the lyrics contain a sense of love and loss that was always palpable for me as a child. She probably heard "Isa Isa" on the radio, next to "God Save Our Gracious Queen," when she was young.[4] After she passed away, I found the lyrics written in

Fijian on a small scrap piece of paper in one of her personal folders. My mother singing "Isa Isa" to me was one of the ways I knew that Fiji was important to her. But also, the song was like a meditation, a way to find a feeling that calmed her, centered her, and grounded her against some of the difficulties and harsh realities she lived through. When I heard it, it triggered the feeling of being hugged by the masi cloth that always covered the walls of my home growing up and that now hangs on the walls of my current home for my children to enjoy and be comforted by. I still felt the sadness, the kind and caring love or loloma, and the calming, centering feelings of the song.

The singers lined up side by side and sang to us to recognize and thank us for our contributions to the Oceania Center. They were recognizing and showing appreciation for my partner's assistance with the lighting design for their first major production in the university's new theater, cataloging the new lighting equipment, and teaching a full-day workshop to train people on the equipment. In addition, the singers were thanking me for teaching weekly contemporary modern dance classes and setting a piece of choreography for their production *Life* that was about to open.[5] Honoring those emergent relations, Logaivau and the artists sang, and we also sang:

> Isa isa vulagi lasa dina
> Nomu lako au na rarawa kina
> Cava beka ko a mai cakava
> Nomu lako au na sega ni lasa.
>
> Isa lei, na noqu rarawa
> Ni ko sana vodo e na mataka
> Bau nanuma, na nodatou lasa
> Mai Suva nanuma tiko ga. [. . .]
>
> [Isa, Isa you are my only treasure
> Must you leave me, so lonely and forsaken?
> As the roses will miss the sun at dawning,
> Every moment my heart for you is yearning
>
> Chorus:
> Isa Lei, the purple shadow falling,
> Sad the morrow will dawn upon my sorrow;

O forget not, when you're far away,
Precious moments at Suva Bay]

We sang together and connected in that moment. But we were also not connected. One of the singers received a text in the middle of the song and texted back. Another singer finished and then, after realizing the others were still singing, joined back in. With these expressed connections/disconnections, the song took on multiple, complex meanings—partly nostalgic while also breaking through my romanticism about the past. These disconnections were also importantly resistive to my family's presence and efforts. My mother's memories of colonial Fiji and Fiji's postindependence realities yielded very different experiences. Our diverse experiences of Fiji in the wake of its fourth coup challenged the feelings I previously associated with Fiji, which my mother had shared with me. So when we were presented with this beautiful song "Isa Isa" on our last day in Fiji as a gift of gratitude, the song felt intimately tied to the uneasy postcolonial politics of bodies in Fiji.

~

This chapter concludes my exploration of the ways in which meke is an emergent space for renegotiations of Fijian identity following the 2006 coup, while remaining attentive to postcolonial tensions embedded within relations between Indigenous and Western notions of reciprocity, responsiveness, and return. My inquiry began with a look at colonial impacts, in which my own family is implicated, that continue to haunt meke. Meke certainly represents postcolonial structures of inequities; however, throughout this book I have also examined how power operates in the governing, spiriting, resistive, migrating, and performative-effective aspects of meke. Power is not static: it governs while also emerging out of the movements of bodies. In this regard, meke reveals a great deal about shifts in power over time and space.

I conclude this book by analyzing my experience of performing and presenting about Logaivau's *Mekhe ni Loloma* and the feedback and criticism I received from respondents in Fiji, in the Canadian Fijian diaspora, and at professional conferences. In its reception, *Mekhe ni Loloma* continues to arouse discomfort and appreciation. Here I focus on the actual meanings and importance of the discomfort created by this meke in terms of my larger arguments about colonial and postcolonial legacies. Ultimately, there is no legitimating or securing way forward that does not include messy and uneasy rhythms. As a dance ethnographer, I used dialogical performance ethnography to represent meke and my work on it in a complex light. Building off of Dwight Conquergood's "Performing as a Moral Act," this chapter explores dialogical performance ethnography in all its complexities, pitfalls, and problems by discussing the responses to *Mekhe ni Loloma*.[6]

Responding to *Mekhe ni Loloma*

My own experiences of performing *Mekhe ni Loloma* are an indicator of uneven relations of power. Logaivau wanted me to feel included as an equal member of the team and to feel strong, proud, joyful, and energetic. Instead, I worried about how my dancing of this meke might impact Indigenous peoples around the globe, who have had their dance practices destroyed and appropriated by colonial processes.

As a performance ethnographer, I struggled with a variety of strategies to approach the meke and my role in its creation and performance. I tried keeping myself detached emotionally. I thought if I distanced myself from any identification with the meke, then I was in less danger of enacting a kind of violence as an appropriator. In other words, I could have a sense of security so long as I thought of myself as an outsider. But this approach also enacted a kind of violence. All of these issues left me somewhere in the middle of loving and despising what I was doing, literally weighing me down and slowing my movement, preventing me from performing the lighting quick, precise, and geometric movements of the meke. When caught in this in-between state, I could not embody a readiness to live life to the fullest that is, for Logaivau, integral to the success of reaching the intended purpose of a meke.

Perhaps it was never Logaivau's intention for me to feel comfortable or secure. As Dr. Mique'l Dangeli, a First Nations Tsimshian scholar (from the Northwest Coast of North America) suggested to me in conversation, maybe he wanted me to know how it feels to have my sense of identity undermined as so many Indigenous peoples around the globe have experienced under colonial rule.[7] Earlier conversations with Logaivau, however, taught me that unknowable and uncertain experiences form an important part of his political perspective. He is invested in trying to move Fiji and Fijians into new uncharted relations of power based on improving social justice and greater equity and widening the parameters of inclusion based on Indigenous values and beliefs rather than colonially imposed concepts. While acknowledging Dr. Dangeli's thoughts, I believe Logaivau's political hopes and desires steered our relations in a different direction. Through his uncertain and uncharted meke process, I believe he wanted me to feel like I was entering an indeterminate zone of possibility built on new power relations and ways of understanding one another through the use of an iTaukei lens. But he was not expecting me to be in this unknown, fluid, and unsettled affective territory alone. This is a territory he challenged himself and those around him to enter through his meke. For him, struggling with a present-day battle with the unknown requires readiness for change in life and for his dancers to move their bodies in relation to quick changes that are not yet charted. So, although the past was a factor in everything that brought us to that moment (including colonialism and my own family's connection to that history), there was no time to refer backward; he was challenging all of us (the dancers and the audience) in the room to move forward and respond to the challenge of not knowing.

Since returning from Fiji, I have presented the video footage of *Mekhe ni Loloma* at two conferences, in two different ways, with very different reception. At the World Dance Alliance Americas 2013 dance studies conference in Vancouver, British Columbia, I did not properly situate my own relationship to the project and left the scholars in the room justifiably troubled by my dancing an Indigenous dance as a non-Indigenous person.[8] In this instance, I was trying to discuss the spirit and energy of the three manu manu ni meke in the footage while ignoring myself in the center of the video frame. I thought if I ignored myself, others would ignore me too. I could not have been more wrong. There have been many times when I wished I could somehow erase my presence from the video. The video would, in some ways, be much easier to explain if I were not in it. But erasing myself feels dishonest. This performance in Suva happened, and the ephemeral memories continue as a kind of uncomfortable durational performance whereby I remain responsive to the consequences.

With a new approach to situating myself within the materials, I attempted to present the material again at a second conference. This time, I presented the video to a group of Indigenous and non-Indigenous Pacific arts scholars at the Pacific Arts Association 2013 International Symposium in Vancouver, British Columbia.[9] The video included excerpts of the rehearsal process and the informal performance in costumes, and in addition, I used a fifteen-minute paper to situate *Mekhe ni Loloma* in relation to Anna

Qumia, loloma, and my family's colonial history in Fiji. One iTaukei scholar came up to me after and gave me a big kiss. She said I did a good job with the dancing, and she appreciated my sharing the story of Qumia. Even more, she volunteered to help me locate Qumia's family (her husband was from the same area in Namosi Province as Qumia). A second response gave me a different perspective. A Canadian artist, who orchestrates collaborative projects with Indigenous artists in Canada and Fiji, said it was "gutsy" of me to show the video. Although she felt that my dancing was sufficiently personal and sanctioned by Logaivau, she was not sure whether or not my dancing would sometimes be read as crossing a boundary into appropriation.

Another audience member at the second conference read the dancing in the video as a text about gender. Concerned about the status of women in Fiji, who are often marginalized and subordinated, this conference participant from Samoa inquired why, in the video, I was rehearsing the vigorous men's sections but performing only the seated women's section. She understood that typical Fijian gender binaries of male and female were in some ways sustained and in other ways temporarily transgressed in the video.

I do not offer these examples as a way to justify my approach to this project, or to undo the critical responses I received at the first conference. Rather, all the responses to *Mekhe ni Loloma* demonstrated that the video alone, like any "text" or single performance, cannot fully represent social formations of power nor sufficiently expose what bodies are doing in relation to culture and identity shifts. Before I situated myself at these conferences, my presence in the video became "the elephant in the room." I needed to address the full context of the relational experiences that led to this meke, and not just the final product, in order to really get to the way power and intention were operating. This larger methodological approach has become key to presenting my research at conferences and, especially when scholars do not necessarily speak Fijian, the social and political intentions of Logaivau. Nevertheless, all the conversations that have resulted in response to this research have been productive in helping me understand my own complex postcolonial relationship to the dance. It is critical that I firmly situate the meke and my presence in it and not assume that respondents will automatically recognize that I have considered the potentially negative, hurtful, and recolonizing ramifications of my dancing.

Ironically, the Fijians and South Pacific Peoples in Canada with whom I have shared the video of *Mekhe ni Loloma* have found my concerns about appropriation to be offensive. For example, in August 2013, the group from the Oceanian community on Vancouver Island that knew my mother and knew me as a child explained that by worrying that I am overstepping my boundaries as non-iTaukei I am perpetuating a divide by thinking of myself as an outsider. They explained that the act of separating myself from them and those in the video is where the violence lies, not in trying to be a part of the group. They assured me that they accept me because of my mother's investment in their lives: her community development work with the South Pacific community on Vancouver Island, her interests and commitment to understanding traditional iTaukei healing practices, and her personal connection to Fiji.[10] Reading the video solely as a representation of power creates a superficial account of relations that may actually impose colonial legacies of governance and control based on categorizing bodies to secure them. Their sentiments do not absolve me of my positionality but instead demonstrate the ways in which such exchanges are messy, indeterminate, and never simple.

Contextualizing my own embodied experience of *Mekhe ni Loloma* has played a crucial role in understanding the political role meke plays in Fiji and Canada. Dwight Conquergood's seminal 2002 essay, "Performance Studies: Intervention in Radical Research," urged me to be critical of distanced perspectives that treat cultural performance as a text ("knowing that" and "knowing about"). Conquergood argued: "Scholarship is so skewed toward texts that even when researchers do attend to extralinguistic human action and embodied events they construe them as texts to be read. . . . This scriptocentrism is a hallmark of Western imperialism."[11] Such dominant epistemologies blind "researchers to meanings that are expressed forcefully through intonation, silence, body tension, arched eyebrows, blank stares, and other protective arts of disguise and secrecy."[12] As a dancer politically invested in the knowledge of the moving body and embodied legacies of colonialism, I took his call for methods "grounded in active, intimate, hands-on participation and personal connection" ("knowing how" and "knowing who") seriously.[13] This approach helped me understand the meanings that were less obvious and direct. This is how I came to know Logaivau was conducting an ontological recentering based on iTaukei knowledge of a responsive and relational, or transcorporeal, body that emerges as it moves and integrates with other human and nonhuman bodies and ephemeral realities, including sounds, costumes, spirits, memories of the past, and future potentials.

The discomforts of performing and presenting *Mekhe ni Loloma* have been just as valuable in understanding the ambivalence of colonial legacies in and around meke. Conquergood advocated for the performance of ethnographic research when he said, "Ethnographers of performance complement their participant observation fieldwork by actually performing for different audiences the verbal art they have studied in situ, they expose themselves to double jeopardy. They become keenly aware that performance does not proceed in ideological innocence and axiological purity."[14] Although this statement reveals Conquergood's investment in verbal communication, the discomforts aroused by my performing and presenting the meke also signal and expose the deep moral implications surrounding dance performance and reception, especially with regard to identity and legacies of colonial and postcolonial conflict. Caught in/between/beside colonial, postcolonial, and post–2006 coup tensions and residues, the meke continues to arouse dialogue.

With such an incongruous response to my inclusion in *Mekhe ni Loloma*, what can the presence of the iTaukei artists from the Oceania Center at the filming of *Mekhe ni Loloma* tell me about the dynamics of those relations? Perhaps it was the complex indeterminacy that attracted the eight artists, who continued to trickle into the space during the filming. Many artists I spoke with were attracted to the Oceania Center because of the guiding philosophy of the center to transcend national boundaries and embrace an Oceanian identity through an awareness of historical and contemporary intersections between peoples of Oceania. Several of the center's artists expressed frustration with external pressures to perform Fijianness in particular ways as authentic, fixed, stable, and knowable (as explored in chapter 2). They resisted such expressions of meke that perpetuate a colonial politics of the body in support of conservative ethnonational iTaukei preeminence. Instead, they were keen to explore more complex notions of identity and indeterminacy. I met artists at the Oceania Center who self-identified as iTaukei, "half caste" (part iTaukei and part European), and Indian as well as homosexual, queer, and transgender. The artists I interviewed sometimes struggled with trying to fit restrictive racialized, sexual, and gendered definitions of iTaukei and were in search of intercultural relations that allowed for greater freedom of expression through cultural fusions, interactions, and transformations. They made apparent the fiction of bodies forming discrete and stable categories of identity. Biopolitical arrangements based on firm categories of race and gender, which Fiji has long relied on, were implausible for some of these artists who inhabit emergent thresholds in their performed expressions. This was perhaps what attracted them to the performance of *Mekhe ni Loloma*—a performance of indeterminacy.

Artists at the Oceania Center were also invested in contemporary art making that decenters colonial legacies. The center's founder and prior director, Tongan philosopher Epeli Hau'ofa, argued that it was imperative that artists take creative authority and control over their own sense of Oceania. They might draw upon Western art and media conventions, but the intention of the art making needed to be for Indigenous peoples of Oceania to create a sense of culture and identity on the basis of their own experiences and perspectives.[15] In this regard, Logaivau was using his creative authority and control to embrace traditional Indigenous art conventions to express contemporary Indigenous perspectives but tactically doing so through an embodied process of translation and transmission to a Western audience via my body. His approach to creating *Mekhe ni Loloma* was to decenter Westernizing colonial conventions, while acknowledging the continued presence of these forces, which I symbolized. This was his embodied way of reconciling multiple and incongruous worldviews on Indigenous terms. Logaivau created an expressive force full of countervailing pressures built from our bodies that became contact zones for negotiating colonial legacies and postcolonial realities of identity.

The performance of *Mekhe ni Loloma* and the responses to it conclude this book as a final example of sensation, experience, and expression in the active process of generating culture and identity. In other words, our bodies, performing a contemporary tradition, were not passive or two-dimensionally fixed as signs, or texts, of the past but generative of emergent meaning. Expressions that generated a sense of security and insecurity were a part of how we shaped ourselves and the world around us: sometimes aligning with dominant beliefs and values, sometimes tearing into the fabric of that dominance.

This book, and all the research and care within it, has always been implicated within a postcolonial story about translocal responsiveness and transmission between bodies. Like *Mekhe ni Loloma*, it is a reminder of the messiness of ongoing postcolonial relations and responses between my own body, the bodies of Fijian, Fiji Canadian, and Oceanian friends and interlocutors, along with our ancestors. Thus, this whole project is a reminder of the complexities of global, postcolonial networks of identification and exchange. The book is intended to keep alive the difficult collaborations and dialogues that express the sometimes uneasy feelings of emergence (in)between Indigenous/postcolonial/colonial worldviews. Despite my best intentions to honor and respect all who have shared their knowledge of Fiji, Fijian meke, and Oceania, the book, like *Mekhe ni Loloma*, is the expressive force of all that has gone into it, including the institutional and personal (though unintentional) colonizing impulses and rhythms (including using English to write this book). With the many political and religious pressures at work in creating a continuum of meke perspectives and practices, it is my hope that the writing up of my experiences serves to open more opportunities to expose and negotiate the complexities of contemporary meke in Fiji and abroad.

Glossary

Terms Related to Social Structure and Exchange

bula	to live, life
kalou vu	a pre-Christian Indigenous term used to describe originary gods
loloma	kindly love
luveniwai	a class of supernatural entities
mana	spiritual efficacy in ritual expression; supernatural power
mataqali	patrilineage—aggregate of small family units
matanitu	large governing confederacies
sevusevu	to present an offering as a token of respect
iTaukei	original and native settlers of Fiji
tabua	oiled and polished tooth of a sperm whale—used in exchange
vinaka vaka levu	deep gratitude and respect
yaqona	a ceremonial and social beverage made from the roots of the piper methysticum plant; also known as kava

Terms Related to Meke

bole	war meke—a challenge to war
cobo	cup-clapping the hands
cibi	war victory meke
curumi konaio ni meke	let the true spirit of meke come in you

daunivucu	meke choreographer/composer
gugu	throwing club used in meke
kiakavo	spurred club for meke
lali	slit drum
masi	patterned bark cloth
meke	to dance; to sing verse with choreographed movement
meke iri	fan meke
meke mata	meke team
meke wau	club meke
meke wesi	spear meke
orei	penalty for infringing on traditional customs
seasea	women's standing dance
sevu ni meke	when the meke is performed for the village chief for the first time
tabu	protocols of restricted behavior in order to increase energy and strength
teivovo	a bole or war meke challenge
ucu ni meke	introductory verse
vakarau	get ready
vakatara	an ensemble of singers who sing the words and provide rhythmic accompaniment for a meke performance

Other Terms

draunikau	"pointing of the leaf"—Indigenous practice associated with a power to heal or harm
drua	double-hulled canoe
io	yes
isa	expressing empathy, solidarity in misfortune, a common vulnerability

Notes

INTRODUCTION

1. Bainimarama (from Kiuva village in the district of Bau and the province of Tailevu) has led two military takeovers in Fiji (2000 and 2006). He briefly held the title of interim prime minister in 2000. In 2006 he became the military head of Fijian governance for eight years until he was democratically elected as Fiji's prime minister in 2014. Bainimarama's stated goals are to create a more equitable and democratic Fiji. His motives and approach to governance are highly controversial and debated within Fiji and abroad. For more about Bainimarama's takeover, see Jon Fraenkel, Stewart Firth, and Brij V. Lal's edited collection, *The 2006 Military Takeover in Fiji: A Coup to End All Coups?* (Canberra: Australian National University Press, 2009).

2. The meke was actually a medley of two mekes: a vakamalolo titled *Rogo Saka na Wekaqu* (Hear Ye O My People) and *Oie na Kula* (A warrior standing up dance from Vuda). Master Lai, email correspondence with the author, December 1, 2018.

3. Indigenous Fijians are to be referred to as "iTaukei" in all official laws and documentation, according to "Fijian Affairs (Amendment) Decree 2010," *Gazette* 11, no. 73, July 2, 2010, accessed February 15, 2019, http://www.paclii.org/fj/promu/promu_dec/fad2010210/.

4. I follow the approach of Marrie Mumford and Jacqueline Shea Murphy, who choose not to italicize words written in Indigenous languages in order to emphasize there is nothing "foreign" about the Indigenous languages being used in the territories discussed. See Jacqueline Shea Murphy, "Editor's Note: Doing Indigenous Dance Today," *Dance Research Journal* 48, no. 1 (April 2016): 7.

5. Vilsoni Hereniko, "Dancing Oceania," in *The 5th Asia-Pacific Triennial of Contemporary Art* (Brisbane: Queensland Art Gallery Publishing, 2006), 32–41.

6. Giorgio Agamben, *Homo Sacer: Sovereign Power and Bare Life*, trans. Daniel Heller-Roazen (Stanford, CA: Stanford University Press, 1998).

7. Brij V. Lal, "Fiji Islands: From Immigration to Emigration," Migration Policy Institute, April 1, 2003, https://www.migrationpolicy.org/article/fiji-islands-immigration-emigration.

8. I have deliberately limited this study in other ways that need to be mentioned. Although Fiji is home to significant Chinese, Rotuman, Banaban, and Tongan populations, I do not address the dances of these groups or the ways in which these populations might influence meke performances.

9. Hereniko, "Dancing Oceania."

10. Nicholas Thomas, *In Oceania* (Durham, NC: Duke University Press, 1997), 65.

11. Susan Leigh Foster, "Choreographies of Gender," *Signs* 24, no. 1 (1998): 1–33; Cindy Garcia, *Salsa Crossings: Dancing Latinidad in Los Angeles* (Durham, NC: Duke University Press, 2013).

12. Including Unaisi Nabobo-Baba, *Knowing and Learning: An Indigenous Fijian Approach* (Suva: Institute of Pacific Studies, University of the South Pacific, 2006); Tupeni L. Baba, 'Okusitino Māhina, Nuhisifa Williams, and Unaisi Nobobo-Baba, eds., *Researching Pacific and Indigenous Peoples: Issues and Perspectives* (Wellington: Center for Pacific Studies, University of Auckland, 2004); Epeli Hau'ofa, *We Are the Ocean* (Honolulu: University of Hawai'i Press, 2008); Hereniko, "Dancing Oceania"; Vilsoni Hereniko, "Dance as a Reflection of Rotuman Culture," in *Rotuma Hanua Pumue: Precious Land* (Suva: Institute of Pacific Studies, University of the South Pacific, 1991), 120–42; Katerina Martina Teaiwa, "Choreographing Difference: The (Body) Politics of Banaban Dance," *Contemporary Pacific* 24, no. 1 (February 12, 2012): 65–95; N. Thomas, *In Oceania*; Matt Tomlinson, *In God's Image: The Metaculture of Fijian Christianity* (Berkeley: University of California Press, 2009); Matt Tomlinson, "Retheorizing Mana: Bible Translation and Discourse of Loss in Fiji," *Oceania* 76, no. 2 (July 1, 2006): 173–85; Karen Stevenson, "The Festival of Pacific Arts: Its Past, Its Future," *Pacific Arts* 25 (December 2002): 31–40; Adrienne Kaeppler, "Dances and Dancing in Tonga: Anthropological and Historical Discourses," in *Dancing from Past to Present: Nation, Culture, Identities*, ed. Theresa Jill Buckland (Madison: University of Wisconsin Press, 2006), 25–51; Wolfgang Kemf and Elfriede Hermann, "Reconfigurations of Place and Ethnicity: Positionings, Performances and Politics of Relocated Banabans in Fiji," *Oceania* 75, no. 4 (September 1, 2005): 368–86.

13. For more on how identity is intricately linked to the staged performance of tradition in national narratives in the South Pacific, see, for example, John Kelly and Martha Kaplan, *Represented Communities: Fiji and World Decolonization* (Chicago: University of Chicago Press, 2001); Adrienne L. Kaeppler, *The Pacific Arts of Polynesia and Micronesia* (Oxford: Oxford University Press, 2008); Hereniko, "Dancing Oceania"; David Murray, "Haka Fracas? The Dialectics of Identity in Discussions of a Contemporary Maori Dance," "The Politics of Dance" special

issue, *Australian Journal of Anthropology* 11, no. 3 (2000): 14–26; Kalissa Alexeyeff, *Dancing from the Heart: Movement, Gender, and Sociality in the Cook Islands* (Honolulu: University of Hawai'i Press, 2009); and Stevenson, "The Festival of Pacific Arts."

14. Beth D. Carell, *South Pacific Dance* (Sydney: Pacific Publications, 1978).

15. Rachmi Diyah Larasati, *The Dance That Makes You Vanish: Cultural Reconstruction in Post-Genocide Indonesia* (Minneapolis: University of Minnesota Press, 2013).

16. Teaiwa, "Choreographing Difference." Dr. Teaiwa is one of the founders (along with Allan Alo) of Oceania Dance Theatre at Oceania Center for Art, Culture and Pacific Studies at University of South Pacific.

17. Katerina Martina Teaiwa, "South Asia Down Under: Popular Kinship in Oceania," *Cultural Dynamics* 19, nos. 2–3 (July 2007): 193–232.

18. Dorothy Sara Lee, "Music Performances and the Negotiation of Identity in Eastern Viti Levu, Fiji" (PhD diss., Indiana University, 1984).

19. This contemporary meke was part of a larger production called *Vaka: The Birth of a Seer*, choreographed by Peter Rockford Espiritu and composed by Igelese Ete with Vilsoni Hereniko as executive producer and advisor on the production.

20. This study does not explore the social structural relationships in Fiji that influence meke. For a greater understanding of the social and structural impacts on the practice of meke, see Dorothy Sara Lee's doctoral dissertation on music performance in Viti Levu, Fiji, "Music Performances and the Negotiation of Identity in Eastern Viti Levu, Fiji." One such relationship is referred to as tauvu ("tau" means friend and "vu" means spirit) and allows audience members to joke with the performers with whom they share the same ancestor spirit (kalou vu). This tauvu relationship came up in many interviews and observations as an aspect of meke performance. Examples of the kinds of joking this relationship permits include audience members putting baby powder or perfume on their tauvu who is dancing, or putting a candy in the performer's mouth as a way to generate laughter toward their tauvu.

21. Kalou vu is a pre-Christian Indigenous term used to describe originary gods. A larger discussion of kalou (spirits and gods) occurs in chapter 1.

22. Claudia Knapman, *White Women in Fiji, 1835–1930: The Ruin of Empire?* (Sydney: Allen and Unwin, 1986).

23. Ibid.

24. Atu Emberson-Bain, *Labour and Gold in Fiji* (Cambridge: Cambridge University Press, 1994).

25. Ibid.

26. Fiji, "Land Tenure," Ministry for Local Government, Urban Development and Public Utilities, Department of Town and Country Planning, 2015, accessed

November 15, 2017, http://www.townplanning.gov.fj/index.php/planning/planning-issues/land-tenure.

27. See Jon Fraenkel and Stewart Firth, "Fiji's Coup Syndrome," in *The 2006 Military Takeover in Fiji: A Coup to End All Coups?*, ed. John Fraenkel, Stewart Firth, and Brij V. Lal (Canberra: Australian National University Press, 2009). See also Kelly and Kaplan, *Represented Communities*.

28. See Rabuka's leadership as an example of how church and state have been interconnected in Fiji in Kelly and Kaplan, *Represented Communities*; and Hirokazu Miyazaki, *The Method of Hope: Anthropology, Philosophy, and Fijian Knowledge* (Stanford, CA: Stanford University Press, 2004). See Nicholas Thomas for more about how Fijian traditions have maintained the hegemonic authority of church and state. Thomas, *In Oceania*, 51.

29. Vanua is a complex concept narrowly defined here as groupings of related yavusa or clans who share an originating ancestor (Adrian Tanner, "Colo Navosa: Local History and the Construction of Region in the Western Interior of Vitilevu, Fiji," *Oceania* 66, no. 3 [March 1996]: 236), and chiefdoms, traditions, customs, beliefs, and values (Martha Kaplan, *Neither Cargo nor Cult: Ritual Politics and the Colonial Imagination in Fiji* [Durham, NC: Duke University Press, 1995], 25), as well as "territory, land (but not soil itself or any specific piece of land), country, nation, place" (Ronald Gatty, *Fijian-English Dictionary: With Notes on Fijian Culture and Natural History* (Ithaca, NY: Cornell University Press, 2012), 296.

30. Tomlinson, *In God's Image*, 23.

31. Jon Fraenkel and Stewart Firth, "Introduction: The Enigmas of Fiji's Good Governance Coup," in *The 2006 Military Takeover in Fiji: A Coup to End All Coups?*, ed. Jon Fraenkel, Stewart Firth, and Brij V. Lal (Canberra: Australian National University Press, 2009), 7.

32. Agamben, *Homo Sacer*.

33. For more critical perspectives on multicultural dance festivals, see Marta Savigliano, "Worlding Dance and Dancing Out There in the World," in *Worlding Dance*, ed. Susan Leigh Foster (New York: Palgrave Macmillan, 2009), 163–90.

34. Piot's analytical tools come from the influential book *Empire* by post-Marxist philosophers Michael Hardt and Antonio Negri. See Michael Hardt and Antonio Negri, *Empire* (Cambridge, MA: Harvard University Press, 2001). See also Charles Piot, *Nostalgia for the Future: West Africa after the Cold War* (Chicago: University of Chicago Press, 2010).

35. For more about Foucault's work on governmentality and new forms of biopolitics, see Hardt and Negri, *Empire*. For more on changes to governance due to a rise in Pentecostalism in Melanesian society, see Richard Eves, "Pentecostal Dreaming and Technologies of Governmentality in a Melanesian Society," *American Ethnologist* 38, no. 4 (2011): 760.

36. Thomas J. Csordas, "Asymptote of the Ineffable: Embodiment, Alterity, and the Theory of Religion," *Current Anthropology* 45, no. 2 (2004):163–68; Thomas J. Csordas, ed., *Embodiment and Experience: The Existential Ground of Culture and Self* (New York: Cambridge University Press, 1994).

37. Recent proponents of affect theory influenced by Baruch Spinoza (such as Massumi, Seigworth and Gregg, Brennan, and Deleuze and Guattari) help me understand affect as a process of exchange and to unpack its political dimensions. See, for example, Brian Massumi, *Parables for the Virtual: Movement, Affect, Sensation* (Durham, NC: Duke University Press, 2002); Melissa Gregg, "An Inventory of Shimmers," in *The Affect Theory Reader*, ed. Greg Seigworth and Melissa Gregg (Durham, NC: Duke University Press, 2010), 1–25; Teresa Brennan, *The Transmission of Affect* (Ithaca, NY: Cornell University Press, 2004); Gilles Deleuze and Félix Guattari, *A Thousand Plateaus: Capitalism and Schizophrenia*, trans. Brian Massumi (Minneapolis: University of Minnesota Press, 1987). These scholars view the body as having the capacity to affect others (causing others to feel and sense) and to be simultaneously affected (to feel and sense). Affect can be shared, communicated, and transmitted between bodies, and as such bodies are no longer self-contained. Bodies are not shaped solely by affects in the present; they have, according to Sara Ahmed, an "affective angle" or affective standpoint composed of one's own unique personal and cultural context and past experiences. Sara Ahmed, "Happy Objects," in *The Affect Theory Reader*, ed. Greg Seigworth and Melissa Gregg (Durham, NC: Duke University Press, 2010), 29–51, 36.

38. Susan Leigh Foster, "Worlding Dance–An Introduction," in *Worlding Dance*, ed. Susan Leigh Foster (New York: Palgrave Macmillan, 2009), 9.

39. José Esteban Muñoz, "Feeling Brown: Ethnicity and Affect in Ricardo Bracho's *The Sweetest Hangover (and Other STDs)*," *Theatre Journal* 52, no. 1 (2000): 67–79.

40. Here I follow the notion of culture set forth by anthropologist Clifford Geertz, who views culture as not substantive or separate from individuals but created at the intersection of competing views, interests, and interpretations of events and is itself expressed and generated through the act of living. See Clifford Geertz, "Deep Play: Notes on the Balinese Cockfight," in *Anthropological Theory: An Introductory History*, 3rd ed., ed. Jon R. McGee and Richard L. Warms (Boston: McGraw Hill, 2004), 553–74.

41. See Tomlinson, "Retheorizing Mana." See also A. M. Hocart, "On the Meaning of Kalou and the Origin of Fijian Temples," *Journal of the Royal Anthropological Institute of Great Britain and Ireland* 42 (December 1912): 437–49.

42. Diana Taylor, "Dancing with Diana: A Study in Hauntology," *TDR: The Drama Review* 43, no. 1 (1999): 59–78, 64.

43. For more on the embodied effects of haunting, ghosts, and specters related to legacies of abusive systems of power and resistance to such legacies, see Avery

Gordon, *Ghostly Matters: Haunting and the Sociological Imagination* (Minneapolis: University of Minnesota Press, 2008); Pierre Nora, "Between History and Memory: Les Lieux de Memoire," in "Memory and Counter-Memory," special issue, *Representations* 26 (1989): 7–24; Taylor, "Dancing with Diana"; Larasati, *The Dance That Makes You Vanish*; Joseph Roach, *Cities of the Dead—Circum-Atlantic Performance* (New York: Columbia University Press, 1996); and Todd R. Ochoa, "Versions of the Dead: Kalunga, Cuban-Kongo Materiality, and Ethnography," *Cultural Anthropology* 22, no. 4 (November 2007): 473–502. For more on haunting as it relates to postcolonial mimesis, see Homi K. Bhabha, "Of Mimicry and Man: The Ambivalence of Colonial Discourse," in *The Location of Culture* (New York: Routledge, 1994); Michael Taussig, *Mimesis and Alterity: A Particular History of the Senses* (New York: Routledge, 1993); and James Ferguson, *Global Shadows: Africa in the Neoliberal World Order* (Durham, NC: Duke University Press, 2006).

44. Jacqueline Shea Murphy has also written about the nuanced understandings of time, efficacy, and links to ancestors in Native American stage dance in relation to violent and oppressive colonial histories. See Jacqueline Shea Murphy, *The People Have Never Stopped Dancing* (Minneapolis: University of Minnesota Press, 2007).

45. 'Okusitino Māhina and Unaisi Nobobo-Baba, "The Issue of Pacific Past and Future: A Challenge for Pacific Students and Academics in the Present," in *Researching Pacific and Indigenous Peoples: Issues and Perspectives*, ed. Tupeni L. Baba, 'Okusitino Māhina, Nuhisifa Williams, and Unaisi Nobobo-Baba (Wellington: Center for Pacific Studies, University of Auckland, 2004), 202–6.

46. See works by Sally Ness for more about the relations between bodily movement and culture, including "Bouldering in Yosemite: Emergent Signs of Place and Landscape," *American Anthropologist* 113, no. 1 (March 2011): 71–87; and "Being a Body in a Cultural Way: Understanding the Cultural in the Embodiment of Dance," in *Cultural Bodies: Ethnography and Theory*, ed. Helen Thomas and Jamilah Ahmed (Malden, MA: Blackwell, 2008), 123–44.

47. Kaplan, *Neither Cargo nor Cult*, 137; see also Thomas, *In Oceania*.

48. For more about the importance of loloma in shaping iTaukei culture and tradition, see Thomas, *In Oceania*, 178.

49. Sefo Avaiki, interview with the author (Victoria, BC, August 2011). Teaiwa has also noted the performance of hyper-heteromasculinity as precolonial warrior in the South Pacific. See Katerina Teaiwa, "Niu Mana, Sport, Media and the Australian Diaspora," in *New Mana: Transformations of a Classic Concept in Pacific Languages and Cultures*, ed. Matt Tomlinson and Ty P. Kāwika Tengan (Acton: ANU Press, 2016), 107–30.

50. José Esteban Muñoz, "Ephemera as Evidence: Introductory Notes to Queer Acts," *Women and Performance* 8, no. 2 (1996): 10.

51. Sociologist Avery Gordon reminds me that the past may haunt the embodied present, but as feminist scholar Elizabeth Grosz has theorized, the embodied

present is indeterminate and plays a role in the future as much as the past. See Gordon, *Ghostly Matters*; and Elizabeth Grosz, *Becomings: Explorations in Time, Memory, and Futures* (Ithaca, NY: Cornell University Press, 1999).

52. Adria L. Imada, *Aloha America: Hula Circuits through the U.S. Empire* (Durham, NC: Duke University Press, 2012), 24.

53. Nabobo-Baba, *Knowing and Learning*, 1–23.

54. Ibid., 25.

55. Damiano Logaivau, interview with the author (Suva, Fiji, September 2012). A lali is a carved wooden drum traditionally and currently used for a number of purposes including meke. Only one lali is traditionally used in the meke.

56. Nabobo-Baba, *Knowing and Learning*, 23.

57. Starting in the late nineteenth century, the British Commonwealth directed state-level forced adoption as a way to populate Australia with racially superior "good white stock." My mother was one of as many as 250,000 cases of inhumane conditions and abuse that the institutionalization of forced adoption enabled. For more on Australia's institutionalization of forced adoption and the resulting trauma, see Australia, Attorney General's Department, "National Apology for Forced Adoption," 2010, accessed June 27, 2017, https://www.ag.gov.au/About/ForcedAdoptionsApology/Pages/default.aspx; and Christine A. Cole, "Stolen Babies—Broken Hearts: Forced Adoption in Australia, 1881–1987" (PhD diss., University of Western Sydney, 2013).

58. Dwight Conquergood, "Performance as a Moral Act: Ethical Dimensions of the Ethnography of Performance," *Literature in Performance* 5, no. 2 (1985): 6.

59. I am grateful to Rebecca Rossen for this insight.

60. For more about love and colonialism, see Elizabeth Povinelli, *The Empire of Love: Toward a Theory of Intimacy, Genealogy, and Carnality* (Durham, NC: Duke University Press, 2006). See also Ann Laura Stoler, *Carnal Knowledge and Imperial Power: Race and the Intimate in Colonial Rule* (Berkeley: University of California Press, 2002).

61. I made two trips to Vancouver and Victoria prior to going to Fiji and a third trip to Canada's west coast after the trip to Fiji to do follow-up interviews and bring gifts of gratitude to my friends and interlocutors.

62. These abuses are echoed in a letter to Commodore Bainimarama from Human Rights Watch and the International Trade Union Confederation dated December 4, 2012. In the letter Bainimarama is criticized for several human rights abuses that include rights abuses that occurred during and after the 2006 coup, such as censorship, control of the media, and limiting freedom of expression, assembly, and association; rights-restricting labor decrees (for example, the Employment Relations Amendment Decree of 2011 and the Essential Industries Decree of 2011); interference in the judiciary, preventing its independence; torture; attacks on journalists; physical abuse of detainees; arbitrary arrest; and detention by security

personnel. See Brad Adams and Sharan Burrow, "Joint Letter to Commodore Bainimarama Regarding Ongoing Rights Abuses in Fiji," *Human Rights Watch* (December 2012), 1–6. On the official policy of censorship, see Media Industry Development Decree 2010. Public Emergency Regulations were in place until weeks after being repealed. Further restrictions on citizens' rights to freedom of speech and assembly were announced in January 2012 with Public Order (Amendment) Decree 2012. The decree enabled increased control over those perceived to be critical of the government. According to this decree, a permit was required for meeting in a public place or building. Police were given power to disperse private gatherings if necessary for maintaining public safety, public order, and essential supplies and services. See also Adams and Burrow, "Joint Letter to Commodore Bainimarama."

63. P. L. T. Smith, *Decolonizing Methodologies: Research and Indigenous Peoples* (New York: Zed Books, 2013).

64. Donna Haraway quoted in Dwight Conquergood, "Performance Studies: Interventions and Radical Research," *TDR: The Drama Review* 46, no. 2 (2002): 146.

65. Deidre Sklar, *Dancing With the Virgin: Body and Faith in the Fiesta of Tortugas, New Mexico* (Berkeley: University of California Press, 2001); Sally Ann Ness, *Body, Movement, and Culture: Kinesthetic and Visual Symbolism in a Philippine Community*, Series in Contemporary Ethnography (Philadelphia: University of Pennsylvania Press, 1992); Priya Srinivasan, *Sweating Saris: Indian Dance as Transnational Labor* (Philadelphia: Temple University Press, 2011); Garcia, *Salsa Crossings*.

66. Foster, "Worlding Dance–An Introduction," 4. Sachs and his contemporaries, such as dance critic John Martin, applied so-called objective scientific theories of social evolution to their ethnographic writing about dance. Their approach used dance to ethnocentrically posit the social evolutionary view that all societies were on parallel paths of development that began with savage and primitive societies and ended with civilized and sophisticated societies.

67. Nabobo-Baba, *Knowing and Learning*, 122.

68. Virginia R. Dominguez, "For a Politics of Love and Rescue," *Cultural Anthropology* 15, no. 3 (2000): 388.

69. Muñoz, "Ephemera as Evidence," 10.

70. Drawing from Diana Taylor's *The Archive and the Repertoire*, I treat the archive not as neutral but, rather, as another site for European imperial control in terms of the way materials are selected, classified, and presented. As such, following cultural studies scholar Ann Cvetkovich, I treat these cultural texts as containing rich deposits of feeling and emotion. See Diana Taylor, *The Archive and the Repertoire: Performing Cultural Memory in the Americas* (Durham, NC: Duke University Press, 2003); and Ann Cvetkovich, *An Archive of Feelings: Trauma, Sexuality, and Lesbian Public Cultures* (Durham, NC: Duke University Press, 2003).

71. Ilaitia S. Tuwere, *Vanua: Towards a Fijian Theology of Place* (Suva: Institute of Pacific Studies, University of the South Pacific, 2002), 155.

72. See Shea Murphy, *The People Have Never Stopped Dancing*; Savigliano, "Worlding Dance"; Srinivasan, *Sweating Saris*; Larasati, *The Dance That Makes You Vanish*; and Garcia, *Salsa Crossings*.

73. See Conquergood, "Performance Studies," 145–56.

74. Larasati, *The Dance That Makes You Vanish*, 9.

75. For more about the larger nation-state and global implications of inclusion and exclusion, see Larasati, *The Dance That Makes You Vanish*.

76. See Narmala Halstead, Eric Hirsch, and Judith Okely, *Knowing How to Know: Fieldwork and the Ethnographic Present* (New York: Berghahn Books, 2008).

77. Logaivau's dialect is from the Macuata province of Vanua Levu (the second-largest island of Fiji, north of Viti Levu) near Seaqaqa. He uses a spelling of meke to denote a different pronunciation that softens the "k" sound used in the Bauan dialect.

Chapter 1. Meke in a Changing Imperial World

1. Dorothy Sara Lee conducted research on the music and traditional religious practices in Verata, Fiji, during the mid-1970s. Through interviews, she found that during the height of luveniwai activity between 1890 and 1930, several powerful daunivucu emerged. She interviewed two daunivucus who were initiated into the soqosoqo vaka luveniwai in the 1920s and notes the persistence of beliefs about the possession of tutelary spirits, who create meke through the entranced daunivucu. Her research suggests the demise of luveniwai activity in the 1940s. See Lee, "Music Performances," 172.

2. G. C. Henderson, *Fiji and the Fijians, 1835–1856* (Sydney: Angus and Robertson, 1931), 300.

3. Ann Laura Stoler, *Along the Archival Grain: Epistemic Anxieties and Colonial Common Sense* (Princeton, NJ: Princeton University Press, 2009), 4.

4. Taylor, *The Archive and the Repertoire*, 19.

5. According to Claudia Knapman, the first European women and children were the families of London Missionary Society missionaries from Tahiti who arrived in 1809–10. See Knapman, *White Women in Fiji*, 1.

6. J. Waterhouse, *The King and People of Fiji* (Honolulu: University of Hawai'i Press, 1997).

7. Although many iTaukei explained to me that the protocols originated in pre-Christian meke performed in relation to ancestor worship, for some daunivucus, many of these protocols still exist, either as Christianized protocols or because of a residual concern about ancestor vengeance.

8. His description suggests the daunivucu is visited in the night by the spirit world and muses (for example, from Nairai [a man] and Thikombia-i-ra [a woman]),

who transmit the meke chant and dance through the daunivucu's dream. In this account, Williams alleges that some Fijians believed the gift of creating meke was hereditary and others believed Fijians gifted, or passed on, the ability to create meke. During my research, Fijians expressed hope that I would learn more about the potential hereditary role of the daunivucu as a mataqali (clan responsible for a certain task), which is a branch of the larger social unit called the yavusa that shares a common ancestral spirit (kalou vu). Other Fijians I interviewed believed that being a daunivucu is a gift. See Rev. Thomas Williams, Rev. James Calvert, and George Stringer Rowe, *Fiji and the Fijians: The Islands and Their Inhabitants* (London: Alexander Heylin, 1858), 113.

9. Waterhouse quoted in Henderson, *Fiji and the Fijians*, 1931.

10. Matt Tomlinson, *In God's Image: The Metaculture of Fijian Christianity* (Berkeley: University of California Press, 2009).

11. Ibid., 39–40. See also Hocart, "On the Meaning of Kalou."

12. Williams, Calvert, and Rowe, *Fiji and the Fijians*.

13. Ibid., 166.

14. Williams also describes some meke as having "a buffoon . . . whose grotesque movements elicit immense applause." Williams, Calvert, and Rowe, *Fiji and the Fijians*, 164.

15. See Fergus Clunie, *Fijian Weapons and Warfare* (Suva: Fiji Times and Herald, 1977), 38. See also Kim Gravelle, *Fiji's Times: A History of Fiji* (Suva: Fiji Times, 1983), 22.

16. These women's war meke were also recorded by early beachcombers in 1809. See Clunie, *Fijian Weapons and Warfare*, 38.

17. Clunie, *Fijian Weapons and Warfare*, 36.

18. Adrienne Kaeppler, personal communication with the author (Toronto, ON, August 2012).

19. Williams, Calvert, and Rowe, *Fiji and the Fijians*, 116.

20. For more details about the war, which began in 1843, and major shifts caused by Cakobau's conversion to Christianity, see Marshall Sahlins, *Islands of History* (Chicago: University of Chicago Press), 1985, 38.

21. Ibid., 39.

22. Ibid., 39–40.

23. Ibid., 37.

24. Ibid., See also Marshall Sahlins, "The Return of the Event, Again; with Reflections on the Beginnings of the Great Fijian War of 1843 to 1855 Between the Kingdoms of Bau and Rewa," *Clio in Oceania: Towards a Historical Anthropology*, ed. Aletta Biersack (Washington, DC: Smithsonian Institution Press, 1991), 37–99.

25. Ibid., 39–40.

26. N. Thomas, *In Oceania*, 198.

27. D. Scarr, *Fragments of Empire: A History of the Western Pacific High Commission, 1877–1914* (Canberra: Australian National University Press, 1967).

28. In his efforts to be recognized as Tui Viti, Cakobau became responsible for increasing debt and the threat of takeover. He initially offered to cede the Fijian Islands to the United Kingdom in 1852 if they would assume responsibility for the debt and he could retain the title of Tui Viti. They initially declined because Cakobau was not recognized as paramount leader of Fiji by his fellow chiefs. Instead, Melbourne's Polynesia Company paid the debt in 1868 in exchange for two hundred thousand acres of land from Cakobau and six chiefs. After the exchange, hundreds of settlers arrived, particularly from Melbourne. See Scarr, *Fragments of Empire*, 14–15.

29. Minutes on Admiralty to C.O., 8 November 1872, CO 83/1, quoted in ibid., 20.

30. Ibid.

31. Ibid.

32. The following is an excerpt from the Instrument of Cession:

INSTRUMENT OF CESSION of the Islands of Fiji by Thakombau, styled Tui Viti and Vunivalu, and by the other high Chiefs of the said Islands, to Her Most Gracious Majesty Victoria, by the Grace of God of the United Kingdom of Great Britain. . . . WHEREAS the Fijian chief Thakombau, styled Tui Viti and Vunivalu, and other high chiefs of the said islands, are desirous of securing the promotion of civilisation and Christianity, and of increasing trade and industry within the said Islands; AND WHEREAS it is obviously desirable in the interests as well of the native as of the white population, that order and good government should be established therein.

Fiji, "Instrument of Cession of the Islands of Fiji," *Gazette* (1874).

33. Kaplan, *Neither Cargo nor Cult*.

34. This allowed chiefs to orient economic production to meet the needs of the colonial government and themselves. Michael C. Howard, *Fiji: Race and Politics in an Island State* (Vancouver: University of British Columbia Press, 1991), 25.

35. Kaplan, *Neither Cargo nor Cult*; Howard, *Fiji: Race and Politics in an Island State*, 25.

36. Structures such as this, along with smaller structures and groupings of people, were to a degree adopted throughout Fiji owing to the influence of the British colonial system of indirect rule. See Tanner, "Colo Navosa," in *Oceania*, 1996.

37. Kirstie Close-Barry, "A National Church Built in 'Primitive' Culture: Communalism, Chiefs and Coins," in *A Mission Divided: Race, Culture and Colonialism in Fiji's Methodist Mission* (Canberra: ANU Press, 2015), 37–52.

38. Ibid.

39. Nicholas Thomas, "Sanitation and Seeing: The Creation of State Power in Early Colonial Fiji," *Comparative Studies in Society and History* 32, no. 1 (1990): 149–70. Missionaries sought to accelerate the evolution of Fijians toward individualism and economic independence in order to receive tithes from Fijian churchgoers and improve the church's system of financial self-support in Fiji. Close-Barry, "A National Church Built in 'Primitive' Culture."

40. For more on British colonial anxieties about iTaukei ritual-authority in the period after annexation, see Kaplan, *Neither Cargo nor Cult*.

41. This is in reference to two CSO Correspondence Files held at the National Archives of Fiji: 109/63 "Crime: Draunikau Practice, Sentence for"; and 109/134 "Draunikau: Reports Regarding Practice of." The files are part of the "F" Series 1 1931–1958 Classification Scheme with correspondences written between 1934 and 1937. I acknowledge the generous permission of the Fiji National Archives to quote these files.

42. Section 64 of the Native Regulation Board was written in 1927, but the colonial administration continued to use it in the 1930s to regulate and criminalize Fijians engaging in non-Christian beliefs and practices.

43. Thomas Williams, quoted in "Provincial Constable v. Niumaia Sorocala—Charge: Kalourere, December 30, 1936," CSO File 109/63, no. 416/36.

44. Fiji, "Draunikau—Reports Regarding Practice Of," Correspondence Files, "F" Series 1 1931–1958 Classification Scheme, File 109/134 (Suva, Fiji: Colonial Secretary's Office, 1934–1937), National Archives of Fiji.

45. On the shark god, see Lee, "Music Performances." The Kauvadra Mountain district in the northern part of Viti Levu was the site of an earlier "Tuka" movement that colonials deemed a threat to colonial governance. The colonial administration removed and relocated the Drauniivi people involved to Kadavu in the late nineteenth century, where colonials believed the worship of ancestors would be eradicated. For more on the "Tuka" movement, see Kaplan, *Neither Cargo nor Cult*.

46. Fiji, "Draunikau—Reports Regarding Practice Of."

47. Ibid.

48. See Kaplan, *Neither Cargo nor Cult*, 132, for more about the links between ritual rites such as luveniwai and anticolonial sentiments. Kaplan also notes that luveniwai prosecutions occurred throughout the 1930s due to fears of anticolonial dissension.

49. See, respectively, Fiji, "Crime: Draunikau Practice, Sentence For," Correspondence Files, "F" Series 1 1931–1958 Classification Scheme, File 109/63 (Suva, Fiji: Colonial Secretary's Office, 1935–1937), National Archives of Fiji; Robert E. Nicole, *Disturbing History: Resistance in Early Colonial Fiji* (Honolulu: University of Hawai'i Press, 2011); Kaplan, *Neither Cargo nor Cult*, 50, 68.

50. Armstrong goes on to give an account of a luveniwai yaqona ceremony:

> Firstly, three men guard the yaqona bowl, and one stands erect to one side of the bowl. Secondly, when the yaqona is ready for drinking, one of the three seated stands up, and faces the leader, salutes and then kneels before the bowl to receive the cup for bearing to the leader. Having received the yaqona he faces the leader fully erect and bears the cup toward him. The leader then decides where the first cup is to be poured out, either at the foot of a post of the house where the meeting is held or outside. The second cup is poured out at the same place. These two cups are for the spirit, so that their wishes may be granted. They do not clap their hands as customary in yaqona ceremonies, but tap the mat as each cup is drunk. After the two cups have been poured out as stated above, the leader drinks the next cup and so on in order of seniority in the Society, until every member or so called members have drunk the yaqona. Then the leader begins to narrate fearsome stories of how the spirit that he serves visited him in his dream and told him several important matters. This is told to the assembly for fear lest they lose their respect for him" (CSO File 109/134, 1934–37).

51. Fiji, "Draunikau—Reports Regarding Practice Of."
52. Fiji, CSO File 25/1, part 2—"Savusavu District Annual Report (Suva, Fiji, 1937), 3.
53. Apolosi Nawai started the Viti Kabani (Fiji Company) in 1913 on behalf of the "itaukei" (people or owners of the land) and in opposition to colonial economic exploitation of Fijians. Colonial administrators viewed his economic leadership and his methods for gaining effectiveness and power (accruing mana) by aligning his actions with the will of Christian God and kalou as threats to colonial and chiefly order because he attained the simultaneous standing of iTaukei and chief in the eyes of Fijians (Kaplan, *Neither Cargo nor Cult*, 136–37). Colonials often compared Apolosi to the "Tuka" movement that was, as Kaplan has put it, a "colonial construction of disorder" involving ancestor worship at the end of the nineteenth century (Kaplan, *Neither Cargo nor Cult*, 2–6).
54. CSO File 109/63 1936–37, "'Luveniwai' and 'Draunikau,'" March 8, 1937.
55. Ibid.
56. Fiji, "Crime: Draunikau Practice, Sentence For."
57. The language colonial authorities used in Fiji demonstrates the borrowing of other British colonial ideas about witchcraft in order to establish Fiji's legal protocols for abolishing worship of ancestral spirits.
58. Kaplan, *Neither Cargo nor Cult*.
59. For example, Sir Basil Thomson, who was a scholar and colonial administrator in Fiji in the late nineteenth century, was critical of missionary bias and wrote "scientifically" about Fijian customs to help preserve them. Sir Basil Thomson,

Bolton Glanvill Corney, and James Stewart, *The Fijians: A Study of the Decay of Custom* (W. Heinemann, 1908).

60. Anthropologist A. M. Hocart explained in 1912 that while initially human, Fijians assigned these founders to bodies of animals, humans, earth, water, mountains, and trees. Hocart, "On the Meaning of Kalou."

61. Ibid.

62. According to Kim Gravelle, the first mentions of the Degei origin story do not appear until 1892. Researcher Peter France has argued the origin story was "born of missionary parentage." See Kim Gravelle, *Fiji's Times*, 7. See also A. Capell and R. H. Lester, "Local Divisions and Movements in Fiji," *Oceania* 11, no. 4 (1941): 313–41.

63. Capell and Lester, "Local Divisions and Movements in Fiji."

64. C. J. Morey, "Wrecked on the Voyage to Lau," *Journal of the Polynesian Society* 41, no. 164 (1932): 310–11.

65. My grandfather was a professor of mining and metallurgical engineering (University of Queensland and McGill University), but he also published and presented on topics related to culture. He was on the Board of Trustees at the Fiji Museum (1938–45) and on the basis of his interests in Fijian culture, according to his CV, gave an address to University of Queensland's Overseas Students Association titled "Fiji and Its Peoples" in 1956. Professor F. T. M. White, Application for Appointment as Vice-Chancellor, University of Queensland (January 28, 1959), in personal possession. In addition to this crossing between colonial administrator and academic, the Suva Rotary Club appears to have been a hub of such intermingling between scientists and colonial administrators. For example, my grandparents retained a condensed copy of a paternalistic address by colonial administrator R. H. Lester to the Suva Rotary Club titled "Effect of War on Fijian Society" in which he used a social evolutionary perspective to outline the dangers of foisting "our democratic ideals on the Fijian, and thereby ruthlessly break[ing] down his organized form of society without giving evolution a chance to complete its job." See R. H. Lester, "Effect of War on Fijian Society," n.d., 5.

66. Lakemba is also heavily influenced by Tongan traditions, including the poetic song-dance called the lakalaka. It is possible the author observed a lakalaka. It is also worth noting the author treats the song-dance in a somewhat ahistorical way. The author recounts a performance he observed in 1929 and uses it as evidence for his arguments about a later time period. Henderson, *Fiji and the Fijians*, 70–71.

67. White, Application for Appointment as Vice-Chancellor, University of Queensland (January 28, 1959).

68. My grandfather, with his family, left Fiji on September 5, 1945, for British Malaya to rehabilitate the tin mines after World War II.

69. Ann Laura Stoler, *Carnal Knowledge and Imperial Power: Race and the Intimate in Colonial Rule* (Berkeley: University of California Press, 2002), 188.

70. Ibid.

71. Tess Marian White, "South Sea Island Memories," n.d., in personal possession. Spelling and punctuation of the original have been maintained.

72. Thomas quoted in Imada, *Aloha America*, 6.

73. Draunikau is translated as "the pointing of the leaf" in my grandmother's memoirs and "leaf of a tree" in the CSO file 109/63 but is defined more recently in a Fijian-English dictionary by Ronald Gatty as "black magic" and "the practice of witchcraft." See Gatty, *Fijian-English Dictionary*, 72. My iTaukei interlocutors also associated draunikau with "black magic" or "witchcraft."

74. Tuwere, *Vanua*.

75. CSO File 25/1 Part 2—"Savusavu Districts Annual Report 1937, Native Affairs: Political and General," January 18, 1938, 3.

76. On the basis of files from the Colonial Secretary's Office housed at the National Archives of Fiji, it is clear that by the 1930s efforts were put in place to control the movements of iTaukei by drawing iTaukei into a tax-paying work force (CSO File 7 1934), providing labor for industry such as tourism, agriculture (CSO File 25/1 1937 and File 83/10 1934), and mining (CSO File 111/28 1938). In the early years of colonization (1879–1916), Indian indentured labor was brought to Fiji to avoid exploiting the labor of the Native population. See Knapman, *White Women in Fiji*.

77. This quote is from a condensed copy of an address by colonial administrator R. H. Lester to the Suva Rotary Club titled "Effect of War on Fijian Society," n.d., 4. While I do not know the exact date of the address, the contents of the address indicate it was made between 1941 and 1945, prior to the end of World War II in the Pacific Theater.

78. Stephanie Lawson, *Tradition versus Democracy in the South Pacific: Fiji, Tonga and Western Samoa* (New York: Cambridge University Press, 1996), 46.

79. Tuwere, *Vanua*, 68.

80. Stoler, *Carnal Knowledge and Imperial Power*.

81. Lynda Newland, "Religion and Politics: The Christian Churches and the 2006 Coup in Fiji," in *The 2006 Military Takeover in Fiji: A Coup to End All Coups?*, ed. Jon Fraenkel, Stewart Firth, and Brij V. Lal (Canberra: Australian National University Press, 2009), 203.

Chapter 2. Governing Meke

1. For more on Fiji's 2006 military coup, see Fraenkel and Firth, "Fiji's Coup Syndrome."

2. iTaukei have rights to between 83 and 87 percent of the land in Fiji. Fraenkel and Firth, "Fiji's Coup System," 451.

3. The Fiji Labor Party based their politics on labor and individual rights (as opposed to communal ones) and common-roll (one person, one vote) electoral

politics. They were opposed to past approaches to communal constituencies whereby electors registered themselves on the basis of ethnicity and then voted for a candidate within their respective ethnic group. The party also opposed the use of Christianity and divinity to inform political decisions. For all of these reasons, the Fiji Labor Party was a serious threat to the chiefly and Christian status quo.

4. N. Thomas, *In Oceania*, 52.

5. Kelly and Kaplan, *Represented Communities*.

6. Agamben, *Homo Sacer*.

7. Tomlinson, *In God's Image*, 8; Lal, "Fiji Islands."

8. Kelly and Kaplan, *Represented Communities*. Fifty-five days later, the coups' leaders had negotiated the release of eighteen hostages (including Chaudhry) on the premise that they would have amnesty and that Fiji's military (led by Voreque Bainimarama) would ensure a revision of the constitution to secure iTaukei as paramount rulers of Fiji with special legal rights and privileges.

9. Newland, "Religion and Politics," 203.

10. Ibid., 190.

11. Ibid.

12. Toni O'Loughlin, "Journalists Expelled as Fiji Coup Leader Cracks Down on Media," *The Guardian*, April 14, 2009.

13. iTaukei men and women wear a sulu (a rectangular cloth wrapped around the waist). The sulu is used by some to identify themselves in opposition to foreigners and as Methodist. I observed that Christian iTaukei men who are Roman Catholic, Seventh-Day Adventist, or from another Pentecostal and evangelical church in Fiji often wear pants.

14. I traveled everywhere with my family because I was still nursing my daughter, Imogen.

15. iTaukei Institute of Language and Culture, email to Ministry of Education, copied to author, July 17, 2012.

16. "Convention for the Safeguarding of the Intangible Cultural Heritage," accessed November 26, 2018, http://portal.unesco.org/en/ev.php-URL_ID=17716&URL_DO=DO_TOPIC&URL_SECTION=201.html.

17. Tuwere, *Vanua*. In his 2002 book, Tuwere writes about two protests: those who see the past as barbarous and evil and the lotu (church) as the new and only way forward (with no past), and those who seek multiracialism and view all defense of any particular racial group or religious persuasion as racist and discriminatory. The iTaukei Institute's safeguarding of culture and heritage constitutes a third, post-2002 protest amid increasing charismatic and multiracial pressures.

18. Lynn Stephen, "The Creation and Re-creation of Ethnicity: Lessons from the Zapotec and Mixtec of Oaxaca," *Latin American Perspectives* 23, no. 2 (Spring 1996): 17–37.

19. "Fiji Cultural Intangible Heritage | Department of Heritage & Art." I received ethical approval from the Institute of iTaukei Language and Culture (under Ministry of iTaukei Affairs) and the Department of Culture and Heritage (under Ministry of Education). These are the government bodies directly responsible for ICH activities in Fiji. Sekove Bigitibau, "Country Reports: Safeguarding Intangible Cultural Heritage—Case 2: Fiji," Meeting Report for the Pacific Sub-regional Network Meeting for Intangible Cultural Heritage Safeguarding Nadi, Fiji (Apia: UNESCO, April 27–28, 2010).

20. Barbara Kirshenblatt-Gimblett, "Intangible Heritage as Metacultural Production," *Museum International* 56, nos. 1–2 (May 2004): 52–65.

21. Adrienne L. Kaeppler, *Lakalaka, A Tongan Masterpiece of Performing Arts* (Nuku'alofa: Vava'u Press, 2012).

22. R. J. Coombe, S. Fish, and F. Jameson, *The Cultural Life of Intellectual Properties: Authorship, Appropriation, and the Law* (Durham, NC: Duke University Press, 1998).

23. Ibid.

24. Kirshenblatt-Gimblett, "Intangible Heritage as Metacultural Production," 61.

25. Park Seong-Yong, "Issues and Tasks of an International Collaboration Regarding the Implementation of the 2003 Convention for the Safeguarding of the Intangible Cultural Heritage," Meeting Report for the Pacific Sub-regional Network Meeting for Intangible Cultural Heritage Safeguarding Nadi, Fiji (Apia: UNESCO, April 2010), 21.

26. Ibid. Safeguarding is viewed as a specific technique that is community based and addresses ethnocentrism resulting from past dichotomies established by cultural heritage preservation between Western "high" culture and "nonhigh" culture from developing regions. See Seong-Yong, "Issues and Tasks of an International Collaboration," 19–20.

27. While the Convention stresses community-based viability and not authenticity (see Seong-Yong, "Issues and Tasks of an International Collaboration," 21), inherent in the convention are dichotomies between past (traditional) practices that need safeguarding and present (contemporary) practices that have emerged from impacts of tourism, urbanization, religious shifts, power shifts, and multi-racialism that are not deemed to be in need of safeguarding.

28. Shea Murphy, *The People Have Never Stopped Dancing*, 29.

29. Ibid., 41.

30. In my meeting with Sekove Degei Bigitibau, he explained that many view the role of chief as being at the top of a hierarchy. He drew me a diagram that exemplified what he felt was a more accurate depiction of the role of chief at the center of a circular construct. He explained that everything a villager iTaukei does is for the chief. But the chief, in turn, must be responsible for the well-being of the

villagers. He argues that the circular image is a better way of depicting the mutual responsibilities. From my observations and what I have read in the National Archive of Fiji, it seems that there is probably not one unilaterally correct image to depict the relationship. Rather, the image would probably shift from village to village, with some chiefs being more or less responsive to villagers needs. See also Bigitibau, "Country Reports: Safeguarding Intangible Cultural Heritage—Case 2: Fiji," 40.

31. Sekove Bigitibau, "The Challenge to Fijian Methodism—the Vanua, Identity, Ethnicity and Change" (master's thesis, University of Waikato, 2007), 88–89.

32. Bigitibau, "Country Reports: Safeguarding Intangible Cultural Heritage—Case 2: Fiji."

33. Dance scholar Rachmi Diyah Larasati makes a similar connection between global attempts to protect diversity (through programs such as UNESCO) and local state violence in Indonesia. See Larasati, *The Dance That Makes You Vanish*, 23–24.

34. iTaukei Institute email to author, November 8, 2012.

35. Ministry of Education email to author, July 24, 2012.

36. Stoler, *Along the Archival Grain*, 28.

37. Ibid., 69.

38. Marcus Banks, *Ethnicity: Anthropological Constructions* (London: Routledge, 1996), 186.

39. Bigitibau, "Country Reports: Safeguarding Intangible Cultural Heritage—Case 2: Fiji."

40. The census demarcates iTaukei as racially separate from Tongans, Samoans, Rotumans, Chinese, Europeans, part Europeans, and other peoples living in Fiji (see, for example, Fiji Bureau of Statistics 2007 Census). However, the idea that iTaukei are themselves of a single line of descent is already problematic, since intermarriage between other Pacific peoples has gone on for generations.

41. Kelly and Kaplan, *Represented Communities*.

42. This question reclaims the sensing and moving body as opposed to asking "what the body is," which serves to define and stabilize bodies in order to govern them. See Erin Manning, *Politics of Touch* (Minneapolis: University of Minnesota Press, 2007), xv.

43. Hereniko, "Dancing Oceania," 32–41.

44. Ibid., 36.

45. Stevenson, "The Festival of Pacific Arts," 32.

46. Laura Marks, *The Skin of the Film: Intercultural Cinema, Embodiment, and the Senses* (Durham, NC: Duke University Press, 2000), 7.

47. After philosopher Epeli Hau'ofa passed away, Dr. Hereniko, who spoke of Hau'ofa as a friend and mentor, came to the Oceania Center to carry out Hau'ofa's vision for the center. Hereniko, interview with the author (Suva, Fiji, June 2012).

48. The production is based on research conducted in Fiji's Lau Islands by Director Dr. Vilsoni Hereniko.

49. Hereniko, personal communication with the author (Nov. 16, 2017). Peter Rockford Espiritu and Igelese Ete went to Honiara to promote the inclusion of the Oceania Center at the festival. They were accepted on the condition they self-produce and self-fund their travel. Hereniko was instrumental in acquiring the funds from the vice president at University of the South Pacific. Espiritu, Skype interview with the author (Dec. 12, 2017).

50. Logaivau, Skype interview with the author (Nov. 25, 2017); Espiritu, Skype interview with the author (Dec. 12, 2017).

51. Hereniko, "Dancing Oceania."

52. Espiritu, Skype interview with the author (Dec.12, 2017).

53. I observed "Teivovo" on three separate occasions in Fiji: the Cultural Center in Pacific Harbour, *Drua: The Wave of Fire* at University of the South Pacific in Suva, and at the Outrigger on the Lagoon resort in Sigatoka. According to the director of the *Drua* production, its use was intended to create a common experience of excitement and recognition. Hereniko, in conversations with the author (Suva, Fiji, June 2012).

54. In 1939 the captain of the rugby team, Ratu Sir George Cakobau (great-grandson of Ratu Seru Cakobau, who unified all of Fiji by the mid-1800s and ceded Fiji to the British in 1874) recommended his team adopt the Teivovo (then referred to as cibi, or war victory dance) when they went for their first tour of New Zealand, so that the Fiji team would have a war dance to match the New Zealand's All Blacks' haka. See blog post by Oceanic Developers, "History," *Official Website of Fiji Rugby Union*, accessed November 24, 2018, https://www.fijirugby.com/rugby-house/history/. Ratu Manoa Rasigatale transformed Teivovo from a cibi to a bole (challenge to war). See KoiNadi and Manoa Rasigatale, "The Bole—Manoa Rasigatale—We Ni Yava," YouTube, March 10, 2013, accessed December 7, 2017, https://www.youtube.com/watch?v=tjg7jeOp-qM.

55. Quoting Manoa Rasigatale, "iTaukei are known warriors. That means we naturally respond to harsh commands with words of deep meaning." See KoiNadi and Rasigatale, *The Bole.*

56. KoiNadi Rasigatale, *The Bole.*

57. Vilsoni Hereniko and Peter Rockford Espiritu codirected the *Drua* production, and Igelese Ete was musical director.

58. According to Fergus Clunie, there are two types of clubs used for club dances, the spurred kiakavo and the gugu. According to Clunie, these clubs were rarely used as fighting weapons but are often carved of heavy hardwoods and sometimes light softwoods stained to resemble hardwoods with bindings of coir sinnet. See Clunie, *Fijian Weapons and Warfare*, 51.

59. The untranslated lyrics were given to me by Logaivau, the daunivucu who staged the Teivovo for *Drua: Wave of Fire*. I have found a translation of the same lyrics by Manoa Rasigatale. See KoiNadi and Rasigatale, *The Bole*.

60. According to Wendy Ratawa, differences in aesthetics align with different regions in Fiji. The Bauan style of meke is linear, whereas the Labasa style from Macuata province is "circular and moving out." See Wendy Margaret Ratawa, "Na Iri Masei: A Preliminary Investigation of Music and Culture in Labasa Fiji" (undergraduate thesis, Deakin University, 1986), 68; Logaivau, interview with the author (Suva, Fiji, October 2012).

61. See introduction, note 3.

62. Peni, interview with the author (Suva, Fiji, October 2012).

63. Ibid.

64. Etueni Tagivakatini, interview with the author (Suva, Fiji, July 2012).

65. Tagivakatini, Sadrishan Velaidan, Epeli Tuibeqa, and Tulevu Soronakadavu, interviews with the author (Suva, Fiji, July 2012).

66. Velaidan, interview with the author (Suva, Fiji, July 2012).

67. Boro, interview with the author (Suva, Fiji, July 2012).

68. Peni, interview with the author (Suva, Fiji, July 2012).

69. Vakarau means "get ready!"

70. Peni, interview with the author (Suva, Fiji, July 2012).

71. Although Fiji has in the past discriminated against men having sex with men, Section 26 (3) (a), page 19, clearly states that the 2013 Constitution of the Republic of Fiji now protects "Right to Equality and Freedom from Discrimination" regardless of "sex, gender, sexual orientation, gender identity and expression." See Fiji, "Section 26: Right to Equality and Freedom from Discrimination—Constitution of the Republic of Fiji," 2013, http://www.fiji.gov.fj/Policy-Dev/Fijian-Constitution.aspx.

72. Manning, *Politics of Touch*, 113.

73. Rasigatale's dance group was referred to as "Dancetheatre of Fiji" in an interview with one of the group's initial performers (Iosefo Kaliova, interview with the author [Deuba, Fiji, August 2012]). However, a photo of the opening day performance of the Cultural Center, housed at the National Archives of Fiji, has the group named "Fiji Dance Group."

74. I attended three full shows at the Cultural Center in July 2012.

75. Beqa is an island off the coast of Viti Levu, not far from Pacific Harbour.

76. In contrast to the idea espoused by the host at the Cultural Center that firewalking is something that only men do, I discovered a picture of a woman performing firewalking on Laucala Island on November 18, 1978, for a cabinet minister tour, courtesy of National Archives of Fiji.

77. Iosefo Kaliova, interview with the author (Pacific Harbour, Fiji, August 2012).

78. Fraenkel and Firth, "Introduction."

79. Ibid.

80. Jonathon Prasad, "The Good, the Bad and the Faithful: The Response by Indian Religious Groups," in *The 2006 Military Takeover in Fiji: A Coup to End All Coups?*, ed. Jon Fraenkel, Stewart Firth, and Brij V. Lal (Canberra: Australian National University Press, 2009); Pacific Islands Forum Secretariat, "Forum Chair on Suspension of Fiji Military Regime from PIF—Pacific Islands Forum Secretariat," *Forumsec*, 2009, http://www.forumsec.org/pages.cfm/newsroom/press-statements/2013/2009/forum-chair-on-suspension-of-fiji-military-regime-from-pif.html.

81. Fraenkel and Firth, "Introduction."

82. Jon Fraenkel and Stewart Firth, "The Fiji Military and Ethno-Nationalism: Analyzing the Paradox," in *The 2006 Military Takeover in Fiji: A Coup to End All Coups?*, ed. Jon Fraenkel, Stewart Firth, and Brij V. Lal (Canberra: Australian National University Press, 2009), 117–38.

83. "Fiji Day Address by H. E. Ratu Epeli Nailatikau," Fijian Government, Suva, Fiji, October 10, 2012.

84. Manning, *Politics of Touch*, xvii.

85. Master Lai Veikoso, interview with the author (Suva, Fiji, September 2012).

86. In addition to observing these meke in Fiji in performance and rehearsal and interviewing some of the dancers and the director of the Conservatorium of Music about the meke, I learned both of these meke at the University of Hawai'i at Mānoa during Oceania Dance Theatre's 2015 Asia Pacific Dance Festival residency. Unfortunately, the meaning of the meke was not clear to the Oceania Dance Theatre dancers or the Conservatorium dancers whom I had interviewed in Fiji.

87. I recognized the Rotuman Tautoga owing to my conversations with my Rotuman mentor and friend Sefo Avaiki and the videos and demonstrations he shared with me on Vancouver Island at various times in my life. I also learned some of the Tautoga from Vilsoni Hereniko at the University of Hawai'i at Mānoa in 2015 during the Asia Pacific Dance Festival.

88. Letila Mitchell, interview with the author (Suva, Fiji, August 2012).

89. Statistically speaking, most iTaukei are Methodist. See Fiji, Bureau of Statistics, 2007.

90. Veikoso, interview with the author (Suva, Fiji, August 2012).

91. Fiji Arts Council (Ministry of Culture and Heritage) organizes projects like exhibitions. Veikoso, interview with the author (Suva, Fiji, September 2012).

92. Veikoso, interview with the author (Suva, Fiji, September 2012).

93. According to the Fiji Bureau of Statistics, tourism earnings in 2010 were 1,194.4 (million Fiji dollars) and in 2011, earnings were 1,286.5 (million Fiji dollars). That is a significant portion of the gross domestic product for those years, at 5,218.3 for 2010 and 5,633.4 for 2011 (current prices million Fiji dollars). See Fiji, Fiji Bureau of Statistics, 2014. Literature prior to independence also shows efforts by the tourism

industry to promote meke as friendly, safe, and reflective of the past. National Archives of Fiji, "Tourist Topics," *Colonial Secretary's Office Correspondence Files, "F" Series 1 1931–1958 Classification Scheme* (File 116/28, Suva, Fiji).

94. The slogan for Tourism Fiji is "Fiji: Where Happiness Finds You." The slogan encourages visitors to come to Fiji to feel welcome, happy, and safe. See Fiji, "PM Bainimarama—2014 National Budget Announcement," November 8, 2013, http://www.fiji.gov.fj/Media-Center/Speeches/2014-NATIONAL-BUDGET-ANNOUNCEMENT.aspx.

95. Imada, *Aloha America*, 10.

96. Veikoso, interview with the author (Suva, Fiji, September 2012).

97. Marshall Sahlins notes that Bauans governed Fiji by war and force. See Marshall Sahlins, "The Return of the Event, Again; with Reflections on the Beginnings of the Great Fijian War of 1843 to 1855 between the Kingdoms of Bau and Rewa," in *Clio in Oceania: Towards a Historical Anthropology* (Washington, DC: Smithsonian Institution Press, 1991), 61; Sahlins, *Islands of History*, 49.

98. Melanesian Spearhead Group is an intergovernmental organization to facilitate trade and economic development negotiations between Fiji, Papua New Guinea, Solomon Islands, and Vanuatu.

Chapter 3. Meke in Multicultural Canada

1. For more on diverse articulations and characterizations of diaspora, see James Clifford, "Diasporas," *Cultural Anthropology* 9, no. 3 (1994): 302.

2. Canada and Fiji have a direct colonial connection via Fiji's first governor, Sir Arthur Hamilton Gordon, who was governor of New Brunswick before Fiji.

3. Canada's GDP was USD 42,157.93 per capita compared with Fiji's GDP per capita at USD 5,153.35. World Bank country profiles (2016), http://databank.worldbank.org/indicator/NY.GDP.PCAP.CD, accessed June 20, 2017. There are limits to this measure of prosperity in that it does not measure nonmonetary wealth.

4. Haunting here links with larger performance studies, postcolonial studies, and anthropological literature on mimesis. See Taylor, "Dancing with Diana"; Larasati, *The Dance That Makes You Vanish*; Bhabha, "Of Mimicry and Man"; Taussig, *Mimesis and Alterity*; Ferguson, *Global Shadows*.

5. Paul Gilroy, *The Black Atlantic: Modernity and Double Consciousness* (Cambridge, MA: Harvard University Press, 1993), 4.

6. Carrie Noland, "Introduction," in *Migrations of Gesture*, ed. Carrie Noland and Sally Ann Ness (Minneapolis: University of Minnesota Press, 2008).

7. Multiculturalism emerged in 1971 out of a prior political awareness of the need for bilingualism and biculturalism to recognize and support Canada's British and French heritage. By the 1980s, however, almost half of Canada's population was not of British or French heritage. Canada adopted multiculturalism as a political,

ideological, and practical tool to recognize and support Canada's increasingly diverse citizenship.

8. Inspired by the work of Laura Marks on intercultural cinema, I use the term intercultural as she does to "indicate a context that cannot be confined to a single culture." It refers to a dialogic process of movement and transformation between cultures. See Marks, *The Skin of the Film*, 6–7.

9. Erik Christensen, "Revisiting Multiculturalism and Its Critics" *The Monist* 95, no. 1 (2012): 33–48.

10. Canada, Canadian Multicultural Act, Section 3 (1) *(d)*, http://laws-lois.justice.gc.ca/eng/acts/C-18.7/FullText.html (accessed June 19, 2017).

11. Canada, Canadian Multicultural Act, Section 5 (1) *(g)*.

12. Bonnie Urciuoli, "Producing Multiculturalism in Higher Education: Who's Producing What and for Whom," *International Journal of Qualitative Studies in Education* 12, no. 3 (July 1, 1999): 287–98, 295.

13. Rugby is a national sport in Fiji and a legacy of the British Empire. For many of the Fijians I spoke with, rugby is intertwined in how they identify as Fijian, regardless of descent.

14. Statistics Canada, Government of Canada, "Immigrant Population by Selected Places of Birth, Admission Category and Period of Immigration, Canada, Provinces and Territories, Census Metropolitan Areas and Areas Outside of Census Metropolitan Areas, 2016 Census," October 27, 2017, http://www12.statcan.gc.ca/census-recensement/2016/dp-pd/dv-vd/imm/index-eng.cfm.

15. This estimated number does not account for subsequent generations born in Canada of Fiji-born parents and those not of Fijian descent who have married Fiji-born immigrants who also identify with this diaspora.

16. Lal, "Fiji Islands.

17. A technique described by Donu. Donu, interview with the author (Vancouver, BC, January 2012).

18. Donu, interview with the author (Vancouver, BC, January 2012).

19. This description of the vakamalolo meke came from observing a recorded performance of the dance, learning the dance myself, and then discussing the movement with Donu. At the time of our interview, Donu had been in Canada for roughly ten years. Donu, interview with the author (Vancouver, BC, January 2012).

20. The dance is being performed to a recorded song titled "Meda Mai Ia." The song is a blend of Fijian culture, Christianity, and Western influences.

21. Damiano Logaivau (dauvivucu and manu manu ni meke) in email correspondence with the author (July 2013).

22. Logaivau, interview with the author (Pacific Harbour, Fiji, July 2012).

23. Donu, interview with the author (Vancouver, BC, January 2012).

24. Donu, interview with the author, and focus group with meke performers (Vancouver, BC, January 2012).

25. Photographs of the event also show the same multicultural cast of female meke dancers wearing saris for the performance of a separate contemporary Indian dance. These dances performed side by side indicate a space within Fiji's Canadian diaspora to articulate Fijian identifications with Indian culture and heritage. Yet, while Fijian Canadians of iTaukei descent performed contemporary Indian dance and Fijian Canadians of Indian descent performed meke, the dance forms remained distinct.

26. Donu, interview with the author (Vancouver, BC, August 2011).

27. Donu, interview with the author (Vancouver, BC, January 2012).

28. See Tamarisi Yabaki's doctoral thesis, "Women's Life in a Fijian Village" (PhD diss., University of Canberra, 2006). Also, for structural violence against women in Fiji, see the World Bank, "Pacific Regional Connectivity Program," 2016, accessed June 20, 2017, http://documents.worldbank.org/curated/en/807961475636945724/pdf/ITM00194-P159297-10-04-2016-1475636942080.pdf.

29. Donu, interview with the author (Vancouver, BC, August 2011).

30. Adrienne Kaeppler, personal communication with the author (Toronto, ON, August 2012).

31. Urciuoli, "Producing Multiculturalism in Higher Education, 289.

32. A. Marguerite Cassin, Tamara Krawchenko, and Madine VanderPlatt, *Racism and Discrimination in Canada Laws, Policies and Practices* (Halifax: Atlantic Metropolis Center, 2007), 8–9.

33. The name "Fiji Cultural Center" is a pseudonym to protect the identities of my interlocutors.

34. Member of Fijian diaspora, interview with the author (Vancouver, BC, August 2011).

35. I refer to this festival as the "first" Fiji Day festival not because it is superior to the second but because it had been an annual event for ten years before the "second" festival was added. The two festival names are pseudonyms, used to maintain anonymity and increase clarity in the discussion.

36. Foster, "Worlding Dance—An Introduction." See also Savigliano, "Worlding Dance," 170.

37. In 2011, Greek Fest, hosted by the Vancouver Island Greek community, took place August 26 to 28 and September 2 to 5 in Victoria, BC. The two weekends offered ongoing dance performances from groups representing regions from around the world.

38. Statistics Canada, "Canada's Ethnocultural Portrait: The Changing Mosaic," 2001, http://www12.statcan.ca/english/census01/products/analytic/companion/etoimm/canada.cfm.

39. Va'a, director and founder of Pearl of the South Pacific Polynesian Dance Group, interview with the author (Victoria, BC, September 2011).

40. Hereniko, "Dance as a Reflection of Rotuman Culture," 135.
41. Ibid., 141.
42. Ibid., 135.
43. Ibid., 138.
44. Peni Tavutonivalu, interview with the author (Victoria, BC, August 2011).
45. Because Black Rose already received permission to alter and contemporize the ancestral chant, others do not need to seek permission to use the Black Rose version of the chant when choreographing new meke to it.
46. Teaiwa, "South Asia Down Under."
47. Va'a, interview with the author (Victoria, BC, August 2011).
48. Canada, "Annual Report on the Operation of the Canadian Multiculturalism Act 2015–2016: Diversity and Inclusion in Action," accessed June 19, 2017, http://canada.pch.gc.ca/eng/1487171871820.
49. "Pacific Peoples' Partnership," accessed November 30, 2017, http://pacificpeoplespartnership.org/.
50. Teaiwa, "South Asia Down Under," 224.
51. Sefo Avaiki, Rotuman member of the Oceanic diaspora on Vancouver Island, in discussion with the author (Victoria, BC, August 2011).
52. Avaiki, interview with the author (Victoria, BC, August 2011).
53. Avaiki, interview with the author (Victoria, BC, August 2011).
54. N. Thomas, *In Oceania*, 4.
55. Vilsoni Hereniko (writer and director), *Drua: The Wave of Fire* (performances at University of the South Pacific, Suva, Fiji), June 14–23, 2012. This history of voyaging for this production was based on research conducted by Hereniko in Fiji's Lau Islands.
56. Kelly and Kaplan, *Represented Communities*. See also Knapman, *White Women in Fiji*.
57. N. Thomas, *In Oceania*, 4.
58. Ibid., 5.
59. Pan-Oceanic relations have recently been revived, supported, and fostered by the work of philosopher Epeli Hau'ofa; scholar, director, and filmmaker Vilsoni Hereniko; Pacific Peoples' Partnership in Victoria, BC, and University of British Columbia's Museum of Anthropology in Vancouver, BC, which hosted the 9th Pacific Arts Symposium held August 5–8, 2013, in partnership with the Musqueam Indian Band, the Pacific Islands Museums Association, and the Pacific Peoples' Partnership.
60. Murray, "Haka Fracas?"
61. Focus group with members of the Fijian diaspora in discussion with author (Victoria, BC, January 2012).
62. Avaiki in discussion with the author (Victoria, BC, January 2012).

63. For more about South Pacific mana in diasporic performances of masculinity in sport, see Teaiwa, "Niu Mana, Sport, Media and the Australian Diaspora."
64. Piot, *Nostalgia for the Future*, 16.
65. Ibid.

Chapter 4. Spiriting Meke

1. Because of the Canadian government's system of parental support, which provided my partner with paternity pay for the duration of our time in Fiji, I was able to travel with my partner, our young son, Eagon, and our newborn daughter, Imogen.
2. During my time in Namatakula, villagers were commenting that the sea levels were rising.
3. Judith Batibasaga, interview with the author (Namatakula, Fiji, July 2012).
4. For more on how the past haunts the embodied present, see Gordon, *Ghostly Matters*; and Nora, "Between History and Memory."
5. The ancestral spirits are only destabilizing in light of such colonial legacies of order and control over bodies.
6. N. Thomas, *In Oceania*, 51.
7. Ibid., 198.
8. This form of political and religious resistance to the dominance of colonial and Methodist authority is well documented by N. Thomas, *In Oceania*; Kaplan, *Neither Cargo nor Cult*; and Nicole, *Disturbing History*.
9. An early colonial example of a rejection of this power structure occurred between 1913 and 1917 when some Fijians rejected custom and tradition in an attempt to install the Viti Kabani (Fiji Company). The Viti Kabani, created by Apolosi R. Nawai, was anticolonial and antichiefly. According to Thomas (*In Oceania*), the aim was to promote native production and sales and remove the white colonizers who were benefiting economically as middlemen. This became known as the Apolosi movement and was an ongoing source of anxiety for the British colonial administration even into the 1930s (see chapter 1).
10. Hereniko, "Dancing Oceania."
11. Piot, *Nostalgia for the Future*, 62.
12. Jacqueline Ryle, *My God, My Land: Interwoven Paths of Christianity and Tradition in Fiji* (Farnham, UK: Ashgate, 2010), 159.
13. Ibid.
14. In two comprehensive theses on meke written over thirty years ago, there is not one mention of meke in relation to devil worship or witchcraft. See, for instance, Linda Good, "Fijian Meke: An Analysis of Style and Content" (master's thesis, University of Hawai'i, 1978); and Ratawa, *Na Iri Masei*. Dorothy Sara Lee, in her doctoral thesis, discusses how meke is feared and revered by some Fijians who associate it with sorcery. See Lee, "Music Performances." It would appear that

language associating meke with devil worship and witchcraft is increasing alongside conversions to evangelical and charismatic Christian churches.

15. Tomlinson, *In God's Image*, 142.

16. The hotel appears to be one of the earliest examples of tourism in Fiji (File 116/28, "Tourist Topics" in CSO files, National Archives of Fiji, Suva).

17. Judith Batibasaga, interview with the author (Namatakula, Fiji, July 2012).

18. N. Thomas, *In Oceania*, 204.

19. Meke are often performed with many dancers (even hundreds) according to some accounts documented at the National Archives of Fiji and from conversations I had with meke dancers and daunivucus.

20. Jiuta Tokula explained that the movements in the dance were precise killing techniques used in warfare. Jiuta Tokula, interview with the author (Komave, Fiji, July 2012).

21. Jiuta Tokula also identifies as "lavo," as part of a tako-lavo traditional moiety relationship that extends familiar kin relations to socially distant individuals. Tokula, interview with the author (Komave, Fiji, July 2012). See Adrian Tanner for more about the tako-lavo relationship in "Colo Navosa."

22. Comedic aspects of meke have been documented by Vilsoni Hereniko in "Polynesian Clowns and Satirical Comedies" (PhD diss., University of the South Pacific, 1990). This particular comedic improvisation added to the dismissive sentiments expressed by some of the members of this group that meke performance is mostly for tourist entertainment and a show.

23. Although they could not perform in the village, I heard the group practicing their meke chants on two occasions, I observed two of their performances at the nearby Warwick Hotel in Navola, and I interviewed three members of the group.

24. Vasutoga, interview with the author (Namatakula, Fiji, July 2012).

25. Tokula, interview with the author (Komave, Fiji, July 2012).

26. Tanner, "Colo Navosa," 232.

27. Ibid.

28. Ibid.

29. Tokula, interview with the author (Komave, Fiji, July 2012).

30. Roach, *Cities of the Dead*, 26.

31. Taylor, *The Archive and the Repertoire*.

32. I use the term "land gods" here because that is the term used by the dancer with whom I was in conversation.

33. Tokula, interview with the author (Komave, Fiji, July 2012).

34. Ibid.

35. Bale, interview with the author (Namatakula, Fiji, July 2012).

36. Tomlinson, *In God's Image*, 9.

37. See Kaplan, *Neither Cargo nor Cult*, for more about how Thurston oversaw the deportation of the Drauniivi people from the north of Viti Levu to Kadavu Island south of Viti Levu for ancestral worship.

38. Sahlins, "The Return of the Event, Again." According to Sahlins, Rewa and Bau were the most powerful states in the Fiji Islands by the mid-nineteenth century. See ibid., 49. Bau eventually won universal hegemonic control but not before the bloody and destructive war that involved the massacre of Suva's Bauan villagers (ibid., 51).

39. Both quotations from Epeli Tuibeqa, interview with the author (Suva, Fiji, July 2012).

40. Jacques Derrida, *Specters of Marx: The State of the Debt, the Work of Mourning, and the New International*, trans. Peggy Kamuf (New York: Routledge, 1994).

41. Three years after having this conversation with a dancer at the Conservatorium of Music, I had the experience of learning this meke in Hawai'i. It was taught by Fiji's Oceania Dance Theatre at Pacific Arts Festival, University of Hawai'i at Mānoa, July 2015. This follow-up experience deepened my understanding of the meke chant and movements.

42. The translation of these lyrics was generously provided by Master Lai Veikoso, email correspondence with the author (November 26, 2018).

43. Selai Eramasi and Anna Masara, interview with the author (Suva, Fiji, July 2012).

44. Several dancers, directors, and daunivucus in Canada and Fiji spoke about sevu ni meke as a key stage of the meke process. It is described as a rite of passage for dancers who are performing meke for the first time and for the village chief. Some Fijians are adapting new approaches to sevu ni meke for urban situations where there is no chief or village structure in place. While in Fiji, I learned of two occasions when the role of the director took the place of village chief in sevu ni meke: for a theatrical performance and for a new meke created by the iTaukei Institute.

45. Vilsoni Hereniko and Peter Rockford Espiritu codirected the production, with Igelese Ete as musical director.

46. A. M. Hocart noted that Seaqaqa ("Senggangga in Mdhuata") was the "scene of the last heathen revolt" against Christianity and colonialism. See Hocart, "On the Meaning of Kalou," 437–49, 438.

47. Damiano Logaivau, interview with the author (Suva, Fiji, June 2012).

48. Logaivau, interview with the author (Suva, Fiji, August 2012).

49. Logaivau, interview with the author (Suva, Fiji, June 2012).

50. Ibid.

51. Ibid.

52. Logaivau, interview with the author (Pacific Harbour, Fiji, October 2012).

53. Logaivau, interview with the author (Pacific Harbour, Fiji, September 2012).

54. "Isa" defined by N. Thomas, *In Oceania*, 185; and by Logaivau, interview with author (Suva, Fiji, September 2012).

55. One of my interview questions asked those I consulted for memories of watching meke that were affectively intense. Without prompting, eight dancers and directors knowledgeable about meke independently brought up Logaivau as an example of evoking such intensity in meke.

56. Meke performer, interview with the author (Suva, Fiji, August 2012).

57. Meke dancer, interview with the author (Suva, Fiji, October 2012).

58. N. Thomas, *In Oceania*, 208.

Chapter 5. Generating Efficacy

1. See Tomlinson, "Retheorizing Mana," for more about how Fiji scholars have addressed verbal expressions producing mana but have not addressed the nonverbal, sonic, rhythmic, and movement-based expressions of the body as sources of mana. For example, in his analysis of the shifts in meaning and usage of mana over time, Tomlinson includes the verbal utterances described in 1830s to 1840s ethnographic accounts of Fiji by the United States Exploring Expedition, which were prior to the translation of the Bible into the Bauan Fijian dialect, and current accounts of contemporary Fijian ritual in Indigenous Fijian discourse. Yet movements, rhythms, and sounds are not absent from the evidence, just absent from analysis. Tomlinson does not analyze, for instance, how cobo (cup-clapping of hands that produces a deep, resonant sound-rhythm-motion), which is also embedded in ritual performance as a feeling of deep gratitude and respect, generates efficacy. Cobo, as sonic movement, puts into motion feelings of gratitude and respect as part of the efficacy mana produces. Anthropologist Andrew Arno has written about cobo and tabua in Fiji as important elements of ritual expression. See Arno, "'Cobo' and 'Tabua' in Fiji: Two Forms of Cultural Currency in an Economy of Sentiment," *American Ethnologist* 32, 1 (2005): 46–62.

2. Logaivau referred to mana in meke as "achieving an intended purpose." Fiji linguist Paul Geraghty has also defined mana in those terms. See Tomlinson, "Retheorizing Mana." Katalina Fotofili, dancer and choreographer with Oceania Dance Theatre, spoke of how mana is generated from meke expressions. Fotofili, interview with the author (Mānoa, Hawaiʻi, August 2015).

3. I thank performance and dance studies scholar Royona Mitra for suggesting a future exploration of the possible relationship between Fijian notions of mana and Hindu concepts of prana as life-giving force, or breath, that may have been brought to Fiji by its Indian immigrant population.

4. Māhina and Nobobo-Baba, "The Issue of Pacific Past and Future."

5. See Shea Murphy, *The People Have Never Stopped Dancing*, for more about the immediacy of achieving an intended purpose in the healing effects of Canadian First Nations dance.

6. Martha Kaplan's research on Fiji water exports in relation to the spirit of the gift demonstrates the complex interconnections between local and global economic systems. See Martha Kaplan, "Fijian Water in Fiji and New York: Local Politics and a Global Commodity," *Cultural Anthropology* 22, no. 4 (2008): 685–706.

7. The notion of Fijian mana as active and effective has a long history of investigation. For sociologist Marcel Mauss, ethnographers Arthur Maurice Hocart, Roger Keesing, Marshall Sahlins, and Tomlinson, Fijian mana denotes a power of bringing-into-existence and action that creates truth. Tomlinson refers to effective action in J. L. Austin's performative sense of accomplishing an action that has been articulated. Tomlinson, "Retheorizing Mana," 176. See also, Marcel Mauss, *The Gift: Forms and Functions of Exchange in Archaic Societies*, trans. Ian Cunnison (Mansfield Center, CT: Martino, 2011); A. M. Hocart, *Lau Islands, Fiji* (Honolulu: Bernice P. Bishop Museum, 1929); Roger M. Keesing, "Conventional Metaphors and Anthropological Metaphysics: The Problematic of Cultural Translation," *Journal of Anthropological Research* 41, no. 2 (1985): 201–17. See also Roger M. Keesing, "Rethinking 'Mana,'" *Journal of Anthropological Research* 40, no. 1 (1984): 137–56; Sahlins, *Islands of History*; Tomlinson, "Retheorizing Mana"; Matt Tomlinson, "Mana in Christian Fiji: The Interconversion of Intelligibility and Palpability," *Journal of the American Academy of Religion* 75, no. 3 (2007): 524–53; and Sahlins, *Islands of History*, 38.

8. Mana in the Fijian Bible was translated as miracles. While ancestor and spirit gods once enriched mana through ritual expression, the adaptation of such concepts into the Bible replaced local spirits with the "one true" Christian God and translated other spirits, specifically tevoro and timoni, into "devils" and "demons." Tomlinson, *In God's Image*, 40; Tomlinson, "Retheorizing Mana." See also Hocart, "On the Meaning of Kalou."

9. N. Thomas, *In Oceania*. Here I also note that things themselves can have a vitality. See Jane Bennett, *Vibrant Matter: A Political Ecology of Things* (Durham, NC: Duke University Press, 2010). Meke costumes, spears, clubs, fans, and the lali were all involved in activating the energy of a meke.

10. Scholars include sociologist Émile Durkheim, anthropologist E. E. Evans-Pritchard, anthropologist Asesela Ravuvu, and theologian Ilaitia Tuwere. Anthropologist Asesela Ravuvu defines mana as "power to effect" and theologian Ilaitia Tuwere writes, "mana is power or influence, not physical and in a way supernatural, but it shows itself in physical force or excellence which a person possesses." Ravuvu and Tuwere quoted in Tomlinson, "Retheorizing Mana," 177.

11. Tomlinson, "Retheorizing Mana," 180.

12. Lynda Newland, "Turning the Spirits into Witchcraft: Pentecostalism in Fijian Villages," *Oceania* 75, no. 4 (September 2004): 1–18. See also Claudia Massey, "Old Gods and New Horizons: Cultural Performance and Religious Syncretism in Modern Fiji" (PhD diss., University of Warwick, 2010).

13. I spoke with one iTaukei Methodist who explained to me that he had left Fiji and moved to Hawai'i because of post-2014 election discrimination against iTaukei Methodists and those of chiefly status. Interview with the author (Honolulu, Hawai'i, July 2015).

14. For more about the complexities of transgressive and resistant forces of social efficacy in performance studies literature, see Jon McKenzie, *Perform or Else: From Discipline to Performance* (Routledge: New York), 2001.

15. Logaivau confirmed that my mother was the subject of the three verses, although the lyrics do not indicate that.

16. Tomlinson, "Retheorizing Mana," 174.

17. Tupeni Baba, "In Search of Yalomatua" (speech, Niusawa Secondary School Prize Giving Ceremony, Niusawa, Fiji, November 26, 1993).

18. Ibid.

19. See Royona Mitra, *Akram Khan: Dancing New Interculturalism* (New York: Palgrave Macmillan, 2015).

20. Logaivau, interview with the author (Suva, Fiji, June 2012).

21. Logaivau, interview with the author (Pacific Harbour, Fiji, October 2012).

22. Ibid.

23. Yabaki, "Women's Life in a Fijian Village."

24. Taylor, *The Archive and the Repertoire.*

25. Logaivau, interview with the author (Pacific Harbour, Fiji, June 2012).

26. Ibid.

27. Ibid.

28. Ibid.

29. Mark Franko, "Given Movement: Dance and the Event," in *Ritual and Event: Interdisciplinary Perspectives* (Milton Park, UK: Taylor & Francis, 2006), 132.

30. Mauss, *The Gift*, 1.

31. Franko, "Given Movement," 132.

32. Mauss, *The Gift*, 6.

33. Franko, "Given Movement," 132.

34. Jacques Derrida, *Given Time: I. Counterfeit Money*, trans. Peggy Kamuf (Chicago: University of Chicago Press, 1994).

35. Mauss, *The Gift*, 12.

36. Logaivau, Skype interview with the author (February 20, 2017).

Chapter 6. Performing Indeterminacy

1. Igelese Ete is also founder and director of Pasifika Voices Choir, a teacher, conductor, and composer. He was choirmaster for Peter Jackson's film *The Lord of the Rings: The Fellowship of the Ring*. He also worked with Pasifika Voices in their role as the official choir for Disney's *Moana* movie soundtrack.

2. Logaivau uses Kajal (or Kohl), a black shade cosmetic, as black face paint instead of face paint made from charcoal. Using Kajal, a South Asian cosmetic, creates a link between meke and Fijians of Indian descent that blurs the geographical and spiritual boundaries of Fijian mana. Thus, the meke is, in a sense, also enriched with the spirit and energy of a South Asian cosmetic.

3. Fumaru Fatiaki, personal communication with the author (Suva, Fiji, October 2012).

4. During British colonial rule in Fiji, the song "Isa Isa" was played with the national anthem "God Save Our Gracious Queen" at the end of radio broadcasts. See "(Fijian Farewell Song) Isa Lei Song 1957," *Matavuvale Network*, accessed June 2017, http://www.matavuvale.com/video/fijian-farewell-songisa-lei.

5. I was invited to teach modern/contemporary dance classes because the dancers were particularly interested in fusing traditions of Oceania with contemporary art practices that sometimes included Western ones. They also invited me to teach a choreographic work by one of my dance mentors, neo-expressionist Canadian choreographer David Earle (who generously gave his permission), for their production called *Life*.

6. Conquergood, "Performance as a Moral Act."

7. Dr. Mique'l Dangeli, personal communication with the author (Vancouver, BC, August 2013).

8. World Dance Alliance Americas, "Evolve + Involve: Dance as a Moving Question...," Scotiabank Dance Center, Vancouver, BC, July 29–August 4, 2013.

9. Pacific Arts Association XI International Symposium, "Pacific Intersections and Cross Currents: Uncharted Histories and Future Trends," August 6–9, 2013, Museum of Anthropology in partnership with the Musqueam Indian Band, the Pacific Peoples' Partnership, and the Pacific Islands Museums Association, University of British Columbia, Vancouver, BC.

10. My mother completed her master's degree in medical anthropology at the University of Victoria on non-Western iTaukei healing practices.

11. Conquergood, "Performance Studies," 145–56, 147.

12. Ibid., 146.

13. Ibid.

14. Conquergood, "Performance as a Moral Act."

15. Peter Brunt, "Art in Oceania Now, 1989–2012," in *Art in Oceania*, ed. Nicholas Thomas (New Haven, CT: Yale University Press, 2012), 410–39.

Bibliography

PRIMARY SOURCES

National Archives of Fiji (NAF) Manuscript Sources

Fiji. "Colonial Office Circular Memorandum—Tourism." File. Colonial Secretary's Office Correspondence Files, "F" Series 1 1931–1958 Classification Scheme. Suva, 1950.

———. "Crime: Draunikau Practice, Sentence For." Correspondence Files. "F" Series 1 1931–1958 Classification Scheme, File 109/63. Suva, Fiji: Colonial Secretary's Office, 1935–1937. National Archives of Fiji.

———. "District Commissioner, Navua—Diary for the Month of October." Monthly Diary in Correspondence Files. "F" Series 1 1931–1958 Classification Scheme. Suva, Fiji: Colonial Secretary's Office, 1934. National Archives of Fiji.

———. "Draunikau—Reports Regarding Practice Of." Correspondence Files. "F" Series 1 1931–1958 Classification Scheme, File 109/134. Suva, Fiji: Colonial Secretary's Office, 1934–1937. National Archives of Fiji.

———. "Quarterly Reports from the Mining Companies." File. Colonial Secretary's Office Correspondence Files, "F" Series 1 1931–1958 Classification Scheme. Suva, 1938.

———. "Savusavu District Annual Reports." Correspondence Files. "F" Series 1 1931–1958 Classification Scheme. Suva, Fiji: Colonial Secretary's Office, 1937. National Archives of Fiji.

———. "Tourist Topics." Colonial Secretary's Office Correspondence Files, "F" Series 1 1931–1958 Classification Scheme, File 116/28. Suva, 1958-02 1956.

Governmental and Nongovernmental Organization (NGO) Sources

Adams, Brad, and Sharan Burrow. "Joint Letter to Commodore Bainimarama Regarding Ongoing Rights Abuses in Fiji." *Human Rights Watch*, December 4,

2012. https://www.hrw.org/news/2012/12/04/joint-letter-commodore-bainima rama-regarding-ongoing-rights-abuses-fiji.

Bigitibau, Sekove. "Country Reports: Safeguarding Intangible Cultural Heritage—Case 2: Fiji." Meeting Report for the Pacific Sub-Regional Network Meeting for Intangible Cultural Heritage Safeguarding Nadi, Fiji. Apia: UNESCO, April 27–28, 2010.

Canada. "Annual Report on the Operation of the Canadian Multiculturalism Act 2015–2016: Diversity and Inclusion in Action." http://canada.pch.gc.ca/eng/148 7171871820.

———. "Canadian Multiculturalism Act." 1988. http://laws-lois.justice.gc.ca/eng/acts/c-18.7/.

———. "Canada's Ethnocultural Portrait: The Changing Mosaic." Statistics Canada, 2001. http://www12.statcan.ca/english/census01/products/analytic/companion/etoimm/canada.cfm.

———. "Ethnic Diversity Survey (EDS)." Statistics Canada, 2002. http://www23.statcan.gc.ca/imdb/p2SV.pl?Function=getSurvey&SDDS=4508.

———. "Immigrant Population by Selected Places of Birth, Admission Category and Period of Immigration, Canada, Provinces and Territories, Census Metropolitan Areas and Areas Outside of Census Metropolitan Areas, 2016 Census." Statistics Canada, October 27, 2017. http://www12.statcan.gc.ca/census-recensement/2016/dp-pd/dv-vd/imm/index-eng.cfm.

"Country Advice: Fiji." *Refugee Review Tribunal*, September 12, 2009. http://www.refworld.org/cgi-bin/texis/vtx/rwmain?page=search&docid=4f1426212&skip=0&query=%20Fiji.

Fiji. "Fijian Affairs (Amendment) Decree 2010." *Gazette* 11, no. 73 (July 2, 2010). Accessed November 26, 2018. http://www.paclii.org/fj/promu/promu_dec/fad2010210/.

———. "Fiji Cultural Intangible Heritage | Department of Heritage & Art." Accessed November 7, 2017. http://www.culture.gov.fj/?page_id=63.

———. "Fiji Government Online Portal—Constitution." Accessed October 25, 2017. http://www.fiji.gov.fj/Govt<HY><HY>Publications/Constitution.aspx.

———. "Instrument of Cession of the Islands of Fiji," *Gazette*, 1874.

———. "Land Tenure." Ministry for Local Government, Urban Development and Public Utilities. Department of Town and Country Planning, 2015. http://www.townplanning.gov.fj/index.php/planning/planning-issues/land-tenure.

———. "2007 Census of Population." Fiji Bureau of Statistics. Accessed October 25, 2017. http://www.statsfiji.gov.fj/index.php/2007-census-of-population.

———. Nailatikau, H.E. Ratu Epeli. "Fiji Day Address." Fijian Government. Suva, Fiji, October 10, 2012.

———. "PM Bainimarama—2014 National Budget Announcement." November 8, 2013. http://www.fiji.gov.fj/Media-Center/Speeches/2014-NATIONAL-BUDGET-ANNOUNCEMENT.aspx.

———. "Section 26: Right to Equality and Freedom from Discrimination—Constitution of the Republic of Fiji." 2013. http://www.fiji.gov.fj/Policy-Dev/Fijian-Constitution.asp.

Pacific Islands Forum Secretariat. "Forum Chair on Suspension of Fiji Military Regime from PIF—Pacific Islands Forum Secretariat." *Forumsec*, 2009. http://www.forumsec.org/pages.cfm/newsroom/press-statements/2013/2009/forum-chair-on-suspension-of-fiji-military-regime-from-pif.html.

"Pacific Peoples' Partnership." Accessed November 30, 2017. http://pacificpeoplespartnership.org/.

Seong-Yong, Park. "Issues and Tasks of an International Collaboration Regarding the Implementation of the 2003 Convention for the Safeguarding of the Intangible Cultural Heritage." Meeting Report for the Pacific Sub-regional Network Meeting for Intangible Cultural Heritage Safeguarding Nadi, Fiji. Apia: UNESCO, April 27–28, 2010.

World Bank. "Country Profile: Canada." World Bank, 2015. http://databank.worldbank.org/data/Views/Reports/ReportWidgetCustom.aspx?Report_Name=CountryProfile&Id=b450fd57&tbar=y&dd=y&inf=n&zm=n&country=CAN.

———. "Country Profile: Fiji." World Bank, 2015. http://databank.worldbank.org/data/Views/Reports/ReportWidgetCustom.aspx?Report_Name=CountryProfile&Id=b450fd57&tbar=y&dd=y&inf=n&zm=n&country=FJI.

———. "Pacific Regional Connectivity Program." World Bank, 2016. http://documents.worldbank.org/curated/en/807961475636945724/pdf/ITM00194-P159297-10-04-2016-1475636942080.pdf.

LATE NINETEENTH AND EARLY TWENTIETH-CENTURY PRINTED SOURCES

Capell, A., and R. H. Lester. "Local Divisions and Movements in Fiji." *Oceania* 11, no. 4 (1941): 313–41.

"The Fijians." In *Handbook of Fiji*. Suva: Fiji Government Press, 1936.

Gordon, Arthur Hamilton. *Letters and Notes Written During the Disturbances in the Highlands (Known as the Devil County) of Viti Levu, Fiji, 1876*. 2 vols. Edinburgh: Privately printed by R. & R Clark, 1876.

Henderson, G. C. *Fiji and the Fijians, 1835–1856*. Sydney: Angus and Robertson, 1931.

Hocart, A. M. *Lau Islands, Fiji*. Honolulu: Bernice P. Bishop Museum, 1929.

———. "On the Meaning of Kalou and the Origin of Fijian Temples." *Journal of the Royal Anthropological Institute of Great Britain and Ireland* 42 (December 1912): 437–49.

Lester, R. H. "Effect of War on Fijian Society." Address to the Suva Rotary Club, n.d. In personal possession.

Mann, Cecil W. "Religion and Symbolism in Fiji." *Journal of General Psychology* 23, no. 1 (1940): 169–84.

Morey, C. J. "Wrecked on the Voyage to Lau." *Journal of the Polynesian Society* 41, no. 164 (1932): 310–11.

Thomson, Basil, Bolton Glanvill Corney, and James Stewart. *The Fijians: A Study of the Decay of Custom*. W. Heinemann, 1908.

Waterhouse, J. *The King and People of Fiji*. Honolulu: University of Hawai'i Press, 1997.

Williams, Reverend Thomas, Reverend James Calvert, and George Stringer Rowe. *Fiji and the Fijians: The Islands and Their Inhabitants*. London: Alexander Heylin, 1858.

Online Video and Popular Sources

Deepika Bandhana. "10th Pacific Festival of Arts—Fiji 2." YouTube, April 13, 2009. Accessed November 8, 2017. https://www.youtube.com/watch?v=cgIWObNVdIk.

Iofinau. "Fiji Dance." YouTube, August 24, 2014. https://www.youtube.com/watch?v=RPYGZWg-N_w.

KoiNadi and Manoa Rasigatale. "The Bole—Manoa Rasigatale—We Ni Yava." YouTube, March 10, 2013. Accessed December 7, 2017. https://www.youtube.com/watch?v=tjg7jeOp-qM.

Oceanic Developers. "History." *Official Website of Fiji Rugby Union*. Accessed November 24, 2018. https://www.fijirugby.com/rugby-house/history/.

Tagata Pasifika. "2012 Festival of Pacific Arts in the Solomon Islands, Part 1." YouTube, August 16, 2012. Accessed November 8, 2017. https://www.youtube.com/watch?v=q65qHPjUoLE&feature=youtu.be.

———. "2012 Festival of Pacific Arts in the Solomon Islands, Part 2." YouTube, August 16, 2012. Accessed November 8, 2017. https://www.youtube.com/watch?v=q-k1kKm3If8&feature=youtu.be.

———. "2012 Festival of Pacific Arts in the Solomon Islands, Part 3." YouTube, August 16, 2012. Accessed November 8, 2017. https://www.youtube.com/watch?v=FQrfiQo2Jbo&feature=youtu.be.

Thumbs Up. "(Fijian Farewell Song) Isa Lei Song 1957." *Matavuvale Network*, 2014. http://www.matavuvale.com/video/fijian-farewell-songisa-lei.

Secondary Sources

Books and Articles

Adams, Tony E., and Stacy Holman Jones. "Telling Stories: Reflexivity, Queer Theory, and Autoethnography." *Cultural Studies ↔ Critical Methodologies* 11, no. 2 (April 2011): 108–16.

Agamben, Giorgio. *Homo Sacer: Sovereign Power and Bare Life*. Translated by Daniel Heller-Roazen. Stanford, CA: Stanford University Press, 1998.

Ahmed, Sara. "Happy Objects." In *The Affect Theory Reader*, edited by Greg Seigworth and Melissa Gregg, 29–51. Durham, NC: Duke University Press, 2010.

Alexeyeff, Kalissa. *Dancing from the Heart: Movement, Gender, and Sociality in the Cook Islands*. Honolulu: University of Hawai'i Press, 2009.

Arno, Andrew. "'Cobo' and 'Tabua' in Fiji: Two Forms of Cultural Currency in an Economy of Sentiment." *American Ethnologist* 32, no. 1 (2005): 46–62.

Baba, Tupeni. "In Search of Yalomatua." Speech presented at the Niusawa Secondary School Prize Giving Ceremony, Niusawa, Fiji, November 26, 1993.

Baba, Tupeni, 'Okusitino Māhina, Nuhisifa Williams, and Unaisi Nobobo-Baba, eds. *Researching Pacific and Indigenous Peoples: Issues and Perspectives*. Wellington: Center for Pacific Studies, University of Auckland, 2004.

Banks, Marcus. *Ethnicity: Anthropological Constructions*. London: Routledge, 1996.

Bennett, Jane. *Vibrant Matter: A Political Ecology of Things*. Durham, NC: Duke University Press, 2010.

Bhabha, Homi. "Of Mimicry and Man: The Ambivalence of Colonial Discourse." In *The Location of Culture*, 85–92. New York: Routledge, 1994.

Bigitibau, Sekove. "The Challenge to Fijian Methodism—the Vanua, Identity, Ethnicity and Change." Master's thesis, University of Waikato, 2007.

———. "Theologies of Mana and Sau in Fiji." In *New Mana: Transformations of a Classic Concept in Pacific Languages and Cultures*, edited by Matt Tomlinson and Ty P. Kāwika Tengan, 237–56. Acton: ANU Press, 2016.

Brennan, Teresa. *The Transmission of Affect*. Ithaca, NY: Cornell University Press, 2004.

Briggs, Charles L. "The Politics of Discursive Authority in Research on the 'Invention of Tradition.'" *Cultural Anthropology* 11, no. 4 (1996): 435–69.

Brown, Wendy. "Specters and Angels: Benjamin and Derrida." In *Politics Out of History*, 138–73. Princeton, NJ: Princeton University Press, 2001.

Brunt, Peter. "Art in Oceania Now, 1989–2012." In *Art in Oceania*, edited by Nicholas Thomas, 410–39. New Haven, CT: Yale University Press, 2012.

Buckland, Theresa Jill. "Dance, History, and Ethnography: Frameworks, Sources, and Identities of Past and Present." In *Dancing from Past to Present: Nation, Culture, Identities*, edited by Theresa Jill Buckland, 3–24. Madison: University of Wisconsin Press, 2006.

Carell, Beth D. *South Pacific Dance*. Sydney: Pacific Publications, 1978.

Cassin, A. Marguerite, Tamara Krawchenko, and Madine VanderPlatt. *Racism and Discrimination in Canada Laws, Policies and Practices*. Halifax, Nova Scotia: Atlantic Metropolis Center, 2007.

Christensen, Erik. "Revisiting Multiculturalism and Its Critics." *The Monist* 95, no. 1 (2012): 33–48.

Clifford, James. "Diasporas." *Cultural Anthropology* 9, no. 3 (1994): 302–38.

———. *Writing Culture: The Poetics and Politics of Ethnography*. Edited by George E. Marcus. Berkeley: University of California Press, 1986.

Close-Barry, Kirstie. "A National Church Built in 'Primitive' Culture: Communalism, Chiefs and Coins." In *A Mission Divided: Race, Culture and Colonialism in Fiji's Methodist Mission*, 37–52. Canberra: ANU Press, 2015.

Clunie, Fergus. *Fijian Weapons and Warfare*. Suva: Fiji Times and Herald, 1977.

Cole, Christine A. "Stolen Babies—Broken Hearts: Forced Adoption in Australia, 1881–1987." PhD diss., University of Western Sydney, 2013.

Conquergood, Dwight. "Performance as a Moral Act: Ethical Dimensions of the Ethnography of Performance." *Literature in Performance* 5, no. 2 (1985): 1–13.

———. "Performance Studies: Interventions and Radical Research." *TDR: The Drama Review* 46, no. 2 (2002): 145–56.

Coombe, R. J., S. Fish, and F. Jameson. *The Cultural Life of Intellectual Properties: Authorship, Appropriation, and the Law*. Durham, NC: Duke University Press, 1998.

Csordas, Thomas J. "Asymptote of the Ineffable: Embodiment, Alterity, and the Theory of Religion." *Current Anthropology* 45, no. 2 (April 2004): 163–85.

———, ed. *Embodiment and Experience: The Existential Ground of Culture and Self*. New York: Cambridge University Press, 1994.

Cvetkovich, Ann. *An Archive of Feelings: Trauma, Sexuality, and Lesbian Public Cultures*. Durham, NC: Duke University Press, 2003.

Deleuze, Gilles, and Félix Guattari. *A Thousand Plateaus: Capitalism and Schizophrenia*. Translated by Brian Massumi. Minneapolis: University of Minnesota Press, 1987.

Derrida, Jacques. *Specters of Marx: The State of the Debt, the Work of Mourning and the New International*. Translated by Peggy Kamuf. New York: Routledge, 1994.

Derrida, Jacques. *Given Time: I. Counterfeit Money*. Translated by Peggy Kamuf. Chicago: University of Chicago Press, 1994.

Dominguez, Virginia R. "For a Politics of Love and Rescue." *Cultural Anthropology* 15, no. 3 (2000): 361–93.

Emberson-Bain, Atu. *Labour and Gold in Fiji*. Cambridge: Cambridge University Press, 1994.

Eves, Richard. "Pentecostal Dreaming and Technologies of Governmentality in a Melanesian Society." *American Ethnologist* 38, no. 4 (2011): 758–73.

Ferguson, James. *Global Shadows: Africa in the Neoliberal World Order*. Durham, NC: Duke University Press, 2006.

Foster, Susan Leigh. "Choreographies of Gender." *Signs* 24, no. 1 (1998): 1–33.

———. "Dance Theory?" In *Teaching Dance Studies*, edited by Judith Chazin-Bennahum and Melinda Jordan, 19–34. New York: Routledge, 2005.

———. "An Introduction to Moving Bodies: Choreographing History." In *Choreographing History*, 3–21. Bloomington: Indiana University Press, 1995.

---. "Worlding Dance—An Introduction." In *Worlding Dance*, edited by Susan Leigh Foster, 1–13. New York: Palgrave Macmillan, 2009.
Foucault, Michel. "Nietzsche, Genealogy, History." In *Language, Counter-Memory, Practice: Selected Essays and Interviews*, edited by Donald F. Bouchard, 139–64. Ithaca, NY: Cornell University Press, 1980.
---. "Panopticon." In *Social Theory: Continuity and Confrontation: A Reader*, edited by Roberta Garner, 440–49. Peterborough, ON: Broadview Press, 2000.
Fraenkel, Jon, and Stewart Firth. "The Fiji Military and Ethno-Nationalism: Analyzing the Paradox." In *The 2006 Military Takeover in Fiji: A Coup to End All Coups?*, edited by Jon Fraenkel, Stewart Firth, and Brij V. Lal, 117–38. Canberra: Australian National University Press, 2009.
---. "Fiji's Coup Syndrome." In *The 2006 Military Takeover in Fiji: A Coup to End All Coups?*, edited by Jon Fraenkel, Stewart Firth, and Brij V. Lal, 449–58. Canberra: Australian National University Press, 2009.
---. "Introduction: The Enigmas of Fiji's Good Governance Coup." In *The 2006 Military Takeover in Fiji: A Coup to End All Coups?*, edited by Jon Fraenkel, Stewart Firth, and Brij V. Lal, 3–20. Canberra: Australian National University Press, 2009.
Fraenkel, Jon, Stewart Firth, and Brij V. Lal, eds. *The 2006 Military Takeover in Fiji: A Coup to End All Coups?* Canberra: Australian National University Press, 2009.
Franko, Mark. "Given Movement: Dance and the Event." In *Ritual and Event: Interdisciplinary Perspectives*, 125–37. Milton Park, UK: Taylor & Francis, 2006.
Garcia, Cindy. *Salsa Crossings: Dancing Latinidad in Los Angeles*. Durham, NC: Duke University Press, 2013.
Gatty, Ronald. *Fijian-English Dictionary: With Notes on Fijian Culture and Natural History*. Ithaca, NY: Cornell University Press, 2012.
Geertz, Clifford. "Deep Play: Notes on the Balinese Cockfight." In *Anthropological Theory: An Introductory History*, 3rd ed., edited by Jon R. McGee and Richard L. Warms, 553–74. Boston: McGraw Hill, 2004.
Gilroy, Paul. *The Black Atlantic: Modernity and Double Consciousness*. Cambridge, MA: Harvard University Press, 1993.
Good, Linda. "Fijian Meke: An Analysis of Style and Content." Master's thesis, University of Hawai'i, 1978.
Gordon, Avery. *Ghostly Matters: Haunting and the Sociological Imagination*. Minneapolis: University of Minnesota Press, 2008.
Gravelle, Kim. *Fiji's Times: A History of Fiji*. Suva: Fiji Times, 1983.
Gregg, Melissa. "An Inventory of Shimmers." In *The Affect Theory Reader*, edited by Greg Seigworth and Melissa Gregg, 1–25. Durham, NC: Duke University Press, 2010.
Grosz, Elizabeth, ed. *Becomings: Explorations in Time, Memory, and Futures*. Ithaca, NY: Cornell University Press, 1999.

Hahn, Tomie. *Sensational Knowledge: Embodying Culture through Japanese Dance.* Middletown, CT: Wesleyan University Press, 2007.

Hall, Stuart. "The Local and the Global: Globalization and Ethnicity." In *Dangerous Liaisons: Gender, Nation, and Postcolonial Perspectives*, edited by Anne McClintock. Minneapolis: University of Minnesota Press, 1997.

Hall, Stuart, and Roberta Garner. "Cultural Identity and Diaspora." In *Social Theory: Continuity and Confrontation: A Reader*, edited by Roberta Garner, 560–72. Peterborough, ON: Broadview Press, 2000.

Halstead, Narmala, Eric Hirsch, and Judith Okely. *Knowing How to Know: Fieldwork and the Ethnographic Present.* New York: Berghahn Books, 2008.

Hardt, Michael, and Antonio Negri. *Empire.* Cambridge, MA: Harvard University Press, 2001.

Hart, Michael Anthony. "Indigenous Worldviews, Knowledge, and Research: The Development of an Indigenous Research Paradigm." *Journal of Indigenous Voices in Social Work* 1, no. 1 (February 2010): 1–16.

Hau'ofa, Epeli. *We Are the Ocean.* Honolulu: University of Hawai'i Press, 2008.

Hereniko, Vilsoni. "Dance as a Reflection of Rotuman Culture." In *Rotuma Hanua Pumue: Precious Land*, 120–42. Suva: Institute of Pacific Studies, University of the South Pacific, 1991.

———. "Dancing Oceania." In *The 5th Asia-Pacific Triennial of Contemporary Art*, 32–41. Brisbane: Queensland Art Gallery Publishing, 2006.

———. "Polynesian Clowns and Satirical Comedies." PhD diss., University of the South Pacific, 1990.

Herzfeld, M. *The Body Impolitic: Artisans and Artifice in the Global Hierarchy of Value.* Chicago: University of Chicago Press, 2004.

Howard, Michael C. *Fiji: Race and Politics in an Island State.* Vancouver: University of British Columbia Press, 1991.

Imada, Adria L. *Aloha America: Hula Circuits through the U.S. Empire.* Durham, NC: Duke University Press, 2012.

Kaeppler, Adrienne L. "Dance Ethnology and the Anthropology of Dance." *Dance Research Journal* 32, no. 1 (2000): 116–25.

———. "Dances and Dancing in Tonga: Anthropological and Historical Discourses." In *Dancing from Past to Present: Nation, Culture, Identities*, edited by Theresa Jill Buckland, 25–51. Madison: University of Wisconsin Press, 2006.

———. *Lakalaka: A Tongan Masterpiece of Performing Arts.* Tonga: Vava'u Press, 2012.

———. *The Pacific Arts of Polynesia and Micronesia.* Oxford: Oxford University Press, 2008.

Kaplan, Martha. "Fijian Water in Fiji and New York: Local Politics and a Global Commodity." *Cultural Anthropology* 22, no. 4 (2008): 685–706.

---. *Neither Cargo nor Cult: Ritual Politics and the Colonial Imagination in Fiji*. Durham, NC: Duke University Press, 1995.
Kealiinohomoku, Joan. "An Anthropologist Looks at Ballet as a Form of Ethnic Dance." In *Moving History/Dancing Cultures: A Dance History Reader*, edited by Ann Dils and Ann Cooper Albright, 33–43. Middletown, CT: Wesleyan University Press, 2001.
Keesing, Roger M. "Conventional Metaphors and Anthropological Metaphysics: The Problematic of Cultural Translation." *Journal of Anthropological Research* 41, no. 2 (1985): 201–17.
---. "Rethinking 'Mana.'" *Journal of Anthropological Research* 40, no. 1 (1984): 137–56.
Kelly, John D., and Martha Kaplan. *Represented Communities: Fiji and World Decolonization*. Chicago: University of Chicago Press, 2001.
Kempf, Wolfgang, and Elfriede Hermann. "Reconfigurations of Place and Ethnicity: Positionings, Performances and Politics of Relocated Banabans in Fiji." *Oceania* 75, no. 4 (September 1, 2005): 368–86.
Kirshenblatt-Gimblett, Barbara. "Intangible Heritage as Metacultural Production." *Museum International* 56, nos. 1–2 (May 1, 2004): 52–65.
Knapman, Claudia. *White Women in Fiji, 1835–1930: The Ruin of Empire?* Sydney: Allen and Unwin, 1986.
Kymlicka, Will. "The Current State of Multiculturalism in Canada and Research Themes on Canadian Multiculturalism, 2008–2010." Citizenship and Immigration Canada, Ottawa, January 2010.
Lal, Brij V. "Fiji Islands: From Immigration to Emigration." Migration Policy Institute, April 1, 2003. https://www.migrationpolicy.org/article/fiji-islands-immigration-emigration.
Larasati, Rachmi Diyah. *The Dance That Makes You Vanish: Cultural Reconstruction in Post-Genocide Indonesia*. Minneapolis: University of Minnesota Press, 2013.
Lawson, Stephanie. *Tradition versus Democracy in the South Pacific: Fiji, Tonga and Western Samoa*. New York: Cambridge University Press, 1996.
Lee, Dorothy Sara. "Music Performances and the Negotiation of Identity in Eastern Viti Levu, Fiji." PhD diss., Indiana University, 1984.
Māhina, 'Okusitino, and Unaisi Nobobo-Baba. "The Issue of Pacific Past and Future: A Challenge for Pacific Students and Academics in the Present." In *Researching Pacific and Indigenous Peoples: Issues and Perspectives*, edited by Tupeni L. Baba, 'Okusitino Māhina, Nuhisifa Williams, and Unaisi Nobobo-Baba, 202–6. Wellington: Center for Pacific Studies, University of Auckland, 2004.
Manning, Erin. *Politics of Touch*. Minneapolis: University of Minnesota Press, 2007.
Marks, Laura. *The Skin of the Film: Intercultural Cinema, Embodiment, and the Senses*. Durham, NC: Duke University Press, 2000.

Massey, Claudia. "Old Gods and New Horizons: Cultural Performance and Religious Syncretism in Modern Fiji." PhD diss., University of Warwick, 2010.

Massumi, Brian. *Parables for the Virtual: Movement, Affect, Sensation*. Durham, NC: Duke University Press, 2002.

Mata, Fernando G. "The Multiculturalism Act and Refugee Integration in Canada." *Refuge* 13, no. 9 (February 1994): 17–20. https://refuge.journals.yorku.ca/index.php/refuge/article/view/21782.

Mauss, Marcel. *The Gift: Forms and Functions of Exchange in Archaic Societies*. Translated by Ian Cunnison. Mansfield Center, CT: Martino, 2011.

Mawyer, Alexander. "The State of Mana, the Mana of the State." In *New Mana: Transformations of a Classic Concept in Pacific Languages and Cultures*, edited by Matt Tomlinson and Ty P. Kāwika Tengan, 203–36. Acton: ANU Press, 2016.

McKenzie, Jon. *Perform or Else: From Discipline to Performance*. New York: Routledge, 2001.

Mendoza, Zoila. *Shaping Society through Dance: Mestizo Ritual Performance in the Peruvian Andes*. Chicago: University of Chicago Press, 2000.

Mitra, Royona. *Akram Khan—Dancing New Interculturalism*. New York: Palgrave Macmillan, 2015.

Miyazaki, Hirokazu. *The Method of Hope: Anthropology, Philosophy, and Fijian Knowledge*. Stanford, CA: Stanford University Press, 2004.

Muñoz, José Esteban. "Ephemera as Evidence: Introductory Notes to Queer Acts." *Women and Performance* 8, no. 2 (1996): 5–16.

———. "Feeling Brown: Ethnicity and Affect in Ricardo Bracho's *The Sweetest Hangover (and Other STDs)*." *Theatre Journal* 52, no. 1 (2000): 67–79.

Murray, David. "Haka Fracas? The Dialectics of Identity in Discussions of a Contemporary Maori Dance." In "The Politics of Dance," special issue, *Australian Journal of Anthropology* 11, no. 3 (2000): 14–26.

Nabobo-Baba, Unaisi. *Knowing and Learning: An Indigenous Fijian Approach*. Suva: Institute of Pacific Studies, University of the South Pacific, 2006.

Ness, Sally Ann. "Being a Body in a Cultural Way: Understanding the Cultural in the Embodiment of Dance." In *Cultural Bodies: Ethnography and Theory*, edited by Helen Thomas and Jamilah Ahmed, 123–44. Malden, MA: Blackwell, 2008.

———. *Body, Movement, and Culture: Kinesthetic and Visual Symbolism in a Philippine Community*. Series in Contemporary Ethnography. Philadelphia: University of Pennsylvania Press, 1992.

———. "Bouldering in Yosemite: Emergent Signs of Place and Landscape." *American Anthropologist* 113, no. 1 (March 2011): 71–87.

———. "Dancing in the Field: Notes from Memory." In *Moving History/Dancing Cultures: A Dance History Reader*, edited by Ann Dils and Ann Cooper Albright, 67–86. Middletown, CT: Wesleyan University Press, 2001.

Newland, Lynda. "Religion and Politics: The Christian Churches and the 2006 Coup in Fiji." In *The 2006 Military Takeover in Fiji: A Coup to End All Coups?*, edited by Jon Fraenkel, Stewart Firth, and Brij V. Lal, 187–208. Canberra: Australian National University Press, 2009.

———. "Turning the Spirits into Witchcraft: Pentecostalism in Fijian Villages." *Oceania* 75, no. 4 (September 2004): 1–18.

Nicole, Robert E. *Disturbing History: Resistance in Early Colonial Fiji*. Honolulu: University of Hawai'i Press, 2011.

Noland, Carrie. "Introduction." In *Migrations of Gesture*, edited by Carrie Noland and Sally Ann Ness, ix–xxviii. Minneapolis: University of Minnesota Press, 2008.

Nora, Pierre. "Between Memory and History: Les Lieux de Mémoire." In "Memory and Counter-Memory," special issue, *Representations* 26 (1989): 7–24.

Norton, Robert. "The Changing Role of the Great Council of Chiefs." In *The 2006 Military Takeover in Fiji: A Coup to End All Coups?*, edited by Jon Fraenkel, Stewart Firth, and Brij V. Lal, 97–116. Canberra: Australian National University Press, 2009.

Novack, Cynthia. *Sharing the Dance: Contact Improvisation and American Culture*. Edited by George F. Marcus and James Clifford. Madison: University of Wisconsin Press, 1990.

Ochoa, Todd R. "Versions of the Dead: Kalunga, Cuban-Kongo Materiality, and Ethnography." *Cultural Anthropology* 22, no. 4 (November 2007): 473–502.

O'Loughlin, Toni. "Journalists Expelled as Fiji Coup Leader Cracks Down on Media." *The Guardian*, April 14, 2009.

O'Shea, Janet. *At Home in the World: Bharata Natyam on the Global Stage*. Middletown, CT: Wesleyan University Press, 2007.

Piot, Charles. *Nostalgia for the Future: West Africa after the Cold War*. Chicago: University of Chicago Press, 2010.

Povinelli, Elizabeth A. *The Empire of Love: Toward a Theory of Intimacy, Genealogy, and Carnality*. Durham, NC: Duke University Press, 2006.

Prasad, Jonathon. "The Good, the Bad and the Faithful: The Response by Indian Religious Groups." In *The 2006 Military Takeover in Fiji: A Coup to End All Coups?*, edited by Jon Fraenkel, Stewart Firth, and Brij V. Lal, 209–36. Canberra: Australian National University Press, 2009.

Ratawa, Wendy Margaret. "Na Iri Masei: A Preliminary Investigation of Music and Culture in Labasa Fiji." Undergraduate thesis, Deakin University, 1986.

Reed, Susan. "The Politics and Poetics of Dance." *Annual Review of Anthropology* 27, no. 1 (1998): 503–32.

Rivera-Servera, Ramón, and Harvey Young. "Introduction: Border Moves." In *Performance in the Borderlands*, edited by Ramón Rivera-Severa and Harvey Young, 1–16. New York: Palgrave Macmillan, 2014.

Roach, Joseph. *Cities of the Dead—Circum-Atlantic Performance*. New York: Columbia University Press, 1996.
Ryle, Jacqueline. *My God, My Land: Interwoven Paths of Christianity and Tradition in Fiji*. Farnham, UK: Ashgate, 2010.
Sahlins, Marshall. *Islands of History*. Chicago: University of Chicago Press, 1985.
———. "The Return of the Event, Again; with Reflections on the Beginnings of the Great Fijian War of 1843 to 1855 between the Kingdoms of Bau and Rewa." In *Clio in Oceania: Towards a Historical Anthropology*, edited by Aletta Biersack, 37–99. Washington, DC: Smithsonian Institution Press, 1991.
Savigliano, Marta. "Worlding Dance and Dancing Out There in the World." In *Worlding Dance*, edited by Susan Leigh Foster, 163–90. New York: Palgrave Macmillan, 2009.
Scarr, D. *Fragments of Empire: A History of the Western Pacific High Commission, 1877–1914*. Canberra: Australian National University Press, 1967.
Seear, Lynne, Suhanya Raffel, and Queensland Art Gallery, eds. *The 5th Asia-Pacific Triennial of Contemporary Art*. Brisbane: Queensland Art Gallery, 2006.
Shea Murphy, Jacqueline. "Editor's Note: Doing Indigenous Dance Today." *Dance Research Journal* 48, no. 1 (April 2016): 1–8.
———. *The People Have Never Stopped Dancing*. Minneapolis: University of Minnesota Press, 2007.
Sklar, Deidre. *Dancing with the Virgin: Body and Faith in the Fiesta of Tortugas, New Mexico*. Berkeley: University of California Press, 2001.
Smith, P. L. T. *Decolonizing Methodologies: Research and Indigenous Peoples*. New York: Zed Books, 2013.
Srinivasan, Priya. *Sweating Saris: Indian Dance as Transnational Labor*. Philadelphia: Temple University Press, 2011.
Stephen, Lynn. "The Creation and Re-Creation of Ethnicity: Lessons from the Zapotec and Mixtec of Oaxaca." *Latin American Perspectives* 23, no. 2 (Spring 1996): 17–37.
Stevenson, Karen. "The Festival of Pacific Arts: Its Past, Its Future." *Pacific Arts* 25 (December 2002): 31–40.
Stewart, Kathleen. "Weak Theory in an Unfinished World." *Journal of Folklore Research* 45, no. 1 (2008): 71–82.
Stimson, Blake. "Gesture and Abstraction." In *Migrations of Gesture*, edited by Carrie Noland and Sally Ann Ness, 69–83. Minneapolis: University of Minnesota Press, 2008.
Stoler, Ann Laura. *Along the Archival Grain: Epistemic Anxieties and Colonial Common Sense*. Princeton, NJ: Princeton University Press, 2009.
———. *Carnal Knowledge and Imperial Power: Race and the Intimate in Colonial Rule*. Berkeley: University of California Press, 2002.

Tanner, Adrian. "Colo Navosa: Local History and the Construction of Region in the Western Interior of Vitilevu, Fiji." *Oceania* 66, no. 3 (March 1996): 230–51.

Taussig, Michael T. *Mimesis and Alterity: A Particular History of the Senses.* New York: Routledge, 1993.

Taylor, Diana. *The Archive and the Repertoire: Performing Cultural Memory in the Americas.* Durham, NC: Duke University Press, 2003.

———. "Dancing with Diana: A Study in Hauntology." *TDR: The Drama Review* 43, no. 1 (1999): 59–78.

Teaiwa, Katerina Martina. "Choreographing Difference: The (Body) Politics of Banaban Dance." *Contemporary Pacific* 24, no. 1 (February 12, 2012): 65–95.

———. "Niu Mana, Sport, Media and the Australian Diaspora." In *New Mana: Transformations of a Classic Concept in Pacific Languages and Cultures*, edited by Matt Tomlinson and Ty P. Kāwika Tengan, 107–30. Acton: ANU Press, 2016.

———. "South Asia Down Under: Popular Kinship in Oceania." *Cultural Dynamics* 19, nos. 2–3 (July 2007): 193–232.

Thomas, Helen. *The Body, Dance and Cultural Theory.* New York: Palgrave Macmillan, 2003.

Thomas, Nicholas. *In Oceania.* Durham, NC: Duke University Press, 1997.

———. "Sanitation and Seeing: The Creation of State Power in Early Colonial Fiji." *Comparative Studies in Society and History* 32, no. 1 (1990): 149–70.

Tomlinson, Matt. *In God's Image: The Metaculture of Fijian Christianity.* Berkeley: University of California Press, 2009.

———. "Mana in Christian Fiji: The Interconversion of Intelligibility and Palpability." *Journal of the American Academy of Religion* 75, no. 3 (2007): 524–53.

———. "Retheorizing Mana: Bible Translation and Discourse of Loss in Fiji." *Oceania* 76, no. 2 (July 1, 2006): 173–85.

Tuwere, Ilaitia S. *Vanua: Towards a Fijian Theology of Place.* Suva: Institute of Pacific Studies, University of the South Pacific, 2002.

Urciuoli, Bonnie. "Producing Multiculturalism in Higher Education: Who's Producing What and for Whom." *International Journal of Qualitative Studies in Education* 12, no. 3 (July 1, 1999): 287–98.

Yabaki, Tamarisi. "Women's Life in a Fijian Village." PhD diss., University of Canberra, 2006.

Index

Adi Cakobau School, 106
adoption, forced, 23, 193n57
affect, 15–20, 23, 27, 35, 78, 107, 125, 146, 155, 179. *See also* haunting; loloma
Agamben, Giorgio, 13
Ahmed, Sara, 191n37
Alo, Allan, 189n16
ancestor spirits. *See* Indigenous spirituality
anticolonialism, 34, 44–45, 63–66, 198n48, 212n9. *See also* colonialism; decolonization; Indigenous rights movements; postcolonialism
Apolosi movement, 44–45, 199n53, 212n9. *See also* Indigenous rights movements
Aporosa, Apo, 71
The Apostles (church), 15
The Archive and the Repertoire (Taylor), 194n70
Armstrong, A. J., 41–44, 56, 61, 199n50
Arno, Andrew, 215n1
Arts Village of Pacific Harbour, 69
Asian Development Bank, 93
Asian Pacific Bank, 15
Assemblies of God, 15, 125–30

Austin, J. L., 216n7
autoethnography, 8, 30–31
Avaiki, Sefo, 100–101, 119–20, 207n87

Baba, Tupeni, 157
Bainimarama, Voreque (Frank), 3, 13, 24, 66–73, 79–80, 92–93, 97–98, 124, 187n1, 193n62, 202n8
Bale, Kelera, 132–33
Banks, Marcus, 79
Baravilala, Livai, 146, 159, 161, 173–75
Batibasaga, Judith, 124–29, 144
Bau, 11, 38–40, 82–86, 97, 127, 206n60, 208n97, 214n38
Bavadra, Timoci, 69
Bigitibau, Sekove Degei, 71–72, 76–77, 203n30
biopolitics, 12–19, 69–70, 78–81, 87. *See also* race
Black Rose, 116, 211n45
bole, 18, 67–68, 82, 205n54. *See also* meke

Cakobau, George, 205n54
Cakobau, Ratu Seru, 38–39, 86, 197n28, 205n54

Canada: economy of, 102, 208n3; exchange between Fiji and, 6–7, 20, 70–71, 208n2, 209n15, 210n25; gender and meke in, 18, 103–9, 112, 115, 118, 121–22; multiculturalism and belonging in, 14, 100–123, 208n7. *See also* diaspora, Fijian

"Canada's Ethnocultural Portrait" (report), 113

Canadian Multicultural Program, 117

Capell, Arthur, 46

Carell, Beth Dean, 9

Catholicism, 49, 65, 127, 202n13. *See also* Christianity

censorship, 24, 70–71, 193n62

cession of Fiji to Britain, 39, 64, 67, 131, 197n32. *See also* colonialism

Chaudry, Mahendra, 70, 202n8

Christianity: biopolitics and, 14–16, 69–70; colonialism and, 5–19, 34–66, 195n7, 197n32, 198n42, 199n53, 214n46; creation of meke in the present and, 147–50, 155–58; governing meke and, 68–72, 76, 88, 96–98, 202n13; meke in Canada and, 20, 105–9, 116; opposition to, 72, 201n3, 214n46; spirituality and meke and, 5, 124–44, 212n14, 216n8. *See also* Catholicism; colonialism; Indigenous spirituality; Methodist Church

The Church War, 131

class, 35, 42, 48–49. *See also* gender; race; sexuality

club meke, 10, 56–59, 83–85, 129–31, 158–59, 162–63, 205n58. *See also* meke

Clunie, Fergus, 205n58

colonialism: cession of Fiji to Great Britain and, 197n28, 197n32; Christianity and, 5–19, 34–66, 195n7, 197n32, 198n42, 199n53, 214n46; creation of meke in the present and legacies of, 4–17, 33, 145–72; criminalization and control of meke through, 31–66, 198n42, 198n45, 198n48, 199n57, 199n59; economics of Fiji and, 18, 29–30, 42–44, 63–66, 127–29, 145–46, 155–56, 197n34, 198n39, 199n53, 201n76; indirect rule, 34, 39–40, 44–45, 63–65, 69, 76, 93, 197n34, 197n36; meke in Canada and, 101–4, 109–12, 118–23, 208n2; performance ethnography and, 3–6, 12, 21–33, 173–84; present governing of meke and, 66–99; pushback against, 12, 29, 34, 44–45, 63–66, 199n53, 212n9, 214n46; race and, 13–16, 34–35, 39–42, 48–55, 63–65, 193n57; social evolution theories and, 17, 35–36, 40, 46, 64–65, 194n66, 200n65; spirituality and meke and, 16–17, 72, 125–44, 212n5. *See also* anticolonialism; Christianity; decolonization; postcolonialism

Colonial Secretary's Office (CSO), 28–29, 32–34, 38–47, 56, 198n41, 201n76

Colonial Sugar Refinery, 12

Commonwealth (organization), 15

Conquergood, Dwight, 23, 30, 178, 181–82

Conservatorium of Music, 3, 94–98, 134

Constitution of the Republic of Fiji, 206n71

Convention for the Safeguarding of Intangible Cultural Heritage, 74–75, 203n27

Convention on Intangible Cultural Heritage, 76

Coombe, Rosemary, 74
Correspondence Files (CSO), 40–45, 198n41
coup (1987), 69–70, 110
coup (2000), 70, 187n1, 202n8
coup (2006), 3, 6, 13, 19, 66–70, 92, 187n1, 193n62
coup d'états in Fiji, 6, 19, 92
"Crime" (CSO Correspondence Files), 198n41
criminalization of meke, 34–66, 198n42. *See also* colonialism; meke; witchcraft, associations of meke with
CSO (Colonial Secretary's Office), 28–29, 32–34, 38–47, 56, 198n41, 201n76
cultural appropriation, 80, 148–49, 160, 178–81
Culture and Pacific Studies, 81
Cvetkovich, Ann, 28, 194n70

dance. *See* meke; performance ethnography
"Dancetheatre of Fiji," 206n73
Dangeli, Mique'l, 178–79
decolonization, 17, 32, 126–35, 143–44, 149–72, 177, 182. *See also* anticolonialism; colonialism; postcolonialism
Deed of Cession, 64, 131
Degei origin story, 46, 200n62
Department of Culture and Heritage, 203n19
Derrida, Jacques, 171
diaspora, Fijian: connections between Fiji and the, 70, 169–74; ethnography in the, 24, 148, 177–84; multiculturalism in Canadian and the, 6–7, 20, 100–123, 209n15, 210n25. *See also* Canada

domestic labor, 48–55, 156
Dominguez, Virginia, 27
draunikau, 41–42, 45, 55, 198n41, 201n73. *See also* Indigenous spirituality; meke
"Draunikau" (CSO Correspondence Files), 198n41
Drua (Oceania Center for Art), 81–84, 136, 141, 205n57, 206n59, 211n55
Durkheim, Émile, 216n10

Earle, David, 218n5
"Effect of War on Fijian Society" (Lester), 64, 200n65, 201n77
Empire (Hardt, Negri), 190n34
Employment Relations Amendment Decree, 193n62
ephemera, 16–23, 27–28, 144, 181
"Ephemera as Evidence" (Muñoz), 28
epistemic violence, 19–31. *See also* performance ethnography
Eramasi, Selai, 135
Erskine, John, 38, 42
Espiritu, Peter Rockford, 189n19, 205n49, 205n57, 214n45
Essential Industries Decree, 193n62
Ete, Tuilagi Igelese, 173, 189n19, 205n49, 205n57, 214n45, 217n1
ethnicity, 6–8, 13–16, 70–89, 94, 104–17, 122, 201n3. *See also* Indo-Fijians; iTaukei; race
ethnonationalism, 9–12, 69–70, 77, 92, 182
Evans-Pritchard, E. E., 216n10
Expo 2012, 98
expression, 8–10, 15–19, 27, 143

Fatiaki, Fumaru, 173–74
Festival of the Pacific Arts, 69, 80–82, 205n49

Fiji. *See* colonialism; Indo-Fijians; iTaukei; meke
Fijian Affairs Bill, 29, 64
"Fijian Affairs Decree 2010," 187n3
Fijian Canadian. *See* Canada
Fijian Cultural Center, 69, 80, 89–92
"Fijian Meke" (Good), 212n14
Fiji Arts Council, 96
Fiji Company, 199n53, 212n9
Fiji Dance Group, 90f, 206n73
Fiji Day, 67–70, 80, 92–98
Fiji Day Fest, 110–11, 210n35
FijiFest, 110–11, 210n35
Fiji First party, 71
Fiji Labor Party, 69, 201n3
Fijiwood (dance group), 95
firewalking, 89–91, 206n76
Folkfest, 100
Fotofili, Katalina, 215n2
Foucault, Michel, 84
France, Peter, 200n62
Franko, Mark, 169–70
"F" Series 1931–1958 Classification Scheme, 198n41
functionalism, 46–47

Garcia, Cindy, 25
Gatty, Ronald, 201n73
Geertz, Clifford, 191n40
gender: colonial perceptions of meke and, 35–38, 41–42, 55–61; creation of meke in the present and, 6, 10–11, 18–19, 163–65; governing of meke and, 84, 86–91, 182, 206n76; meke in Canada and, 106–9, 114–15, 118–22; performance ethnography and, 23, 174, 180. *See also* class; race; sexuality
Geraghty, Paul, 155, 215n2
gift giving, 12, 18, 21–25, 145–50, 155–58, 167–71, 175–77

"God Save Our Gracious Queen" (song), 218n4
Good, Linda, 212n14
Gordon, Arthur Hamilton, 39–40, 63, 208n2
Gordon, Avery, 192n51
Gravelle, Kim, 200n62
Great Council of Chiefs, 14, 39, 63–65, 69–70, 73, 79, 93–94, 150
Greek Fest, 113–16, 210n37
Grosz, Elizabeth, 192n51
Gucake, Netani, 19–21
Gucake Donu, Lavonne, 19–20, 106–8, 209n19

Haraway, Donna, 25
Hardt, Michael, 190n34
haunting: about, 8, 17, 192n51; governing meke and, 66–67, 76, 98; meke in Canada and, 102, 109–10, 122; performance ethnography and, 4, 146, 177; spirituality and, 126–28, 131–33, 144. *See also* affect; anticolonialism; colonialism; Indigenous spirituality; postcolonialism
Hau'ofa, Epeli, 25, 81, 183, 204n47, 211n59
Henderson, G. C., 47, 55, 200n66
Hereniko, Vilsoni, 25, 80–82, 115, 120, 136, 189n19, 204–5nn47–49, 205n57, 207n87, 211n55, 211n59, 213n22, 214n45
hierarchical power formation, 13–14, 34–40, 48–49, 63–68, 89, 93, 98. *See also* colonialism; horizontal power formation
Hocart, Arthur Maurice, 200n60, 214n45, 216n7
homophobia, 88–89, 206n71. *See also* sexuality

horizontal power formation, 14–15, 68, 81, 89, 98. *See also* hierarchical power formation
Human Rights Watch, 193n62

ICH, 72–77. *See also* safeguarding of iTaukei culture
Imada, Adria, 21
Implementation of the 2003 UNESCO Convention in the Pacific with Special Emphasis on Multinational Nominations, 72
indentured labor, 12, 109, 172, 201n76
Indigenous peoples. *See* iTaukei
Indigenous rights movements, 12, 29, 44–45, 63–66, 198n45, 199n53, 202n8, 212n9. *See also* iTaukei
Indigenous spirituality: colonialism and, 34–46, 55, 66, 199n57; creation of meke in the present and, 147–75, 195n7, 213n32; draunikau, 41–42, 45, 55, 198n41, 201n73; kalou vu and, 11, 36–46, 82, 90–91, 107, 134, 189nn20–21, 195n8, 200n60; luveniwai, 41–45, 64, 195n1, 198n48, 199n50; mana and, 17, 96, 133, 138–41, 216n8, 218n2; origin stories of, 46, 200n62; power dynamics and meke and, 16–19, 72, 124–44, 212n5. *See also* iTaukei
indirect rule, 34, 39–40, 44–45, 63–65, 69, 76, 93, 197n34, 197n36. *See also* colonialism
Indo-Fijians: in Canada, 14, 20, 105, 110–11, 210n25; history of, 12–13, 201n76, 215n3; meke and, 19, 77–84, 87, 95, 182, 218n2; tensions between Indigenous and, 6, 68–70, 77–79, 92, 110–11
In Oceania (Thomas), 212n9, 215n54

Instrument of Cession, 39, 197n32
intangible cultural heritage (ICH), 72–77. *See also* safeguarding of iTaukei culture
interculturalism, 81, 96, 209n8. *See also* multiculturalism
International Trade Union Confederation, 193n62
"Isa Isa," 175–77, 218n4
iTaukei: in Canada, 20, 103–11, 114–16, 210n25; colonialism and, 8, 12–13, 32–66, 197n34, 198n39, 198n42, 199n57, 201n76; creation of meke in the present and, 5–9, 146–72; designation of, 13–14, 86, 187n3, 204n40; gender and, 18–19, 84–91, 115, 164–65, 182; governing of meke and, 67–99, 182, 205n55; land ownership and, 68–69, 77, 92, 108, 199n53, 201n2; Methodist, 13, 24, 76–79, 93, 96, 125–44, 202n13, 207n89, 217n13; performance ethnography and, 12, 21–24, 174–84; power structure of, 38, 66–78, 92–98, 127, 203n30; rights movements of, 12, 29, 44–45, 63–66, 198n45, 199n53, 202n8, 212n9; safeguarding of the culture of, 12, 39–40, 68, 73–78, 82, 89–92, 96–98, 202n17, 203nn26–27; spirituality and, 124–44, 189n21, 195nn7–8. *See also* colonialism; meke
iTaukei Institute of Language and Culture, 68, 71–80, 98, 202n17, 203n19

Jackson, Peter, 217n1

Kabu ni Vanua (meke group), 3, 94–97, 134

kalou vu, 11, 36–46, 82, 90–91, 107, 134, 189nn20–21, 195n8, 200n60. *See also* Indigenous spirituality
Kaplan, Martha, 18, 39, 198n48
Keesing, Roger, 216n7
Kelly, Aaron, 83, 114, 136, 161
kinesthetic, 8, 11, 15, 31, 169–72
Knapman, Claudia, 195n5

Labor Party, Fiji, 69, 201n3
lakalaka, 74, 200n66
land ownership, 5, 13, 22, 68–70, 77–80, 92, 108, 130–33, 150, 199n53, 201n2. *See also* iTaukei
land spirits. *See* ancestor spirits; Indigenous spirituality
Larasati, Rachmi Diyah, 9, 30, 204n33
Lavaki, Dave, 165
Lee, Dorothy Sara, 189n20, 195n1, 212n14
Lester, R. H., 46, 64–65, 200n65, 201n77
Life (production), 176, 218n5
Ligairi, Ilisoni, 70
Logaivau, Damiano, 33, 83–86, 137–83, 206n59, 215n2, 215nn54–55, 217n15, 218n2
loloma, 11, 18, 146–48, 155–56, 168–70. *See also* meke
London Missionary Society, 195n5
The Lord of the Rings, 217n1
luveniwai, 41–45, 64, 195n1, 198n48, 199n50. *See also* Indigenous spirituality; meke

Māhina, 'Okusitino, 17, 148
mana: academic treatment of, 169–70, 215nn1–2, 216n7, 216n10; colonialism and, 17, 149–51, 155–56, 199n53, 216n8; and creation of meke in the present, 17, 24, 121, 147–73, 218n2; efficacy and, 17, 148, 156–57, 169–72, 185, 215n1; spirituality and, 17, 96, 133, 138–41, 216n8, 218n2. *See also* Indigenous spirituality; meke
Manning, Erin, 88
Marks, Laura, 209n8
Martin, John, 194n66
"Masterpieces of Oral and Intangible Heritage of Humanity" (UNESCO), 74
Mauss, Marcel, 169–71, 216n7
"Meda Mai Ia" (Raikoro), 116
meke: Bauan, 29, 82–86, 206n60; club, 10, 56–59, 83–85, 129–31, 158–59, 162–63, 205n58; colonialism and, 3–18, 31–66, 195n7, 196n14, 198n48, 200n66, 201n73; comedy and, 129, 213n22; governing of, 15–16, 67–99, 207n93; historic performances of, 34–66, 84–85, 90–91, 213n19; iri, 10, 59–60, 112–18, 158–59; and multiculturalism in Canada, 6–7, 100–123, 210n25; ni yaqona, 29, 107; performance ethnography and, 3, 8, 20–33, 173–84; present creation processes of, 10–19, 145–72, 215n2, 216n7, 218n2; sevu ni, 96, 136, 139, 214n44; spirituality and, 11, 16–18, 32, 124–44, 195n1, 195n8, 199n50, 212n14, 216n8; vakamalolo, 57–58, 94, 105–9, 187n2, 209n19; war, 18–19, 37–38, 67–69, 82–92, 114–15, 136–37, 205n54, 213n20; wau, 10, 56–59, 83–85, 129–31, 158–59, 162–63, 205n58; wesi, 9–10, 116, 129, 141, 158–59. *See also* iTaukei
Mekhe ni Loloma: creation of, 32–33, 146–72, 217n15; performance ethnography and, 32–33, 173–84

Melanesian Spearhead Group, 3, 97, 208n98
Methodist Church: colonial influence of the, 34–40, 65, 69–70, 93, 149–50, 207n89; Fijians in Canada and the, 20, 105; perceptions of meke and the, 96, 126–29, 144; power system of Fiji and the, 13, 24, 79, 93–94, 217n16; safeguarding iTaukei culture and the, 76–77, 96; spirituality in meke and the, 126–27, 130. *See also* Christianity
migration: colonialism and, 46, 63–66; Fijian culture and, 46, 75; between Fiji and Canada, 6–7, 18–20, 70, 102–8, 114–15, 122, 209n15 (*see also* diaspora, Fijian); performance ethnography and, 24
Ministry of Education (Fiji), 69, 77–80, 98, 203n19
Ministry of Foreign Affairs (Fiji), 97–98
Ministry of Industry, Trade, and Tourism (Fiji), 97
Ministry of iTaukei Affairs (Fiji), 71–73, 77, 203n19
Ministry of Tourism (Fiji), 96–98
missionaries: accounts of meke by, 34–40, 46–47, 56, 61, 149–50, 199n59; arrival of, 13, 127, 195n5; colonialism and, 8, 13, 16–18, 34–40, 46–47, 120, 127, 198n39, 200n62; governing of meke in the present and legacies of, 66, 72, 75. *See also* Christianity; colonialism
Mitra, Royona, 215n3
Mix and Match (group), 95
Moana, 217n1
Morey, C. J., 46
movement. *See* meke; migration
Multicultural Act (Canada), 103–4, 117
multiculturalism, 14, 18, 100–123, 208n7. *See also* interculturalism
multiracial ideology: Fijian policy of, 4–6, 13–16, 66–73, 105, 150, 202n17; governing of meke and, 67–73, 78–82, 86, 92–98; performance ethnography and, 27, 31, 157, 162
Mumford, Marrie, 187n4
Muñoz, José Esteban, 16, 27–28
Murphy, Jacqueline Shea, 75, 187n4
"Music Performances and the Negotiation of Identity in Eastern Viti Levu, Fiji" (Lee), 189n20

Nabobo-Baba, Unaisi, 17, 21–22, 148
NAF, 28, 31, 34, 55
Nailatikau, Epeli, 93–94
Na Iri Maesi (Ratawa), 212n14
Nasikawa Meke Group, 129–32, 213n23
National Archives of Fiji (NAF), 28, 31, 34, 55
Native Administration, 39, 63–64
Native Regulation Board, 39–41, 44–45, 198n42
Nawai, Apolosi R., 199n53, 212n9
Negri, Antonio, 190n34
neoliberalism, 10, 18, 42, 93, 149, 155, 169, 198n39. *See also* colonialism; postcolonialism
Ness, Sally, 25
New Methodists, 15
New Zealand, 117
Noland, Carrie, 102
Nunn, Hilary White, 50–51

Oceania Center for Art, Culture, and Pacific Studies (OCACPS), 81–82, 182–83, 189n16, 205n49
Oceania Dance Theatre, 11, 24, 81, 189n16, 214n41

Oceanic community, 25, 102–3, 112–21, 211n59
Oie na Kula (meke), 187n2
One Wave Gathering, 118

Pacific Arts Association, 179
Pacific Arts Symposium, 211n59
Pacific Islands Forum, 15, 93
Pacific Peoples' Partnership, 118, 211n59
Pasifika Voices Choir, 217n1
Pearl of the South Pacific Polynesian Dance Group, 113–14
Peni, Ledua, 173–75
Pentecostal Church, 19–20, 105, 127–28, 202n13. *See also* Christianity
performance ethnography, 20–21, 32–33, 173–84
"Performance Studies" (Conquergood), 181
"Performing as a Moral Act" (Conquergood), 178
Piot, Charles, 14, 122, 127, 190n29
Polynesia Company, 197n28
"Polynesian Clowns and Satirical Comedies" (Hereniko), 213n22
postcolonialism: coups and, 19, 177; creation of meke in the present and, 10, 12, 156–62, 170–72, 177; meke in Canada and, 110–12; performance ethnography and, 147–48, 151, 180–84; race and, 79, 102; spirituality in meke and, 16–17, 126–28. *See also* anticolonialism; colonialism; decolonization
Public Order Decree, 193n62

Qaraniqio, Ratu, 133
Qarase, Laisenia, 70

Qumia, Valeriana (Anna), 20–23, 48–55, 61, 65–66, 145–46, 152–56, 163, 168–69, 180

Rabuka, Sitiveni, 69–70, 94, 190n28
race: colonialism and, 13–16, 34–35, 39–42, 48–55, 63–65, 193n57; creation of meke in the present and, 6–11, 16–19, 150–51, 154, 162–64; designation of iTaukei and, 13–14, 86, 187n3, 204n40; Fijian policy of multiracialism and, 4–6, 13–16, 66–73, 78–82, 105, 150, 202n17; governing of meke and, 67–70, 78–89, 96, 182; meke and multiculturalism in Canada and, 20, 102–15, 122, 210n25; performance ethnography and, 3–4, 27–31, 146, 178–83. *See also* class; ethnicity; gender; iTaukei; sexuality
racism, 23, 39, 70, 89, 105, 110, 193n57, 194n66, 202n17. *See also* colonialism; race; social evolution theories
Ragg, Hugh, 128
Raikoro, Sekove, 116
Rasigatale, Manoa, 82, 89, 205n55, 206n59, 206n73
Ratawa, Wendy, 206n60, 212n14
"Raude" (Black Rose), 116
Ravuvu, Asesela, 216n10
reciprocity, 8, 21–25, 30, 147–49, 155–56, 167–72, 177
Reproductive and Family Health Association of Fiji, 89
"Retheorizing Mana" (Tomlinson), 215n1
Roach, Joseph, 131
Rogo Saka na Wekaqu (Hear Ye O My People) (meke), 94–95, 187n2, 207n86

Rose, Nikolas, 122
rugby, 82–83, 105, 121, 205n54, 209n13
Ryle, Jacqueline, 128

Sachs, Curt, 27, 194n66
safeguarding of iTaukei culture, 12, 39–40, 68, 73–78, 82, 89–92, 96–98, 202n17, 203nn26–27. *See also* Indigenous spirituality; iTaukei
Sahlins, Marshall, 38, 133, 208n97, 216n7
Said, Edward, 30
Sa Lutu a Caucau Vanua (meke), 95, 134, 207n86
Sawesawe, Elia, 137
Scarr, Deryck, 39
Seaqaqa, 214n45
seasea meke, 10, 61f, 95, 134, 174. *See also* meke
Section 26 (Constitution of the Republic of Fiji), 206n71
Section 64 (Native Regulation Board), 41, 44–45, 198n42
sevu ni meke, 96, 136, 139, 214n44. *See also* meke
sexism. *See* gender
sexuality, 38–42, 56, 88–89, 182, 206n71
Sklar, Deidre, 25
Smith, Linda Tuhiwai, 25
social evolution theories, 17, 35–36, 40, 46, 64–65, 194n66, 200n65. *See also* colonialism; racism
"South Sea Island Memories" (White), 35, 49–55, 65
Speight, George, 70
spirituality. *See* Indigenous spirituality
Srinivasan, Priya, 25
Stoler, Ann Laura, 35, 49–51, 66, 78
Sukuna, Ratu Sir Lala, 65

sulu, 42, 52, 61, 93, 100, 109, 202n13
Suva Rotary Club, 200n65, 201n77

Tagivakatini, Etueni, 86
Takyo, Naoki, 11f
Tanner, Adrian, 131
Tautoga (sang/dance), 95, 207n87
Taylor, Diana, 17, 28, 35, 194n70
Teaiwa, Katerina, 9–10, 117, 189n16
Teaiwa, Teresia, 97
Teivovo, 80–91, 205nn53–54, 206n59. *See also* meke
Thomas, Nicholas, 9, 54, 120, 127–29, 144, 212n9, 215n54
Thomson, Basil, 199n59
Thurston, John Bates, 39, 133
Tikoitoga, Mosese, 71
Todorov, Tzvetan, 23
Tokula, Jiuta, 129–32, 213nn20–21
Tomlinson, Matt, 37, 133, 149–50, 170, 215n1, 216n7
tourism: colonialism and meke and, 62–63; economic benefits of, 18, 30, 96–97, 127–29, 207n93, 213n16; performance of meke for, 3–4, 12, 91–92, 128–35
Tourism Fiji, 97, 208n94
Tuibeqa, Epeli, 133–34
Tuka movement, 198n45, 199n53. *See also* Indigenous rights movements
Tuwere, Ilaitia, 216n10

UNESCO, 12, 74–77, 204n33
United States Exploring Expedition, 215n1
University of the South Pacific, 81–82
Urciuoli, Bonnie, 104, 109

Va'a, Mua, 113–18, 210n39
Vaka (production), 189n19

vakamalolo, 57–58, 94, 105–9, 187n2, 209n19. *See also* meke
vanua, 13, 39, 76, 108, 116, 127, 190n29. *See also* iTaukei
Vanua (Tuwere), 202n17
Vasutoga, Asesela, 130
Veikoso, Lai, 3–4, 96–97, 135, 187n2, 214n42
Velaidan, Sadi, 87
vertical power formation, 13–14, 34–40, 48–49, 63–68, 89, 93, 98. *See also* colonialism; horizontal power formation
Viti Kabani, 199n53, 212n9

war dances, 18–19, 37–38, 67–69, 82–92, 114–15, 119–21, 129–31, 136–37, 205n54, 213n20. *See also* meke
Waterhouse, Joseph, 36–37

Wesleyan Methodist Church, 13, 34, 39, 127, 149. *See also* Methodist Church
White, Frank Thomas Matthews, 6, 13, 21–22, 48, 50–51, 200n65, 200n68
White, Tess, 13, 35, 48–57, 61, 65
Williams, Thomas, 36–38, 41, 47, 195n8, 196n14
witchcraft, associations of meke with, 34–35, 41–47, 55, 62, 66, 123, 128, 138–39, 167, 199n57, 201n73, 212n14. *See also* colonialism
Witchcraft Ordinance, 45, 47
World Dance Alliance Americas, 179

Yabaki, Tamarisi, 164
yaqona, 29, 36, 42–44, 72, 107–8, 126, 132, 139, 167, 175, 199n50

STUDIES IN DANCE HISTORY
Published under the auspices of the Dance Studies Association

Titles in Print

The Origins of the Bolero School, edited by
JAVIER SUÁREZ-PAJARES and XOÁN M. CARREIRA

Carlo Blasis in Russia
by ELIZABETH SOURITZ, with preface by SELMA JEANNE COHEN

Of, By, and For the People: Dancing on the Left in the 1930s,
edited by LYNN GARAFOLA

Dancing in Montreal: Seeds of a Choreographic History
by IRO TEMBECK

*The Making of a Choreographer: Ninette de Valois and
"Bar aux Folies-Bergère"*
by BETH GENNÉ

*Ned Wayburn and the Dance Routine:
From Vaudeville to the "Ziegfeld Follies"*
by BARBARA STRATYNER

Rethinking the Sylph: New Perspectives on the Romantic Ballet,
edited by LYNN GARAFOLA (available from the
University Press of New England)

Dance for Export: Cultural Diplomacy and the Cold War
by NAIMA PREVOTS, with introduction by ERIC FONER
(available from the University Press of New England)

José Limón: An Unfinished Memoir,
edited by LYNN GARAFOLA, with introduction by DEBORAH JOWITT,
foreword by CARLA MAXWELL, and afterword by NORTON OWEN
(available from the University Press of New England)

Dancing Desires: Choreographing Sexualities on and off the Stage,
edited by JANE C. DESMOND

Dancing Many Drums: Excavations in African American Dance,
edited by THOMAS F. DEFRANTZ

Writings on Ballet and Music,
by FEDOR LOPUKHOV, edited and with an introduction by
STEPHANIE JORDAN, translations by DORINDA OFFORD

Liebe Hanya: Mary Wigman's Letters to Hanya Holm,
compiled and edited by CLAUDIA GITELMAN,
introduction by HEDWIG MÜLLER

*The Grotesque Dancer on the Eighteenth-Century Stage:
Gennaro Magri and His World,*
edited by REBECCA HARRIS-WARRICK and BRUCE ALAN BROWN

Kaiso! Writings by and about Katherine Dunham,
EDITED BY VÈVÈ A. CLARK and SARA E. JOHNSON

Dancing from Past to Present: Nation, Culture, Identities,
edited by THERESA JILL BUCKLAND

Women's Work: Making Dance in Europe before 1800,
edited by LYNN MATLUCK BROOKS

Dance and the Nation: Performance, Ritual, and Politics in Sri Lanka
by SUSAN A. REED

*Urban Bush Women: Twenty Years of African American Dance Theater,
Community Engagement, and Working It Out*
by NADINE GEORGE-GRAVES

*Directing the Dance Legacy of Doris Humphrey: Politics and
the Creative Impulse of Reconstruction*
by LESLEY MAIN

The Body of the People: East German Dance since 1945
by JENS RICHARD GIERSDORF

Dramaturgy in Motion: At Work on Dance and Movement Performance
by KATHERINE PROFETA

Contemporary Directions in Asian American Dance,
edited by YUTIAN WONG

*Dancing Spirit, Love, and War:
Performing the Translocal Realities of Contemporary Fiji*
by EVADNE KELLY

www.ingramcontent.com/pod-product-compliance
Lightning Source LLC
Chambersburg PA
CBHW020835160426
43192CB00007B/653